21st Workshop on Multiword Expressions (MWE 2025)

Albuquerque, New Mexico, USA
4 May 2025

ISBN: 979-8-3313-1924-3

Printed from e-media with permission by:

Curran Associates, Inc.
57 Morehouse Lane
Red Hook, NY 12571

CURRAN ASSOCIATES INC.
proceedings
.com

Some format issues inherent in the e-media version may also appear in this print version.

Association for Computational Linguistics
209 N. Eighth Street
Stroudsburg, Pennsylvania 18360

Phone: 1-570-476-8006
Fax: 1-570-476-0860

acl@aclweb.org

Additional copies of this publication are available from:

Curran Associates, Inc.
57 Morehouse Lane
Red Hook, NY 12571 USA
Phone: 845-758-0400
Fax: 845-758-2633
Email: curran@proceedings.com
Web: www.proceedings.com

MWE 2025

The 21st Workshop on Multiword Expressions (MWE 2025)

Proceedings of the Workshop

May 4, 2025

The MWE organizers gratefully acknowledge the support from the following organizations.

Gold

Introduction

The 21st Workshop on Multiword Expressions (MWE 2025) took place on May 4, 2025, in Albuquerque, New Mexico, USA, and online, as a satellite event of the 2025 Annual Conference of the Nations of the Americas Chapter of the Association for Computational Linguistics (NAACL 2025). The workshop was organized and sponsored by the Special Interest Group on the Lexicon (SIGLEX) (http://www.siglex.org) of the Association for Computational Linguistics (ACL)(https://www.aclweb.org/portal/).

The notion of multiword expressions (MWEs), i.e., word combinations that exhibit lexical, syntactic, semantic, pragmatic, and/or statistical idiosyncrasies, encompasses closely related phenomena: idioms, compounds, light-verb constructions, phrasal verbs, rhetorical figures, collocations, institutionalized phrases, etc. Given their irregular nature, MWEs often pose complex problems in linguistic modeling (e.g. annotation), NLP tasks (e.g. parsing), and end-user applications (e.g. natural language understanding and Machine Translation), hence still representing an open issue for computational linguistics.

For this 21st edition of the workshop, our call for papers focused particularly on the following topics:

- MWE processing to enhance end-user applications;
- MWE processing and identification in the general language, as well as in specialized languages and domains;
- MWE processing in low-resourced languages;
- MWE identification and interpretation in LLMs
- new and enhanced representation of MWEs in language resources and computational models of compositionality as gold standards for formative intrinsic evaluation.

For this edition, all submitted papers were peer-reviewed by international experts and 75% of the submitted papers were accepted. Barbu Mititelu et al. paints the current state of the art of MWE lexica designed for NLP purposes. A diachronic perspective is adopted by Alves et al. when investigating the syntagmatic productivity of MWEs in English scientific writing.

The interest in endangered and low-resourced languages is still visible in the papers that report the development of new resources, dedicated to such languages. Thus, the paper authored by Adkins et al. focuses on Irish and on the recognition of named entities in this language, for which a tool is developed, while also producing a small gold-standard corpus annotated with named entities. Galician is the language for which a dataset of 240 ambiguous noun-adjective MWEs, contextualized in two sets of sentences, is manually rated for compositionality at token level, being also added information about frequency, ambiguity, and productivity. Markantonatou et al. propose the first Standard Modern Greek Universal Dependencies treebank annotated with Verbal MWEs, while also using it to evaluate the performance of models in MWEs identification tasks. A new resource for European Portuguese, namely a corpus annotated for verbal idioms, is reported by Antunes et al.

The development of multilingual resources is also an area of research represented in this workshop: Sentsova et al. introduce MultiCoPIE, a multilingual corpus of potentially idiomatic expressions in Catalan, Italian, and Russian, as well as the cross-lingual transfer of the potentially idiomatic expressions disambiguation task from English to the three languages in this new resource.

LLMs are found in several tasks: Kissane et al. examine how LLMs capture lexical and syntactic properties of phrasal verbs and prepositional verbs at different neural network layers. Adkins et al. compare both monolingual and multilingual BERT models fine-tuned on named entity recognition task. LLMs are also used to generate synthetic idiom datasets and to evaluate their effectiveness in training task-specific models for idiomaticity detection.

Verginica Barbu Mititelu, Mathieu Constant, A. Seza Doğruöz, Voula Giouli, Gražina Korvel, Atul Kr. Ojha, Alexandre Rademaker (MWE-2025 Organizers and Co-Chairs)

Organizing Committee

Workshop Chairs

Mathieu Constant, Université de Lorraine, CNRS, ATILF
A. Seza Doğruöz, Ghent University
Voula Giouli, Aristotle University of Thessaloniki and ILSP - "Athena" Research Center
Gražina Korvel, Vilnius University
Verginica Barbu Mititelu, Romanian Academy Research Institute for Artificial Intelligence
Atul Kr. Ojha, Insight Research Ireland Centre for Data Analytics, DSI, University of Galway, Ireland and Panlingua Languague Processing LLP, India
Alexandre Rademaker, School of Applied Mathematics of Getulio Vargas Foundation

Program Committee

Agata Savary, Université Paris-Saclay
Beata Trawinski, Leibniz Institute for the German Language
Carlos Ramisch, LIS - Laboratoire d'Informatique et Systèmes
Chikara Hashimoto, Rakuten Institute of Technology
Cvetana Krstev, University of Belgrade, Faculty of Philology
Eric G C Laporte, Université Gustave Eiffel
Francis Bond, Palacký University Olomouc
Gaël Dias, University of Caen Normandy
Gražina Korvel, Vilnius University
Irina Lobzhanidze, Ilia Chavchavadze State University
Ismail El Maarouf, Imprevicible
Ivelina Stoyanova, Deaf Studies Institute
Jan Odijk, Utrecht University
John Philip McCrae, University of Galway
Kenneth Church, Northeastern University
Manfred Sailer, Johann Wolfgang Goethe Universität Frankfurt am Main
Mathieu Constant, Université de Lorraine, CNRS, ATILF
Matthew Shardlow, The Manchester Metropolitan University
Meghdad Farahmand, University of Genoa
Miriam Butt, Universität Konstanz
Paul Cook, University of New Brunswick
Pavel Pecina, Charles University
Petya Osenova, Sofia University St. Kliment Ohridski
Ranka Stanković Stanković, University of Belgrade
Sabine Schulte im Walde, University of Stuttgart
Shiva Taslimipoor, University of Cambridge
Stan Szpakowicz, University of Ottawa
Stella Markantonatou, ATHENA RIC
Tiberiu Boros, Adobe Systems
Tunga Gungor, Bogazici University

Keynote Talk: Meaning Construction at the Syntax-Lexis Nexus

Nathan Schneider
Associate Professor of Linguistics and Computer Science at Georgetown University (USA)

Abstract: When words and grammar come into contact, things sometimes get messy: idiosyncratic expressions and patterns disobey ordinary principles of regularity and compositionality. A useful point of reference is the theoretical perspective of Construction Grammar, which exhorts us to view linguistic knowledge in terms of form-function mappings—at all levels of granularity. How can this perspective inform a broad-coverage, multilingual approach to lexicosyntactic conundrums? First, I will discuss implications for corpus annotation: while some multiword expressions and names (e.g. "at least", "in order to", "Chapter 1") test the limits of categorical annotation standards like Universal Dependencies, UD treebanks nevertheless enable empirical investigation of some functionally-defined constructions across languages. Second, I will discuss efforts to interpret the latent representations of constructional form and meaning in transformer language models, with the NPN construction (noun-preposition-noun, as in "face to face") as a case study.

Bio: Nathan Schneider is a computational linguist. As Associate Professor of Linguistics and Computer Science at Georgetown University, he leads the NERT lab, looking for synergies between practical language technologies and the scientific study of language, with an emphasis on how words, grammar, and context conspire to convey meaning. He is the recipient of an NSF CAREER award to study NLP vis-à-vis metalinguistic enterprises like language learning, linguistics, and legal interpretation. Recently, he has weighed in on specific interpretive debates in U.S. law; one of these analyses was cited by U.S. Supreme Court justices in a major firearms case. He is active in the NLP community—especially ACL's SIGANN and SIGLEX—and the Universal Dependencies project; and cofounded the SOLID forum for empirical research on legal interpretation. Prior to Georgetown, he inhabited UC Berkeley, Carnegie Mellon University, and the University of Edinburgh. Apart from annotation scheming and computational modeling, he enjoys classical music and chocolate chip cookies.

Table of Contents

Program

Sunday, May 4, 2025

09:15 - 09:30 *Welcome and Introduction to 21st MWE Workshop*

09:30 - 10:30 *Invited Talk*

10:30 - 11:00 *Coffee Break*

11:00 - 12:30 *Oral Session-I*

Survey on Lexical Resources Focused on Multiword Expressions for the Purposes of NLP
Verginica Mititelu, Voula Giouli, Gražina Korvel, Chaya Liebeskind, Irina Lobzhanidze, Rusudan Makhachashvili, Stella Markantonatou, Aleksandra Markovic and Ivelina Stoyanova

Named Entity Recognition for the Irish Language
Jane Adkins, Hugo Collins, Joachim Wagner, Abigail Walsh and Brian Davis

Gathering Compositionality Ratings of Ambiguous Noun-Adjective Multiword Expressions in Galician
Laura Castro and Marcos Garcia

VMWE identification with models trained on GUD (a UDv.2 treebank of Standard Modern Greek)
Stella Markantonatou, Vivian Stamou, Stavros Bompolas, Katerina Anastasopoulou, Irianna Linardaki Vasileiadi, Konstantinos Diamantopoulos, Yannis Kazos and Antonios Anastasopoulos

12:30 - 14:00 *Lunch*

14:00 - 15:00 *Oral Session-II*

A European Portuguese corpus annotated for verbal idioms
David Antunes, Jorge Baptista and Nuno J. Mamede

MultiCoPIE: A Multilingual Corpus of Potentially Idiomatic Expressions for Cross-lingual PIE Disambiguation
Uliana Sentsova, Debora Ciminari, Josef Van Genabith and Cristina España-Bonet

Probing Internal Representations of Multi-Word Verbs in Large Language Models
Hassane Kissane, Achim Schilling and Patrick Krauss

	Syntagmatic Productivity of MWEs in Scientific English Diego Alves, Stefan Fischer and Elke Teich
15:30 - 16:00	*Coffee Break*
16:00 - 18:00	*Oral Session III, panel and community discussion*
	Using LLMs to Advance Idiom Corpus Construction Doğukan Arslan, Hüseyin Anıl Çakmak, Gulsen Eryigit and Joakim Nivre
16:21 - 17:20	*Panel: Tokenization in the era of LLMs*
17:21 - 17:50	*Community discussion*
17:51 - 18:00	*Best Paper Awards and Concluding Remarks*

Syntagmatic Productivity of MWEs in Scientific English

Diego Alves[1], Stefan Fischer[2], Elke Teich[3]

Saarland University, Saarbrücken - Germany

diego.alves@uni-saarland.de, stefan.fischer@uni-saarland.de, e.teich@mx.uni-saarland.de

Abstract

This paper presents an analysis of the syntagmatic productivity (SynProd) of different classes of multiword expressions (MWEs) in English scientific writing over time (mid 17th to 20th c.). SynProd refers to the variability of the syntagmatic context in which a word or other kind of linguistic unit is used. To measure SynProd, we use entropy. The study reveals that, similar to single-token units of various parts of speech, MWEs exhibit an increasing trend in syntagmatic productivity over time, particularly after the mid-19th century. Furthermore, when compared to similar parts of speech (PoS), MWEs show a more pronounced increase in SynProd over time.

1 Introduction

In this paper, we examine the syntagmatic productivity of multiword expressions (MWEs) in English scientific writing, focusing on diachronic changes from the mid-17th century to the present. The syntagmatic productivity of a word refers to its ability to combine with other words in various syntactic contexts to form meaningful and coherent expressions. We use entropy to measure how often and in which ways a word can appear in different syntagmatic (sequential) relationships within larger constructions.

From a communicative perspective, multiword expressions play an important role in language efficiency because they are usually highly conventionalized. MWEs consist of combinations of words that are mutually highly predictable and often processed as single chunks, providing a significant processing advantage for language users. Their use in scientific writing is particularly noteworthy, given the high informational load typical of the scientific domain, where MWEs function as tools to smooth the information density over a message (Conklin and Schmitt, 2012).

It has been shown that scientific writing becomes increasingly conventionalized over time (see e.g., Degaetano-Ortlieb and Teich (2019) and Teich et al. (2021)), and that different classes of MWEs exhibit distinct diachronic tendencies in terms of association measures (Alves et al., 2024b) and discourse functions (Alves et al., 2024a).

In this study, our aim is to use entropy as a measure to analyze changes in the syntagmatic productivity of different classes of MWEs over time, comparing them to changes in individual tokens within similar parts of speech (e.g., compounds compared to nouns, and phrasal verbs compared to single-token verbs). Our hypothesis is that, due to a conventionalization process regarding the usage of MWEs, the syntagmatic productivity of these constructions presents a more pronounced increase over time when compared to their single-token counterparts.

The remainder of the paper is organized as follows. In Section 2, we discuss related work on the characterization of MWEs in English scientific writing. Sections 3 and 4 present our methods and results, respectively. We conclude with a summary of our findings and perspectives for future work in Section 5.

2 Related Work

From a linguistic standpoint, numerous corpus-based studies have explored MWEs across various registers, including the scientific domain (e.g., Biber and Barbieri (2007); Hyland (2008); Liu (2012)). Some of these studies provide lists of MWEs used in academic texts, which are extracted using corpus-based methods such as frequency and mutual information (e.g., Simpson-Vlach and Ellis (2010)). However, these studies primarily focus on synchronic analysis and provide valuable data for manuals aimed at improving writing skills.

Regarding NLP research, most studies focus on

Proceedings of the 21st Workshop on Multiword Expressions (MWE 2025), pages 1–6
May 4, 2025 ©2025 Association for Computational Linguistics

the correct identification and extraction of MWEs (Ramisch et al., 2023). The PARSEME initiative (Savary et al., 2015) provides valuable corpora and guidelines for annotating MWEs, however, their approach is restricted to verbal MWEs and the available corpora concern only recent texts.

A characterization of different classes of MWEs in scientific English, based on dimensions of information (i.e., dispersion and association), was proposed by Alves et al. (2024a). The authors demonstrated that specific formulaic expressions commonly used in scientific writing exhibit a stronger diachronic tendency to increase the association between the units forming the MWEs.

Moreover, Alves et al. (2024b) demonstrated that different types of MWEs, used for specific discourse functions (e.g., referential expressions and discourse organizers), exhibit distinct diachronic changes that are linked to the linguistic needs of different time periods.

As shown by Ramisch et al. (2023), the identification and evaluation of MWEs can be highly problematic, especially when dealing with specific registers, as is the case in our study. The studies in the last two paragraphs demonstrate that the methods used in our analysis are quite robust for identifying MWEs in a diachronic scientific corpus of English.

Regarding the syntagmatic productivity of different parts of speech in scientific writing, it has been shown that from 1660 to 1920, all parts of speech exhibit an increasing tendency, with a more pronounced slope starting around 1840 (Fankhauser, 2025). However, in this study, MWEs were not considered.

3 Methods

3.1 Data

In our analysis, we use the Royal Society Corpus (RSC) 6.0[1], a diachronic corpus of scientific English spanning the period from 1665 to 1996. This resource consists of 47,837 texts (295,895,749 tokens), primarily scientific articles from various fields, including mathematics, physical sciences, and biology. It is based on the Philosophical Transactions and Proceedings of the Royal Society of London (Fischer et al., 2020). The distribution of texts per discipline over time was not controlled in this analysis; this issue will be addressed in future work.

The corpus was parsed with the Stanza tool (Qi et al., 2020) using the combined model for the English language trained on different UD corpora (i.e., EWT, GUM, GUMReddit, PUD, and Pronouns). To identify the different classes of MWEs in the RSC, we followed the methodology proposed by Alves et al. (2024a). Once identified, the MWEs were combined into a single token (with spaces between tokens replaced by a character not seen in the corpus: ||) and labelled according to the classes described below.

- compound - combinations of tokens that morphosyntactically behave as single words (e.g., *water content, sea waves*)
- flat - this relation combines elements of an expression where none of the immediate components can be identified as the sole head using standard substitution tests. For example: *Hillary Clinton and San Francisco*
- phrasal verb (e.g., *shut down* and *find out*)
- fixed - used for certain fixed grammaticalized expressions which tend to behave like function words (e.g., *because of, in spite of, as well as*).
- Academic Formulas List (AFL) - list of formulaic expressions proposed by Simpson-Vlach and Ellis (2010) automatically extracted from academic texts (e.g., *in terms of, at the end of, whether or not*)

In total, 3,147,703 types of MWEs were identified in our corpus. The distribution of these types across the different classes is presented in Table 1.

Class	Number of Types
`compound`	2,523,696
`flat`	604,057
`phrasal verb`	16,337
`fixed`	3,107
`AFL`	506

Table 1: Distribution of the MWEs types in the RSC according to their MWE class.

3.2 Syntagmatic Productivity

As previously mentioned, the syntagmatic productivity of a word refers to its ability to combine

[1] `https://fedora.clarin-d.uni-saarland.de/rsc_v6/`

with other words in various syntactic contexts and form meaningful and coherent expressions. This can be measured using entropy as described by Fankhauser (2025): The syntagmatic productivity of a term is the entropy over all syntagmatic neighbours of a word x within a contextual window C_x of +/- 3 (see Formula 1).

$$SynProd(x) = - \sum_{c_i \in C_x} p(c_i|x) log(p(c_i|x)) \quad (1)$$

Entropy is a measure of uncertainty or variability in a system, and in the context of syntagmatic productivity, it quantifies the diversity of words that co-occur with a given term. A higher entropy value indicates that a word appears in a wide range of syntactic contexts with many different neighbors, suggesting greater syntagmatic flexibility. On the other hand, lower entropy implies that the word tends to co-occur with a more limited set of words, reflecting restricted combinatory potential. By capturing the distributional diversity of a word's syntagmatic associations, entropy provides a numerical representation of how productively a word participates in different constructions within a given corpus.

For each class of MWEs, we calculated the average syntagmatic productivity per decade of the RSC. Using a contextual window of 3, we define L3 as the syntagmatic productivity in the left context of each textual unit (single tokens and MWEs), and R3 as the syntagmatic productivity in the right context of each textual unit.

4 Results

4.1 Overall Syntagmatic Productivity

Figure 1 shows the average syntagmatic productivity of different classes of MWEs identified in the RSC, analyzed per decade. These results are compared to the average overall syntagmatic productivity of all other tokens in the text (i.e., tokens that are not part of MWEs, labelled as *All*).

As expected, all classes of MWEs exhibit an increasing tendency regarding both R3 and L3, with a more pronounced rise beginning in the mid-19th century. This pattern aligns with the observations reported by Fankhauser (2025) in their analysis of different parts of speech up to 1920. The graphs show that this rapid increase continues throughout the entire 20th century, not only for the different classes of MWEs but also for all other parts of speech. This suggests an expansion in the range of contexts where MWEs are employed.

Moreover, we observe that, although not identical, the R3 and L3 curves exhibit similar patterns across all analyzed cases. When compared to the curve representing the syntagmatic productivity of other parts of speech, it becomes evident that fixed and AFL MWEs display higher SynProd values, indicating more diverse usage. This can be attributed to the domain-independent, functional nature of these expressions, as they do not refer to a specific entity or action and can therefore be used in a wider variety of contexts. Additionally, from the mid-18th century onward, the average SynProd values of these two classes diverge even further from the *All* values, suggesting a growing conventionalization in the usage of these expressions in the scientific register.

Compounds and flat expressions, due to their more restricted meanings, exhibit lower SynProd values compared to other parts of speech. However, the difference between these two classes of MWEs and the *All* curve becomes less pronounced, especially in the 20th century.

It is interesting to note that phrasal verbs, often described as less common in academic prose (see, e.g., Biber et al. (2021) and Brown et al. (2015)), exhibit lower average values of L3 and R3 compared to other parts of speech (*All*) until the mid-19th century. However, they show an increasing trend in the more recent decades, surpassing the *All* curve in the final decades of the 20th century.

4.2 Syntagmatic Productivity per Class

To better understand the diachronic changes in syntagmatic productivity across different classes of MWEs, we compared them to the average SynProd of single-token units with comparable parts of speech. Figures 2 and 3 present the L3 and R3 graphs, comparing: a) phrasal verbs to other verbs; b) compounds and flat expressions to nouns and proper nouns; c) fixed and AFL MWEs to function words.

In all cases, changes are observed around the mid-19th century. Regarding phrasal verbs, their syntagmatic productivity is generally lower than that of other verbs. However, there is a reduction in the SynProd difference in more recent texts.

Compounds exhibit the lowest SynProd values up to 1730, being used in more specific contexts. However, after this decade, their average SynProd value increases, bringing it much closer to the pro-

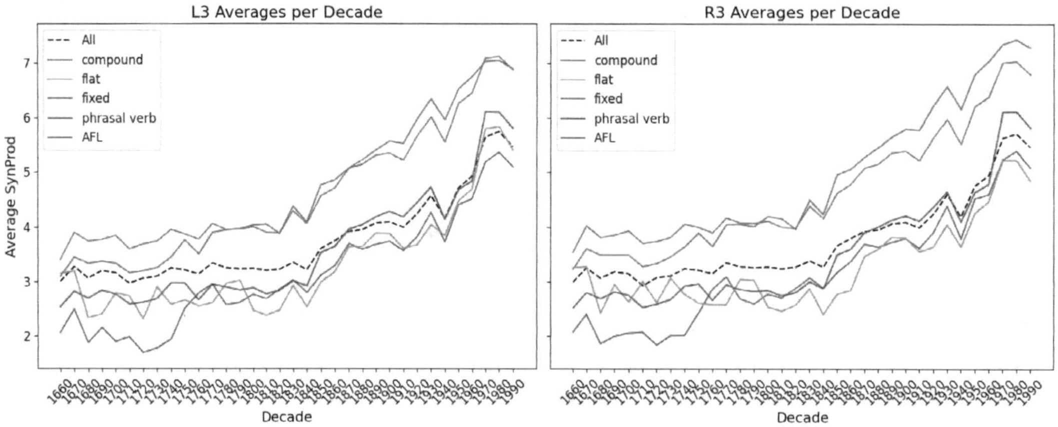

Figure 1: Average syntagmatic productivity of the different classes of MWEs per decade of the RSC.

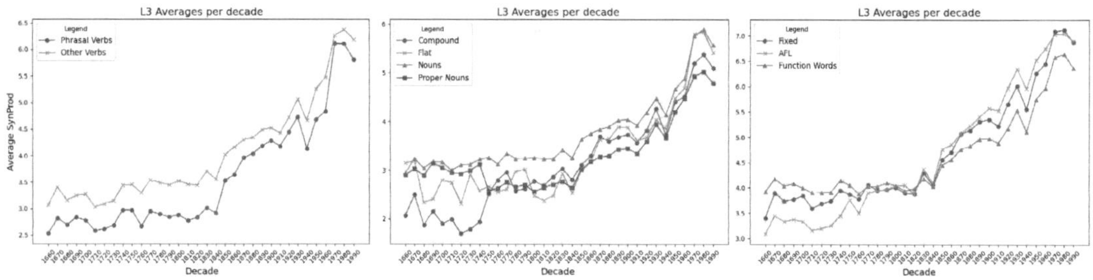

Figure 2: Average syntagmatic productivity considering the left context (L3) comparing MWEs with similar PoS.

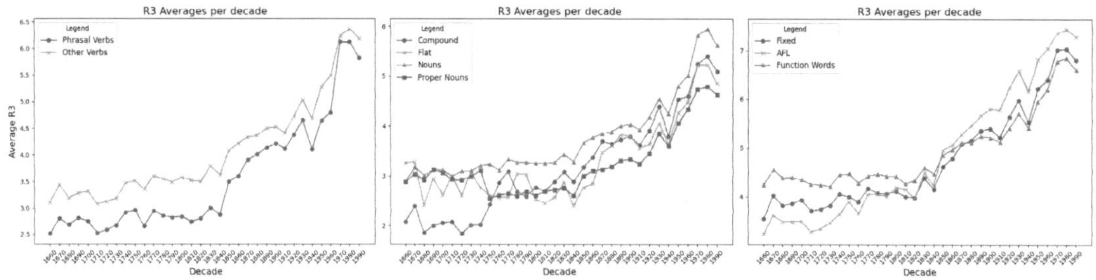

Figure 3: Average syntagmatic productivity considering the right context (R3) comparing MWEs with similar PoS.

ductivity of nouns in the RSC. In contrast, flat expressions start with higher SynProd averages but do not show a significant increase until the mid-19th century. When compared to proper nouns, flat expressions have higher SynProd values from the mid-19th century onward, even approaching the L3 SynProd of nouns in the final decades of the 20th century.

Finally, fixed and AFL expressions are the classes that surpass similar parts of speech in terms of SynProd after the mid-19th century, confirming the widespread conventionalized usage of these constructions in this register. In the later periods, we observe that, with regard to L3 values, fixed and AFL expressions exhibit quite similar averages. However, this is not the case for R3, where AFL expressions show higher syntagmatic productivity.

These results demonstrate that the use of MWEs in scientific English broadens in terms of context over time, exhibiting stronger increasing tendencies compared to similar parts of speech. Furthermore, they confirm the conventionalized and recurrent usage of fixed and formulaic expressions in this register.

It is important to mention that the size of the sub-corpora representing each time period was not controlled, which may affect the entropy values. As future work, we intend to conduct the same analysis using equal-sized samples for each period.

5 Conclusion and Future Work

In this paper, we have presented an analysis of the syntagmatic productivity of different classes of MWEs in scientific writing. Our investigation reveals that, like other single-token units with comparable parts of speech, MWEs exhibit an increasing tendency in SynProd, especially after the mid-19th century, considering both left and right contexts. We have also shown that, when comparing each class of MWE with corresponding parts of speech, MWEs tend to exhibit a more considerable increase in syntagmatic productivity over time. In most cases, the average SynProd values for MWEs are lower; however, over time, the delta decreases, or even reverses, as is the case for AFL and fixed expressions. In future work, we intend to compare the tendencies regarding syntagmatic productivity of MWEs to other information-theoretical measures such as paradigmatic variability (i.e., the sets of linguistic options available in a given or similar syntagmatic contexts) and typicality.

Acknowledgements

This research is funded by *Deutsche Forschungsgemeinschaft* (DFG, German Research Foundation) – Project-ID 232722074 – SFB 1102.

References

Diego Alves, Stefania Degaetano-Ortlieb, Elena Schmidt, and Elke Teich. 2024a. Diachronic analysis of multi-word expression functional categories in scientific English. In *Proceedings of the Joint Workshop on Multiword Expressions and Universal Dependencies (MWE-UD) @ LREC-COLING 2024*, pages 81–87.

Diego Alves, Stefan Fischer, Stefania Degaetano-Ortlieb, and Elke Teich. 2024b. Multi-word expressions in English scientific writing. In *Proceedings of the 8th Joint SIGHUM Workshop on Computational Linguistics for Cultural Heritage, Social Sciences, Humanities and Literature (LaTeCH-CLfL 2024)*, pages 67–76.

Douglas Biber and Federica Barbieri. 2007. Lexical bundles in university spoken and written registers. *English for specific purposes*, 26(3):263–286.

Douglas Biber, Stig Johansson, Geoffrey N Leech, Susan Conrad, and Edward Finegan. 2021. *Grammar of spoken and written English*. John Benjamins.

David West Brown, Chris C Palmer, Michael Adams, Laurel J Brinton, and Roger D Fulk. 2015. The phrasal verb in American English: Using corpora to track down historical trends in particle distribution, register variation, and noun collocations. *Studies in the history of the English language VI: Evidence and method in histories of English*, 85:71–97.

Kathy Conklin and Norbert Schmitt. 2012. The Processing of Formulaic Language. *Annual Review of Applied Linguistics*, 32:45–61.

Stefania Degaetano-Ortlieb and Elke Teich. 2019. Toward an Optimal Code for Communication: The Case of Scientific English. *Corpus Linguistics and Linguistic Theory*, 0(0):1–33.

Peter Fankhauser. 2025. Measuring and visualizing diachronic word use. Accessed: 2025-01-26.

Stefan Fischer, Jörg Knappen, Katrin Menzel, and Elke Teich. 2020. The Royal Society Corpus 6.0: Providing 300+ years of scientific writing for humanistic study. In *Proceedings of the Twelfth Language Resources and Evaluation Conference*, pages 794–802.

Ken Hyland. 2008. As can be seen: Lexical bundles and disciplinary variation. *English for specific purposes*, 27(1):4–21.

Dilin Liu. 2012. The most frequently-used multi-word constructions in academic written English: A multi-corpus study. *English for Specific Purposes*, 31(1):25–35.

Peng Qi, Yuhao Zhang, Yuhui Zhang, Jason Bolton, and Christopher D Manning. 2020. Stanza: A Python natural language processing toolkit for many human languages. *arXiv preprint arXiv:2003.07082*.

Carlos Ramisch, Abigail Walsh, Thomas Blanchard, and Shiva Taslimipoor. 2023. A survey of MWE identification experiments: the devil is in the details. In *Proceedings of the 19th workshop on multiword expressions (MWE 2023)*, pages 106–120.

Agata Savary, Manfred Sailer, Yannick Parmentier, Michael Rosner, Victoria Rosén, Adam Przepiórkowski, Cvetana Krstev, Veronika Vincze, Beata Wójtowicz, Gyri Smørdal Losnegaard, et al. 2015. Parseme–parsing and multiword expressions within a European multilingual network. In *7th Language & Technology Conference: Human Language Technologies as a Challenge for Computer Science and Linguistics (LTC 2015)*.

Rita Simpson-Vlach and Nick C Ellis. 2010. An academic formulas list: New methods in phraseology research. *Applied linguistics*, 31(4):487–512.

Elke Teich, Peter Fankhauser, Stefania Degaetano-Ortlieb, and Yuri Bizzoni. 2021. Less is More/More Diverse: On The Communicative Utility of Linguistic Conventionalization. *Frontiers in Communication*, 5.

Probing Internal Representations of Multi-Word Verbs in Large Language Models

Hassane Kissane[1,2], Achim Schilling[2,3], Patrick Krauss[2,3]
[1]Chair of English Philology and Linguistics, University Erlangen-Nuremberg, Germany
[2]Cognitive Computational Neuroscience Group, University Erlangen-Nuremberg, Germany
[3]Neuroscience Lab, University Hospital Erlangen, Germany
*

Abstract

This study investigates the internal representations of verb-particle combinations, called multi-word verbs, within transformer-based large language models (LLMs), specifically examining how these models capture lexical and syntactic properties at different neural network layers. Using the BERT architecture, we analyze the representations of its layers for two different verb-particle constructions: phrasal verbs like *give up* and prepositional verbs like *look at*. Our methodology includes training probing classifiers on the model output to classify these categories at both word and sentence levels. The results indicate that the model's middle layers achieve the highest classification accuracies. To further analyze the nature of these distinctions, we conduct a data separability test using the Generalized Discrimination Value (GDV). While GDV results show weak linear separability between the two verb types, probing classifiers still achieve high accuracy, suggesting that representations of these linguistic categories may be *non-linearly separable*. This aligns with previous research indicating that linguistic distinctions in neural networks are not always encoded in a linearly separable manner. These findings computationally support usage-based claims on the representation of verb-particle constructions and highlight the complex interaction between neural network architectures and linguistic structures.

1 Introduction

1.1 The linguistic problem

Multi-word verbs or verb-particle combinations are a linguistic category presented in the English language in which the lexical verb is combined with a particle to form an independent unit. It is called a phrasal verb when the lexical verb is combined with an adverbial particle like *work out*. It is a prepositional verb when the verb is combined with a prepositional particle like *rely on* (Carter and McCarthy, 2006). Usually, the prepositional verbs are followed by a noun phrase. Rather than the nature of the following particle, there are several differences between phrasal verbs and prepositional verbs. One main difference between the two categories is the particle placement in phrasal verbs and the foxed order in prepositional verbs. Where in phrasal verbs, the particle can sometimes be separated from the verb and placed after the object. In contrast, the only grammatical form in prepositional verbs is the V+prepostion+object.

- *Turn off the light. (phrasal)*
- *Turn the light off. (phrasal)*
- *Look at the painting. (prepositional)*
- **Look the painting at.(prepositional)*

Several studies explored the mental storage of these verb-particle constructions, specifically phrasal verbs, to see in which way they are stored and processed in the brain. For instance Cappelle et al. (2010) and further discussed by Pulvermüller et al. (2013) that phrasal verbs are processed as single lexical units, as evidenced by MEG. However, prepositional verbs remain unexplored, which are still treated similarly to phrasal verbs in terms of both the verb and the particle form a single lexical unit called verb, for example the prepositional verbs *look at*, and the phrasal verb *turn off* (Quirk et al., 1985; Carter and McCarthy, 2006). From a constructional point of view, Herbst and Schüller (2008) proposed what is called the valency model for the distinction between phrasal verbs and prepositional verbs, assuming that prepositions function as integral parts of the complement rather than the verb itself in prepositional verbs. This valency-based approach emphasizes the syntactic relationship between the verb and its complements, analyz-

*Correspondence: patrick.krauss@fau.de

Proceedings of the 21st Workshop on Multiword Expressions (MWE 2025), pages 7–13
May 4, 2025

ing prepositional verbs like *look at* as the verb *look* and the complement *at*.

1.2 probing-based methods for linguistic tasks

Probing methods analyze the linguistic properties encoded in the representations of the NLP model. Probes are supervised models trained to predict linguistic properties or other categories, such as parts of speech or word meanings, from model representations such as BERT embeddings (Immertreu et al., 2024; Ramezani et al., 2024b). These probes have achieved high accuracy on various linguistic tasks, demonstrating their utility in understanding how models encode features such as syntax and semantics (Conneau et al., 2018). The search classifiers are trained on the activations to identify predefined concepts or linguistic properties, such as syntactic tags or semantic meanings, from the model output embeddings (Hupkes and Zuidema, 2018; Sajjad et al., 2022). Furthermore, layer-wise analysis (Tenney et al., 2019a; Ramezani et al., 2024b; Krauss et al., 2024; Banerjee et al., 2025; Ramezani et al., 2024a) investigates how linguistic knowledge is distributed across the layers of transformer-based models, providing insights into the hierarchical organization of encoded knowledge.

The internal representations of LLMs are frequently analyzed using probing approaches. Tenney et al. (2019a) employ probing tasks to investigate the linguistic information that BERT gathers and discover that various layers encode different kinds of linguistic properties. A set of probes is presented by Tenney et al. (2019b) to examine the representations acquired by contextualized word embeddings and to determine the distribution of syntactic and semantic information among layers.

While prior studies (e.g., Cappelle et al. (2010); Pulvermüller et al. (2013)) have suggested that phrasal verbs function as single lexical units, and Herbst and Schüller (2008) proposed a valency-based linguistic distinction for prepositional verbs, it remains unclear whether these distinctions are reflected in the internal representations of neural language models. This study aims to investigate how neural language models encode and differentiate between these two linguistically distinct categories of multi-word verbs. Specifically, we examine whether internal representations capture key syntactic, lexical, and compositional differences. To achieve this, we apply probing classifiers to measure classification accuracy across layers and data separability methods to assess how distinctly these verb categories are organized within the representational space of a neural language model.

2 Methods

2.1 Data

The dataset consists of sentences containing phrasal and prepositional verbs, extracted from the British National Corpus (BNC, 2001). Sequences were selected based on syntactic variability using part-of-speech (PoS) tag patterns:

- *Phrasal verbs were identified using the pattern "V + ADV + Det + N", where the output is like* ***look up the word.***
- *Prepositional verbs followed the pattern "V + PREP + Det + N", where the the output is like* ***look after the child.***

The dataset was manually divided to ensure that each verb appearing in the training set does not appear in the test set. This was done to prevent overlap in representation and ensure that the classifiers generalize beyond memorization. The training set includes 1920 examples of phrasal verbs and 2070 of prepositional verbs. The test set contains 522 phrasal verb examples and 623 prepositional verb examples, with a total of 2442 for phrasal verbs and 2693 for prepositional verbs, as shown in Table 1. Since our study focuses on probing analysis rather than optimizing a model, we did not require hyperparameter tuning, which typically demands a development set. Before using the dataset as input for the model, we applied several cleaning steps, which are detailed in Table 2.

2.2 Model (Embedding Extraction)

We use transformer-based model (Vaswani et al., 2017) BERT (Devlin et al., 2019) as the feature extraction model for generating contextual embeddings. Specifically, we use the *bert-base-uncased* version, consisting of 12 layers, each producing 768-dimensional contextual embeddings for input tokens. For each sample, we extract embeddings at two levels:

Token-Level Embeddings For verb-specific analysis, we extract the embedding corresponding to the main token of the verb (e.g., *give* in *give up*). These embeddings focus on the localized representation of the verb within the sentence.

Sentence-Level Embeddings To capture the entire context of the sentence, we compute the average of all token embeddings in the sentence. This

Phrasal	#	Prepositional	#
		Training	
blow_up	52	break_into	147
break_down	134	call_on	138
close_down	54	come_across	168
fill_up	54	do_without	76
find_out	243	get_off	184
finish_off	46	care_for	150
give_away	35	cope_with	150
give_up	239	get_into	150
hand_in	229	get_on	150
hold_up	56	go_into	150
look_up	67	lead_to	148
put_off	57	listen_to	153
shut_down	57	look_at	154
throw_away	58	look_for	152
turn_down	75		
wake_up	31		
take_over	102		
work_out	101		
sort_out	230		
Total	1920	Total	2070
		Test	
take_up	100	depend_on	150
carry_on	184	look_after	154
bring_up	115	deal_with	153
check_out	123	get_over	111
		approve_of	55
Total	522	Total	623
Grand Total	2442	Grand Total	2693

Table 1: Distribution of phrasal and prepositional verbs in training and test sets with their frequencies.

approach aggregates information across all tokens, providing a representation of the sentence without relying solely on the [CLS] token embedding.

Our study focuses on *bert-base-uncased* as a widely used transformer model, but we acknowledge that different LLM architectures may encode linguistic categories differently. Future research could extend this analysis to other models, such as *roberta-base* or *bert-large*, to assess whether the observed patterns generalize across architectures.

2.3 Classification Models

Logistic Regression (LR) is a linear model used in modeling the probabilities of possible outcomes given an input variable.

Support Vector Machines (SVM) perform well on smaller datasets by optimizing data transformations based on predefined classes. They are based on the principle of Structural Risk Minimization from Statistical Learning Theory (Boser et al., 1992). In their fundamental form, SVMs learn linear discrimination that separates positive examples from negative ones with a maximum margin. This margin, defined by the distance of the hyperplane to the nearest positive and negative examples, has proven to have good properties in terms of generalization bounds for the induced classifiers.

2.4 Generalized Discrimination Value (GDV)

We used the GDV to calculate cluster separability as published and explained in detail in Schilling et al. (2021). Briefly, we consider N points $\mathbf{x_{n=1..N}} = (x_{n,1}, \cdots, x_{n,D})$, distributed within D-dimensional space. A label l_n assigns each point to one of L distinct classes $C_{l=1..L}$. In order to become invariant against scaling and translation, each dimension is separately z-scored and, for later convenience, multiplied with $\frac{1}{2}$:

$$s_{n,d} = \frac{1}{2} \cdot \frac{x_{n,d} - \mu_d}{\sigma_d}. \tag{1}$$

Here, $\mu_d = \frac{1}{N}\sum_{n=1}^{N} x_{n,d}$ denotes the mean, and $\sigma_d = \sqrt{\frac{1}{N}\sum_{n=1}^{N}(x_{n,d} - \mu_d)^2}$ the standard deviation of dimension d. Based on the re-scaled data points $\mathbf{s_n} = (s_{n,1}, \cdots, s_{n,D})$, we calculate the *mean intra-class distances* for each class C_l

$$\bar{d}(C_l) = \frac{2}{N_l(N_l - 1)} \sum_{i=1}^{N_l - 1} \sum_{j=i+1}^{N_l} d(\mathbf{s}_i^{(l)}, \mathbf{s}_j^{(l)}), \tag{2}$$

and the *mean inter-class distances* for each pair of classes C_l and C_m

$$\bar{d}(C_l, C_m) = \frac{1}{N_l N_m} \sum_{i=1}^{N_l} \sum_{j=1}^{N_m} d(\mathbf{s}_i^{(l)}, \mathbf{s}_j^{(m)}). \tag{3}$$

Here, N_k is the number of points in class k, and $\mathbf{s}_i^{(k)}$ is the ith point of class k. The quantity $d(\mathbf{a}, \mathbf{b})$ is the euclidean distance between **a** and **b**. Finally, the Generalized Discrimination Value (GDV) is calculated from the mean intra-class distances

$$\langle \bar{d}(C_l) \rangle = \frac{1}{L} \sum_{l=1}^{L} \bar{d}(C_l) \tag{4}$$

and the mean inter-class distances

$$\langle \bar{d}(C_l, C_m) \rangle = \frac{2}{L(L-1)} \sum_{l=1}^{L-1} \sum_{m=l+1}^{L} \bar{d}(C_l, C_m) \tag{5}$$

as follows:

$$\mathrm{GDV} = \frac{1}{\sqrt{D}} \left[\langle \bar{d}(C_l) \rangle - \langle \bar{d}(C_l, C_m) \rangle \right] \tag{6}$$

<table>
<tr><th>Character</th><th>Pre-processing step</th></tr>
<tr><td>Punctuations
(!"#$%&'()*+,-./:;<=>?@[\]\^_
\`{}|\~)</td><td>Removed</td></tr>
<tr><td>Leading and trailing whitespaces</td><td>Removed</td></tr>
<tr><td>Extra whitespaces</td><td>Replaced with a single space</td></tr>
<tr><td>Uppercase characters</td><td>Converted to lowercase</td></tr>
</table>

Table 2: Text pre-processing steps applied to the dataset.

whereas the factor $\frac{1}{\sqrt{D}}$ is introduced for dimensionality invariance of the GDV with D as the number of dimensions.

Note that the GDV is invariant with respect to a global scaling or shifting of the data (due to the z-scoring), and also invariant concerning a permutation of the components in the N-dimensional data vectors (because the euclidean distance measure has this symmetry). The GDV is zero for completely overlapping, non-separated clusters, and it becomes more negative as the separation increases. A GDV of -1 signifies already a very strong separation.

3 Results

Token-based classification

The results of the lexical verb token classification task using logistic regression and linear SVM have shown distinct trends across the 12 layers of the BERT model Figure 1. For the Logistic Regression classifier, accuracy starts at 0.87 in the input layer, remains stable around 0.84 - 0.80 through layers 2 to 4, and then increases significantly, reaching 0.99 in layer 6 before slightly decreasing in the late layers of the model. Similarly, the linear SVM classifier achieves an accuracy of 0.63 in the input layer. Then 0.84, through layers 2 to 4. To start improving from layer 5 onward, reaching its highest accuracy of 0.99 at layer 8. Both classifiers show the best accuracy in the middle layers (layers 6–9, suggesting that these layers encode the most significant linguistic features to distinguish between phrasal verbs and prepositional verbs. Therefore, the accuracies decrease slightly in the late layers, which indicates a shift towards task-specific representations less suited for this classification task.

Sentence-Based Classification

For the sentence-based classification task, both Logistic Regression and Linear SVM show distinct trends across the 12 BERT layers Figure 1. However, the accuracies in the token-based classification were higher than those based on sentence embeddings. The Logistic Regression classifier begins with an accuracy of 0.80 in the input layer and improves to 0.85 in layers 6 and 7. Then, accuracy decreases in the late layers, dropping to 0.69 in layers 11 and 12. Similarly, the linear SVM classifier starts with an accuracy of 0.77 and 0.76 in the input and first layer respectively, to 0.84 in layer 6, then decreases to the lowest accuracy of 0.66 in the final layer of the model. With these results, it is suggested that the middle layers (layers 5–7) of the model are the best to capture linguistic information at sentence-level representations to distinguish phrasal verbs and prepositional verbs, while the higher layers, likely focused on task-specific semantics, encode features less suited to these properties predictions.

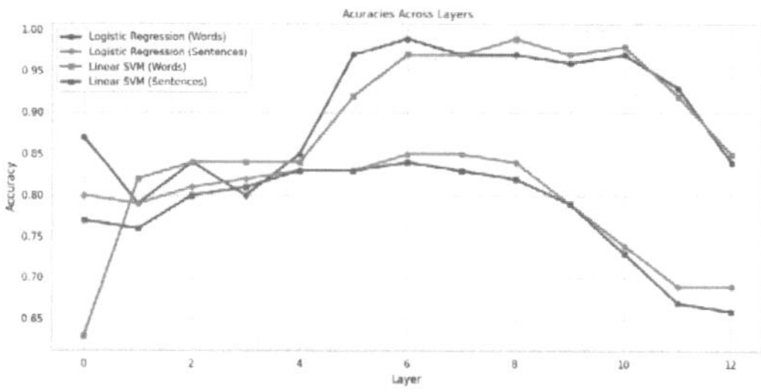

Figure 1: Classification accuracies

GDV Values for Data Separability

The GDV calculations for both token-based and sentence-based embeddings has shown non-strong separation between between the phrasal and prepositional verbs across BERT layers Figure 2. For the token-based embeddings, GDV values start at equivalent of 0.00 in the input layer which is responsible for converting tokens into dense vector representations before they are processed by the transformer layers. Then, the GDV has shown an improvement (less negative) across the layers, reaching their strongest separability at layers 3 and 4 with a value of -0.049 and -0.048 respectively.

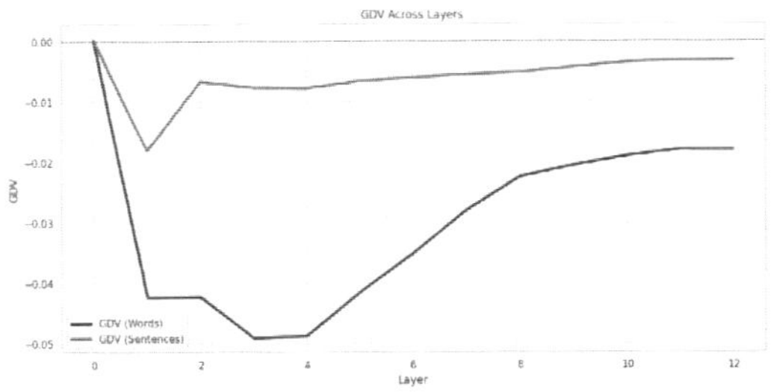

Figure 2: GDV values for data separability between the two multi-word verbs classes across BERT layers

This improvement indicates that BERT's middle layers may encode more discriminative features for distinguishing between the two verb types in word embeddings.

After we ran a normality test on the classification accuracies and GDV scores across BERT layers, we found that the data was not normally distributed, which justified the use of Spearman's rank correlation as a non-parametric test Figure 3. The analysis showed no statistically significant correlation between the variables. For words, the correlation between Logistic Regression and GDV was r_s = 0.32, p = 0.285, and between Linear SVM and GDV, r_s = 0.26, p = 0.383. For sentences, the correlation between Logistic Regression and GDV was r_s = -0.44, p = 0.128, while Linear SVM and GDV showed a negative correlation of r_s = -0.52, p = 0.069, approaching significance. Overall, no strong or significant associations were observed.

4 Discussion

Our findings indicate that while probing classifiers and GDV provide some investigations into how BERT encodes differences between linguistic categories, they may not fully capture the complexities of linguistic representations. Particularly, when distinguishing between phrasal and prepositional verbs based on token-level embeddings. As proposed by Goldberg (1995), lexico-semantic elements convey a portion of linguistic information, but they do not embody all structural and functional aspects present in a text. This limitation is particularly relevant in the case of the investigated cases in the study, where distinctions often emerge from interactions between lexical, syntactic, and semantic factors rather than being determined by individual token representations.

Our study focuses on bert-base-uncased as a widely used transformer model, but we acknowledge that different LLM architectures may encode linguistic categories differently. Future research could extend this analysis to other models, such as roberta-base or bert-large, to assess whether the observed patterns generalize across architectures.

This perspective aligns with the constructionist approach to language processing (Madabushi et al., 2020), which challenges the traditional separation of lexical and grammatical elements. Instead, it proposes a continuum of constructions—where linguistic representations arise from learned pairings of form and meaning rather than being strictly lexical or grammatical only. From this point, phrasal and prepositional verbs might be better understood as integrated constructions, rather than purely lexical or syntactic units. Consequently, probing classifiers, which primarily capture lexical or semantic properties in token-based classification tasks, may fail to fully account for the grammatical and contextual information that shapes the representation of these constructions. This is evident in the mismatch between classification accuracies and GDV values, suggesting that different methods may capture other dimensions of representation.

Several studies have discussed the limitations of probing classifiers (Belinkov, 2022; Sajjad et al., 2022). One major limitation is the disconnect between probing accuracy and the original model's internal processing. While probing classifiers can detect correlations between model embeddings and linguistic features, they do not necessarily indicate whether the model actively uses these properties for linguistic processing. This limitation is apparent in our findings: while probing classifiers achieved high accuracies, GDV analysis showed weak linear separability between phrasal and prepositional verbs, as indicated by the lack of significant correlation between classification accuracies and GDV values.

This observed Disagreement between classifier accuracies and GDV values aligns with previous research suggesting that internal representations in neural networks and large language models are not necessarily linearly separable (Hewitt and Liang, 2019; Kissane et al., 2024; Zhang and Bowman, 2018; Banerjee et al., 2025; Hildebrandt et al., 2025; Krauss et al., 2024; Ramezani et al., 2024b). Since GDV measures linear separability, it does not capture non-linearly structured representations. In contrast, probing classifiers can still detect nonlinearly separable distinctions, allowing them to identify linguistic categories that may be encoded

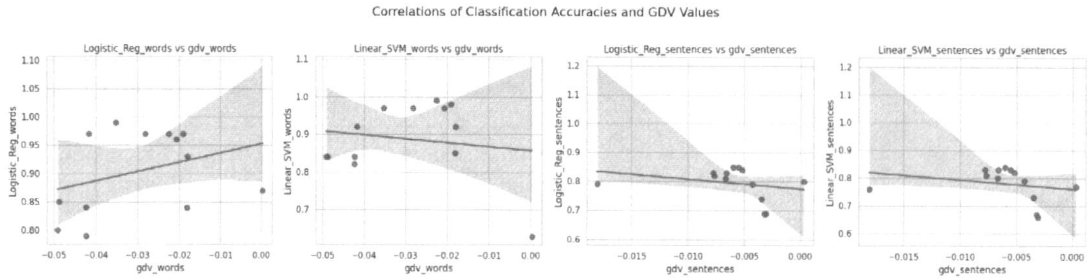

Figure 3: The correlation between probing classifier accuracy and Generalized Discrimination Value (GDV) scores across BERT layers. While probing classifiers achieve high accuracy in distinguishing phrasal and prepositional verbs, GDV values remain close to zero, indicating that these categories are not linearly separable in BERT's representation space.

in high-dimensional space. Therefore, the low GDV scores do not suggest that BERT fails to encode multi-word verb distinctions, but rather that these representations may require non-linear transformations to be fully distinguished. This Point up the need for comprehensive analytical methods when investigating how LLMs structure linguistic knowledge and suggests that linear separability should not be the only one criterion for assessing learned representations.

Acknowledgments

This work was funded by the Deutsche Forschungsgemeinschaft (DFG, German Research Foundation): KR 5148/3-1 (project number 510395418), KR 5148/5-1 (project number 542747151), and GRK 2839 (project number 468527017) to PK, and grant SCHI 1482/3-1 (project number 451810794) to AS.

References

Awritrojit Banerjee, Achim Schilling, and Patrick Krauss. 2025. Exploring narrative clustering in large language models: A layerwise analysis of bert. *arXiv preprint arXiv:2501.08053*.

Yonatan Belinkov. 2022. Probing classifiers: Promises, shortcomings, and advances. *Computational Linguistics*, 48(1):207–219.

BNC. 2001. The British National Corpus, version 2 (BNC World). Distributed by Oxford University Computing Services on behalf of the BNC Consortium.

Bernhard E. Boser, Isabelle M. Guyon, and Vladimir N. Vapnik. 1992. A training algorithm for optimal margin classifiers. In *Title*, COLT '92, page 144–152, New York, NY, USA. Association for Computing Machinery.

Bert Cappelle, Yury Shtyrov, and Friedemann Pulvermüller. 2010. Heating up or cooling up the brain: MEG evidence that phrasal verbs are lexical units. *Brain and Language*, 115(3):189–201.

R. Carter and M. McCarthy. 2006. *Cambridge Grammar of English: A Comprehensive Guide*. Cambridge Grammar of English Series. Cambridge University Press.

Alexis Conneau, German Kruszewski, Guillaume Lample, Loïc Barrault, and Marco Baroni. 2018. What you can cram into a single $&!#* vector: Probing sentence embeddings for linguistic properties. In *Proceedings of the 56th Annual Meeting of the Association for Computational Linguistics (Volume 1: Long Papers)*, pages 2126–2136, Melbourne, Australia. Association for Computational Linguistics.

Jacob Devlin, Ming-Wei Chang, Kenton Lee, and Kristina Toutanova. 2019. BERT: Pre-training of deep bidirectional transformers for language understanding. In *Proceedings of the 2019 Conference of the North American Chapter of the Association for Computational Linguistics: Human Language Technologies, Volume 1 (Long and Short Papers)*, pages 4171–4186, Minneapolis, Minnesota. Association for Computational Linguistics.

Adele E Goldberg. 1995. *Constructions: A construction grammar approach to argument structure*. University of Chicago Press.

Thomas Herbst and Susen Schüller. 2008. *Introduction to Syntactic Analysis: A Valency Approach*. Narr Francke Attempto Verlag.

John Hewitt and Percy Liang. 2019. Designing and interpreting probes with control tasks. In *Proceedings of the 2019 Conference on Empirical Methods in Natural Language Processing and the 9th International Joint Conference on Natural Language Processing (EMNLP-IJCNLP)*, pages 2733–2743, Hong Kong, China. Association for Computational Linguistics.

Fabian Hildebrandt, Andreas Maier, Patrick Krauss, and Achim Schilling. 2025. Refusal behavior in large language models: A nonlinear perspective. *arXiv preprint arXiv:2501.08145*.

Dieuwke Hupkes and Willem H. Zuidema. 2018. Visualisation and 'diagnostic classifiers' reveal how recurrent and recursive neural networks process hierarchical structure (extended abstract). In *International Joint Conference on Artificial Intelligence*.

Mathis Immertreu, Achim Schilling, Andreas Maier, and Patrick Krauss. 2024. Probing for consciousness in machines. *arXiv preprint arXiv:2411.16262*.

Hassane Kissane, Achim Schilling, and Patrick Krauss. 2024. Analysis and visualization of linguistic structures in large language models: Neural representations of verb-particle constructions in bert. *arXiv preprint arXiv:2412.14670*.

Patrick Krauss, Jannik Hösch, Claus Metzner, Andreas Maier, Peter Uhrig, and Achim Schilling. 2024. Analyzing narrative processing in large language models (llms): Using gpt4 to test bert. *arXiv preprint arXiv:2405.02024*.

Harish Tayyar Madabushi, Laurence Romain, Petar Milin, and Dagmar Divjak. 2020. Cxgbert: Bert meets construction grammar. In *Proceedings of the 28th International Conference on Computational Linguistics*, pages 4020–4032. International Committee on Computational Linguistics.

Friedemann Pulvermüller, Bert Cappelle, and Yury Shtyrov. 2013. 397 brain basis of meaning, words, constructions, and grammar. In *The Oxford Handbook of Construction Grammar*. Oxford University Press.

Randolph Quirk, Sidney Greenbaum, and Geoffrey Leech. 1985. *A Comprehensive Grammar of the English Language*. Longman.

Pegah Ramezani, Achim Schilling, and Patrick Krauss. 2024a. Analysis of argument structure constructions in a deep recurrent language model. *arXiv preprint arXiv:2408.03062*.

Pegah Ramezani, Achim Schilling, and Patrick Krauss. 2024b. Analysis of argument structure constructions in the large language model bert. *arXiv preprint arXiv:2408.04270*.

Hassan Sajjad, Nadir Durrani, and Fahim Dalvi. 2022. Neuron-level interpretation of deep NLP models: A survey. *Transactions of the Association for Computational Linguistics*, 10:1285–1303.

Achim Schilling, Andreas Maier, Richard Gerum, Claus Metzner, and Patrick Krauss. 2021. Quantifying the separability of data classes in neural networks. *Neural Networks*, 139:278–293.

Ian Tenney, Dipanjan Das, and Ellie Pavlick. 2019a. BERT rediscovers the classical NLP pipeline. In *Proceedings of the 57th Annual Meeting of the Association for Computational Linguistics*, pages 4593–4601, Florence, Italy. Association for Computational Linguistics.

Ian Tenney, Patrick Xia, Berlin Chen, Alex Wang, Adam Poliak, R. Thomas McCoy, Najoung Kim, Benjamin Van Durme, Samuel R. Bowman, Dipanjan Das, and Ellie Pavlick. 2019b. What do you learn from context? probing for sentence structure in contextualized word representations. In *International Conference on Learning Representations*.

Ashish Vaswani, Noam M. Shazeer, Niki Parmar, Jakob Uszkoreit, Llion Jones, Aidan N. Gomez, Lukasz Kaiser, and Illia Polosukhin. 2017. Attention is all you need. In *Neural Information Processing Systems*.

Kelly Zhang and Samuel Bowman. 2018. Language modeling teaches you more than translation does: Lessons learned through auxiliary syntactic task analysis. In *Proceedings of the 2018 EMNLP Workshop BlackboxNLP: Analyzing and Interpreting Neural Networks for NLP*, pages 359–361, Brussels, Belgium. Association for Computational Linguistics.

VMWE identification with models trained on GUD (a UDv.2 treebank of Standard Modern Greek)

Stella Markantonatou[1,2], Vivian Stamou[1], Stavros Bompolas[1], Katerina Anastasopoulou[3], Irianna Vasileiadi Linardaki[3], Konstantinos Diamantopoulos[3], Yannis Kazos[1,4], Antonios Anastasopoulos[1,5]
[1]Archimedes, Athena Research Center, Greece
[2]ILSP, Athena Research Center [3]Department of Informatics and Telecommunications, NKUA
[4]National Technical University of Athens, NTUA [5]George Mason University, USA
Correspondence: marks@athenarc.gr

Abstract

UD_Greek-GUD (GUD) is the most recent *Universal Dependencies* (UD) treebank for *Standard Modern Greek* (SMG) and the first SMG UD treebank to annotate *Verbal Multiword Expressions* (VMWEs). GUD contains material from fiction texts and various sites that use colloquial SMG. We describe the special annotation decisions we implemented with GUD, the pipeline we developed to facilitate the active annotation of new material, and we report on the method we designed to evaluate the performance of models trained on GUD as regards VMWE identification tasks.

1 Introduction

Multiword expressions (MWEs) pose significant challenges in both linguistic annotation and computational processing due to their semantic and structural idiosyncratic properties. Previous research on MWEs in Modern Greek has explored their theoretical properties (2024) and led to the development of lexical resources documenting their semantic and syntactic behavior (Markantonatou et al., 2019). Lexicographic and annotation studies have examined various semantic, pragmatic, and methodological aspects of MWE (Giouli et al., 2019). Computational approaches have also contributed to MWE processing, focusing on MWE extraction (Stamou et al., 2020b) and multilingual parsing (Michou and Seretan, 2009; Foufi et al., 2019), as well as the evaluation of MWE discovery methods (Stamou et al., 2020a). However, despite these advancements, systematic treatments of MWEs within syntactic parsing adapted to Modern Greek remain relatively rare, with existing studies employing symbolic frameworks such as *Lexical Functional Grammar* (LFG; Samaridi and Markantonatou, 2014).

To address this gap, we introduce UD_Greek-GUD (GUD)—a new Universal Dependencies (UD v2) treebank (de Marneffe et al., 2021) for SMG. GUD integrates rich morphological and syntactic annotations with explicit *verbal MWEs* (VMWEs) annotation, in the spirit of the PARSEME guidelines (Savary et al., 2018). We outline specific linguistic decisions regarding tokenization, contractions, functional words, and diminutives/augmentatives, and propose a novel annotation strategy that integrates VMWEs information directly into the syntactic layer of the CoNLL-U format.

Building on this, we experiment with an annotation method that eventually encodes VMWEs as dependency sub-relations, facilitating automatic identification through syntactic parsing. The approach is shown to be promising for computational processing; open issues are the identification of nested, or overlapping expressions and of discontinuous MWEs (Constant et al., 2017).

This paper explores these challenges, evaluates their implications, and outlines ongoing efforts toward improved evaluation and their practical integration into syntactic parsing frameworks, offering new perspectives for linguistic annotation and computational processing in Greek and beyond.

2 Materials and annotation method

UD_Greek-GDT (henceforth GDT; Prokopidis and Papageorgiou (2017)) is the first UD treebank for SMG. Both GUD and GDT have been manually annotated for morphology and syntax, with GUD additionally annotated for VMWEs.

To develop GUD, a total of 1,807 sentences (25,493 tokens) were randomly selected from fiction texts in SMG. Additionally, 723 sentences (13,111 tokens), annotated specifically for VMWEs, were retrieved from IDION (Markantonatou et al., 2019), an open-source web database of SMG VMWEs, resulting in a combined corpus of 2,530 sentences. These VMWE usage examples

Proceedings of the 21st Workshop on Multiword Expressions (MWE 2025), pages 14–20
May 4, 2025

have been collected over the past 15 years through Google searches from social media, football sites, and other sources where colloquial SMG is used. The ArboratorGrew tool[1] was used to implement the annotation.

The annotation of GUD was carried out by graduate students in Language Technology (2021-2024) under the supervision of two of the authors. It proceeded in three rounds during this period. In the first round, students edited morphological and syntactic annotations obtained from models trained on GDT, developed morphological guidelines from scratch, and revised and enriched the syntactic guidelines originally produced by the GDT annotators. In the second round, one of the authors reviewed all annotated material and unified the guidelines. In the third round, the authors re-edited GUD and refined the material exemplifying VMWEs based on the established guidelines. Annotation decisions were reached through discussions and consensus among the annotators.

3 What is new about GUD

GUD and GDT share the same tokenization and word segmentation guidelines but differ notably in terms of morphological and syntactic annotation.

Morphological annotation: The main differences in the morphological annotation of the two treebanks are:

1. να *na* 'to', που *pou* 'that' (occurring $\geq$ 300 and $\leq$ 200 in GUD, respectively) introduce sentential complements of verbs. Additionally, *pou* introduces relative clauses and certain types of adverbial clauses, while *na* is also used to form periphrastic imperatives, express wishes and curses, and in other constructions, such as pointing to something. In GDT *pou* is tagged as PRON, and *na* as AUX. As shown in example (1a), GUD tags *pou* as SCONJ when it introduces sentential complements of verbs (Joseph and Philippaki-Warburton, 1987; Joseph, 1981) and as PRON (1b) when it introduces relative clauses. For *na*, GUD uses the tag SCONJ when it introduces sentential complements of verbs (2a), the tag AUX when it introduces main clauses expressing orders, wishes, curses, etc. (2b), and the tag PART in clauses with deixis (2c).

(1a)	Χαίρομαι	που	ήρθες
	chairomai	pou	irthes
	be.glad.1SG.PRS	that.SCONJ	come.2SG.PST
	'I'm glad you came.'		
(1b)	Αυτός	που	ήρθε
	aftos	pou	irthe
	he.NOM	that.PRON	come.3SG.PST
	'The one who came.'		
(2a)	Ελπίζω	να	έρθεις
	elpizo	na	erthis
	hope.1SG.PRS	to.SCONJ	come.2SG
	'I hope you come.'		
(2b)	Να	έρθεις	
	na	erthis	
	to.AUX	come.2SG	
	'You should come.'		
(2c)	Να	ήρθαν	
	na	irthan	
	there.PART	come.3SG.PST	
	'Here they are, they've arrived.'		

2. GUD adheres closely to the UD.v2 morphological guidelines and assigns the DET tag to 39 lemmas, whereas GDT assigns it to 17.

3. Unlike GDT, GUD annotates diminutives and augmentatives on nouns, adjectives, and adverbs. As shown in example (3), GUD assigns the lemma without a diminutive (or augmentative) affix to both forms with (3a) and without (3b) a diminutive (or augmentative) affix.

(3a)	λαμπάκι	(3b)	λάμπα
	Lemma=λάμπα		Lemma=λάμπα
	UPOS=NOUN		UPOS=NOUN
	Case=Nom		Case=Nom
	Gender=Neut		Gender=Fem
	Number=Sing		Number=Sing
	Degree=Dim		

4. GUD tags passive participles as VERB and GDT as ADJ. In GUD, participles not related to a verb in use are tagged as ADJ.

5. GUD does not use the case DAT tag because the dative belongs to the diachrony of Greek (Anagnostopoulou and Sevdali, 2020); spoken SMG uses the dative only in fixed expressions.

6. GUD tags fossilized forms from the diachrony of Greek with the UPOS X.

7. At the time of GUD's development, GDT and GUD used different sets of auxiliaries.

8. Unlike GDT, GUD provides an exhaustive annotation of both periphrastic and morphological degrees of comparison in SMG, following the established UD guidelines for comparative constructions.[2]

Syntactic annotation: The relations

[1] https://arborator.github.io/

[2] https://universaldependencies.org/workgroups/newdoc/comparatives.html

advcl:relcl, dislocated, and nsubj:outer are specific to GUD. Unlike GDT, GUD does not employ the dep relation.

GUD, but not GDT, analyzes the contracted forms *ston*, *stin*, *sto*, *stous*, *stis*, *sta*, which arise from the fusion of two pronouns: one in the genitive case and another in the accusative case. This phenomenon is linked to the broader loss of the dative-genitive distinction in SMG (Anagnostopoulou and Sevdali, 2020), where the genitive has been extended across various functions, while the accusative serves as the direct object. Although these contracted forms are formally identical to those formed by the combination of the adposition *se* and the definite article, they are structurally distinct (see Figure 1).

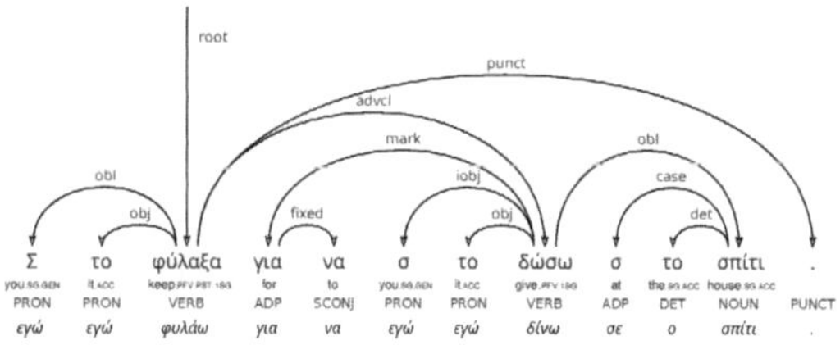

Figure 1: Dependency tree illustrating GUD's analysis of the Greek sentence 'I kept it for you so that I could give it to you at home'. The contractions (στο *sto*) differ in their underlying structure: the first two instances represent contracted pronoun forms (σου το *sou to*), combining a genitive pronoun and a direct object pronoun, while the last instance represents a contraction of the adposition (σε *se*) with a definite article (το *to*). For further details, see the main text.

4 Verbal MWE annotation

GUD contains material from fiction texts and additional 723 sentences (28% of the total GUD sentences) featuring 100 VMWEs, primarily of the verbal idiom type, along with some light verb constructions and verb-particle combinations. This classification of VMWEs follows the PARSEME typology (Savary et al., 2018). The sentences exemplify flexible usages of VMWEs in terms of morphology, word order permutations of the lexicalized parts of the VMWEs, insertion, and lexical variant pairs.

Our VMWE annotation strategy is in the spirit of the guidelines proposed by Savary et al. (2023) and incorporates suggestions from D. Zeman. In our setup, VMWE annotations are initially integrated into the MISC column (10th column) of the standard CoNLL-U format. Although the PARSEME project utilizes an additional 11th column in alignment with CoNLL-U Plus specifications,[3] widely-used annotation tools such as ArboratorGrew and parsing frameworks like Stanza currently support only the standard ten-column CoNLL-U format. Notably, the DEPS (9th) and MISC (10th) columns are generally excluded from dependency parsing training procedures (Qi et al., 2020).

To effectively bridge this gap, we created a preprocessing script, move_mwes.py, which transfers VMWE annotations from the MISC column to the DEPREL (8th) column by appending them as subrelation labels to the existing syntactic dependency labels. This transformation allows models such as Stanza to directly predict VMWE subrelations as part of their syntactic parsing task.

The VMWE annotation pipeline is clearly illustrated in Examples 1–3 (see Appendix):

- Example 1 shows the original treebank annotation prior to applying move_mwes.py.
- Example 2 illustrates the annotation after applying move_mwes.py, with VMWE annotations integrated into the DEPREL column.
- Example 3 presents a correct model prediction from Stanza, precisely identifying tokens that constitute an MWE.

Additionally, the move_mwes.py script supports reversing the annotation transformation, enabling the removal of VMWE subrelation labels from the DEPREL column and their restoration back into the MISC column. For systematic evaluation of VMWE predictions, we employ the evaluate_mwes.py script, which computes performance metrics detailed in Section 5. In this evaluation procedure, the annotations in the MISC column (10th column) serve as the gold standard reference against which the model predictions (encoded in the 8th column) are compared. Our integrated pipeline—[move_mwes.py → Model Prediction → move_mwes.py (reversal) → evaluate_mwes.py]—facilitates the efficient integration of VMWE predictions into active annotation workflows, thereby promoting continuous improvement in annotation accuracy and model performance.[4]

[3] https://universaldependencies.org/ext-format.html

[4] https://github.com/JohnKaz/mwes

5 Experiments and evaluation

We trained Stanza models in four experimental settings: three models combined the full GUD corpus (1,807 sentences) with additional subsets of 723, 500, and 300 sentences from IDION, each featuring $\geq$ 1 VMWE; the fourth model was trained exclusively on the 723 IDION sentences, each featuring $\geq$ 1 VMWE, without including the original GUD corpus. (Embeddings: GUD+GreekBert). We used only one test set, consisting of 200 sentences, each featuring $\geq$ 1 VMWE, with a total of 242 VMWE occurrences. Importantly, while many test VMWEs were not identical to those in the training set, a large portion were lexical variants of seen VMWEs. To ensure a diverse test set, sentences were selected to include different morphological forms of the head verb, as well as variations in word order and lexicalized component distance.

Table 1 presents the models' evaluation results, obtained using standard UD metrics.[5] These metrics assess general syntactic parsing performance. The observed differences between the original GUD and the expanded GUD+723 dataset suggest potential variability. A possible cause of this variability is the difference in annotation quality between GUD and the VMWE material, or the increased structural complexity introduced by the additional VMWE-rich sentences.

Since VMWEs are encoded as subrelations within the syntactic structure, their correct identification depends on the model's ability to accurately recover syntactic dependencies (as reflected in the UAS and LAS measures).

Setting[†]	Lemma	UPOS	UFEATS	UAS	LAS
GUD+723	90.99	94.78	87.18	88.03	81.62
GUD+500	90.99	94.97	87.80	87.94	82.27
GUD+300	90.23	94.69	86.93	88.03	81.25
723	90.12	94.01	86.39	86.67	78.94

Table 1: Performance metrics for four settings. [†]723/500/300 sentences each one featuring at least one VMWE.

We provide a targeted evaluation of VMWE identification. In CoNLL-U, a sentence is represented as a table with 10 columns and a set of rows numbered from 1 to m, $m > 1$. The representation of a VMWE with $l, l \leq m$ lexicalized components in column 8 consists of a set of not necessarily contiguous table cells containing information about the VMWE (a sentence may contain ≥ 1 VMWE): $\text{VMWE}_x^{C8} = \{r_{i_1}^{C8}, r_{i_2}^{C8}, ..., r_l^{C8}\}$ and in column 10: $\text{VMWE}_x^{C10} = \{r_{i_1}^{C10}, r_{i_2}^{C10}, ..., r_l^{C10}\}$, where in both cases $i_1 < i_2 < \ldots < l \wedge i_n, l, n \in \{1, 2, 3, \ldots, m\}$. These simplified definitions allow to evaluate the model's ability to discover/identify a VMWE but not its ability to classify it by type (e.g., idiom, light-verb construction, etc.).

We measure recall (R=TP/(TP+FN)) and precision (P=TP/(TP+FP)) of the model trained in four settings in two ways (see Table 2):

1. **Per-token**. Taking advantage of the tabular format of CoNLL-U, we use the following definitions (see also Savary et al. 2018,38):
TP if $r_i^{C8} \in \text{VMWE}_x^{C8} \wedge r_i^{C10} \in \text{VMWE}_x^{C10}$
FP if $r_i^{C8} \in \text{VMWE}_x^{C8} \wedge r_i^{C10} \notin \text{VMWE}_x^{C10}$
FN if $r_i^{C8} \notin \text{VMWE}_x^{C8} \wedge r_i^{C10} \in \text{VMWE}_x^{C10}$ (for all cases above $1 \leq i \leq l \leq m$).
2. **Per-unit**. A per-VMWE TP occurs if for all $r_i^{C10} \in \text{VMWE}_x^{C10}$ there is a Per-token TP. A Per-VMWE FN occurs when there is at least one $r_i^{C10} \in \text{VMWE}_x^{C10}$ that has a Per-token FN. Per-VMWE FP cannot be defined because we can only identify VMWEs represented in column 10.

Setting	PTR	PTP	PUR
GUD+723	0.813	0.867	0.606
GUD+500	0.807	0.847	0.655
GUD+300	0.791	0.850	0.588
723	0.827	0.880	0.624

Table 2: Performance evaluation metrics, including *per-token recall* (PTR), *per-token precision* (PTP), and *per-unit recall* (PUR) for four settings.

It should be noted that our models recognize both contiguous and non-contiguous VMWEs.

The performance analysis of our models, presented in Table 2, reveals interesting patterns regarding the effectiveness of different training configurations. The highest per-token precision (0.88) and recall (0.827) were observed in the 723-only training setting, suggesting that models trained exclusively on VMWE-rich data perform better at accurately identifying multiword expressions. However, the best per-unit recall (0.655) was achieved in the GUD+500 setting, indicating that larger training corpora can improve complete MWE identification, despite minor trade-offs in precision.

The GUD+300 setting consistently underper-

[5] https://github.com/UniversalDependencies/tools/blob/master/eval.py

formed, with the lowest per-token recall (0.791) and per-unit recall (0.588), reinforcing the importance of sufficient VMWE-specific training data. Interestingly, while GUD+723 and 723-only performed similarly in precision and recall, the latter showed a slight advantage in correctly predicting token-level VMWE components. Future work should explore larger, more diverse datasets and fine-tune MWE subrelations to further enhance identification accuracy.

6 Future plans

We intend to expand our experiments by using larger test sets and corpora that encompass a wider variety of MWE types. Another direction for future research and experimentation is exploring the dissociation of MWE subrelations from syntactic annotation, potentially by encoding them in the (currently empty) XPOS column. Additionally, we aim to develop more informative evaluation metrics to better assess system performance.

The GUD treebank remains a valuable linguistic resource for facilitating knowledge transfer across Greek dialects, contributing to an ongoing contrastive study of low-resource language varieties. Furthermore, the integration of MWE into the treebank could prove beneficial for various downstream applications that rely heavily on idiomatic expressions, such as offensive language detection.

7 Limitations

A key limitation of our approach is that the indexes encoded in the MISC column are not interpretable by the model, as they indicate VMWE units rather than POS tags, morphological features, or dependency relations. This results in at least two major consequences:

1. The model cannot distinguish between nested VMWEs, such as those shown in the manually annotated Appendix/Example 1. Additionally, the model itself does not generate VMWE indexes. We are working on a solution to this issue.

2. To integrate VMWE annotation into the active annotation cycle, we have developed a script that transfers VMWE annotations from subrelations in the dependency relations column (8th column) to the MISC column. However, since the model does not generate indexed VMWE annotations, the resulting MISC column lacks indexes. Consequently, manual annotation is required during the active annotation phase for newly parsed data.

Moreover, per-token evaluation is not entirely informative, as it does not indicate how many lexicalized elements of a VMWE unit are correctly recognized. We are currently exploring evaluation methods that better capture these nuances.

The test set included both seen and partially unseen VMWEs. The unseen instances shared only their fixed components with the seen ones but contained different verbal elements. In other words, the test set included lexical variants of the seen VMWEs. Ideally, our evaluation methods should differentiate between identification and discovery performance; however, this distinction is not currently made. We plan to address this issue in future work.

Acknowledgements

This work was been partially supported by project MIS 5154714 of the National Recovery and Resilience Plan Greece 2.0 funded by the European Union under the NextGenerationEU Program. It also received support from the CA21167 COST action UniDive, funded by COST (European Cooperation in Science and Technology).

References

Elena Anagnostopoulou and Christina Sevdali. 2020. Two modes of dative and genitive case assignment: Evidence from two stages of greek. *Natural Language & Linguistic Theory*, 38(4):987–1051.

Mathieu Constant, Gülşen Eryiğit, Johanna Monti, Lonneke van der Plas, Carlos Ramisch, Michael Rosner, and Amalia Todirascu. 2017. Multiword Expression Processing: A Survey. *Computational Linguistics*, 43(4):837–892. _eprint: https://direct.mit.edu/coli/article-pdf/43/4/837/1808392/coli_a_00302.pdf.

Marie-Catherine de Marneffe, Christopher D. Manning, Joakim Nivre, and Daniel Zeman. 2021. Universal Dependencies. *Computational Linguistics*, 47(2):255–308.

Vasiliki Foufi, Luka Nerima, and Eric Wehrli. 2019. Multilingual parsing and mwe detection. *Representation and parsing of multiword expressions: Current trends*, pages 217–237.

Voula Giouli, Vasiliki Foufi, and Aggeliki Fotopoulou. 2019. Annotating greek vmwes in running text: A piece of cake or looking for a needle in a haystack? In *Proceedings of the 13th International Conference on Greek Linguistics*. The University of Westminster, St. John's College, University of Cambridge, The H. M. Chadwick Fund, Cambridge University Press.

Brian D. Joseph. 1981. On the Synchrony and Diachrony of Modern Greek NA. *Byzantine and Modern Greek Studies*, 7:139–154.

Brian D. Joseph and Irene Philippaki-Warburton. 1987. *Modern Greek*. Routledge Kegan Paul, Oxfordshire, UK.

Panagiota Kyriazi and Aggeliki Fotopoulou. 2024. Multiword expressions of greek language: A case study of non-referential clitics in mwes. In Vojkan Stojičić, Ana Elaković-Nenadović, and Martha Lampropoulou, editors, *Proceedings of the 15th International Conference on Greek Linguistics. Vol. 2*, volume 15 of *International Conference on Greek Linguistics*, chapter 17, pages 292–309. University of Belgrade – Faculty of Philology, Belgrade, Serbia. Available online at http://doi.fil.bg.ac.rs/volume.php?pt=eb_ser&issue=icgl-2024-15-2&i=17.

Stella Markantonatou, Panagiotis Minos, George Zakis, Vassiliki Moutzouri, and Maria Chantou. 2019. IDION: A database for Modern Greek multiword expressions. In *Proceedings of the Joint Workshop on Multiword Expressions and WordNet (MWE-WN 2019)*, pages 130–134, Florence, Italy. Association for Computational Linguistics.

Athina Michou and Violeta Seretan. 2009. A tool for multi-word expression extraction in Modern Greek using syntactic parsing. In *Proceedings of the Demonstrations Session at EACL 2009*, pages 45–48, Athens, Greece. Association for Computational Linguistics.

Prokopis Prokopidis and Haris Papageorgiou. 2017. Universal Dependencies for Greek. In *Proceedings of the NoDaLiDa 2017 Workshop on Universal Dependencies (UDW 2017)*, pages 102–106, Gothenburg, Sweden. Association for Computational Linguistics.

Peng Qi, Yuhao Zhang, Yuhui Zhang, Jason Bolton, and Christopher D. Manning. 2020. Stanza: A python natural language processing toolkit for many human languages. In *Proceedings of the 58th Annual Meeting of the Association for Computational Linguistics: System Demonstrations*, pages 101–108, Online. Association for Computational Linguistics.

Niki Samaridi and Stella Markantonatou. 2014. Parsing Modern Greek verb MWEs with LFG/XLE grammars. In *Proceedings of the 10th Workshop on Multiword Expressions (MWE)*, pages 33–37, Gothenburg, Sweden. Association for Computational Linguistics.

Agata Savary, Marie Candito, Verginica Barbu Mititelu, Eduard Bejček, Fabienne Cap, Slavomír Čéplö, Silvio Ricardo Cordeiro, Gülşen Eryiğit, Voula Giouli, Maarten Van Gompel, Yaakov HaCohen-Kerner, Jolanta Kovalevskaitė, Simon Krek, Chaya Liebeskind, Johanna Monti, Carla Parra Escartín, Lonneke Van Der Plas, Behrang QasemiZadeh, Carlos Ramisch, Federico Sangati, Ivelina Stoyanova, and Veronika Vincze. 2018. PARSEME multilingual corpus of verbal multiword expressions. In Stella Markantonatou, Carlos Ramisch, Agata Savary, and Veronika Vincze, editors, *Multiword expressions at length and in depth: Extended papers from the MWE 2017 workshop*, pages 87–147. Language Science Press, Berlin. 10.5281/ZENODO.1471591.

Agata Savary, Sara Stymne, Verginica Barbu Mititelu, Nathan Schneider, Carlos Ramisch, and Joakim Nivre. 2023. Parseme meets universal dependencies: Getting on the same page in representing multiword expressions. *The Northern European Journal of Language Technology (NEJLT)*, 9(1).

Vivian Stamou, Marilena Malli, Penny Takorou, Artemis Xylogianni, and Stella Markantonatou. 2020a. Evaluation of Verb Multiword Expressions discovery measurements in literature corpora of Modern Greek. In *Lexicography for Inclusion: Proceedings of the 19th EURALEX International Congress, 7-9 September 2021, Alexandroupolis, Vol. 1*, pages 295–301, Alexandroupolis. Democritus University of Thrace.

Vivian Stamou, Artemis Xylogianni, Marilena Malli, Penny Takorou, and Stella Markantonatou. 2020b. VMWE discovery: a comparative analysis between literature and Twitter corpora. In *Proceedings of the Joint Workshop on Multiword Expressions and Electronic Lexicons*, pages 66–72, online. Association for Computational Linguistics.

A Appendix

που	μας	έχεις	αφήσει
pou	mas	echis	afisi
because	us	have.2.SING	left
σύξυλους	στους	πέντε	δρόμους
sixilous	stous	pente	dromous
petrified	in.the	five	roads

'because you have astounded and abandoned us'

text = που μας έχεις αφήσει σύξυλους στους πέντε δρόμους.
18 που που SCONJ _ _ 21 mark _ _
19 μας εγώ PRON _ Case=Acc|Number=Plur|Person=1|PronType=Prs 21 obj _ _
20 έχεις έχω AUX _ Mood=Ind|Number=Sing|Person=2|Tense=Pres |VerbForm=Fin |Voice=Act 21 aux _ _
21 αφήσει αφήνω VERB _ Aspect=Perf|Mood=Ind|VerbForm=Inf|Voice=Act 2 advcl _ mwe=1,2:VID
22 σύξυλους σύξυλος ADJ _ Case=Acc|Gender=Masc|Number=Plur 21 xcomp _ mwe=1
23 στους στου ADP _ Case=Acc|Gender=Masc|Number=Plur 25 case _ mwe=2
24 πέντε πέντε NUM _ Case=Acc|Gender=Masc|Number=Plur |NumType=Card 25 nummod _ mwe=2
25 δρόμους δρόμος NOUN _ Case=Acc|Gender=Masc|Number=Plur 21 obl _ mwe=2:VID
26 . . PUNCT _ _ 2 punct _ PunctType=Peri

Example 1: Annotation of 2 conflated VMWEs with the same verb head (afisei) and different lexicalized parts (sixilous, pente dromous).

Δεν	βγήκε	ποτέ	από	το	μυαλό
den	vgike	pote	apo	to	mialo
it	never	left.3.SING	from	the	mind
μου	και	ούτε	πρόκειται		
mou	kai	oute	prokeitai		
my	and	neither	will.happen		

'It never left my mind and it will not'

```
# text = Δεν βγήκε ποτέ από το μυαλό μου και ούτε πρόκειται.
1 Δεν δεν PART PtNg Polarity=Neg 2 advmod _ _
2 βγήκε βγαίνω VERB _ As-
pect=Perf|Mood=Ind|Number=Sing|Person=3|Tense=Past|VerbForm=Fin|Voice=Act
0 root:vid _ mwe=1:VID
3 ποτέ ποτέ ADV _ _ 2 advmod _ None=Yes
4 από από ADP _ _ 6 case:vid _ mwe=1|None=Yes
5 το ο DET _ Case=Acc|Definite=Def|Gender=Neut|Number=Sing|PronType=Art
6 det:vid _ mwe=1
6 μυαλό μυαλό NOUN _ Case=Acc|Gender=Neut|Number=Sing 2
obl:vid _ mwe=1
7 μου εγώ PRON _ Case=Gen|Number=Sing|Person=1|Poss=Yes|PronType=Prs
6 nmod _ _
8 και και CCONJ _ _ 10 cc _ None=Yes
9 ούτε ούτε PART _ Polarity=Neg 10 advmod _ None=Yes
10 πρόκειται πρόκειται VERB _ As-
pect=Imp|Mood=Ind|Number=Sing|Person=3|Tense=Pres|VerbForm=Fin|Voice=Pass
2 conj _ _
11 . . PUNCT _ _ 2 punct _ PunctType=Peri
```

Example 2: Output produced by the script.

ο	πήχυς	για	φέτος
o	pichis	gia	fetos
the	bar	for	this.year
έχει	ανέβει	πολύ	ψηλά
echi	anevi	poli	psila
has	risen	very	high

'The bar for this year has risen very high'

```
# text = Ο πήχυς για φέτος έχει ανέβει πολύ ψηλά
1 Ο ο DET _ Case=Nom|Definite=Def|Gender=Masc|Number=Sing
|PronType=Art 2 det:vid _ _
2 πήχυς πήχης NOUN _
Case=Nom|Gender=Masc|Number=Sing 6 obj:vid _
_
3 για για ADP _ _ 6 case _ None=Yes
4 φέτος φέτος ADV _ _ 3 fixed _ _
5 έχει έχω AUX _
Mood=Ind|Number=Sing|Person=3|Tense=Pres|VerbForm=Fin
6 aux _ _
6 ανέβει ανέβω VERB _ As-
pect=Perf|Mood=Ind|Number=Sing|Person=3|VerbForm=Fin|Voice=Act
0 root:vid _ _
7 πολύ πολύ ADV _ _ 8 advmod _ None=Yes
8 ψηλά ψηλά ADV _ _ 6 advmod _ _
```

Example 3: Output produced by the Stanza model.

Using LLMs to Advance Idiom Corpus Construction

Doğukan Arslan[*] and **Hüseyin Anıl Çakmak**[*] and **Gülşen Eryiğit**[*] and **Joakim Nivre**[†]
[*]ITU NLP Research Group, Istanbul Technical University, Türkiye;
[†]Department of Linguistics and Philology, Uppsala University, Sweden
[*]{arslan.dogukan, cakmakh19, gulsen.cebiroglu}@itu.edu.tr
[†]joakim.nivre@lingfil.uu.se

Abstract

Idiom corpora typically include both idiomatic and literal examples of potentially idiomatic expressions, but creating such corpora traditionally requires substantial expert effort and cost. In this article, we explore the use of large language models (LLMs) to generate synthetic idiom corpora as a more time- and cost-efficient alternative. We evaluate the effectiveness of synthetic data in training task-specific models and testing GPT-4 in few-shot prompting setting using synthetic data for idiomaticity detection. Our findings reveal that although models trained on synthetic data perform worse than those trained on human-generated data, synthetic data generation offers considerable advantages in terms of cost and time. Specifically, task-specific idiomaticity detection models trained on synthetic data outperform the general-purpose LLM that generated the data when evaluated in a zero-shot setting, achieving an average improvement of 11 percentage points across four languages. Moreover, synthetic data enhances the LLM's performance, enabling it to match the task-specific models trained with synthetic data when few-shot prompting is applied.

1 Introduction

An idiom is a linguistic expression the meaning of which cannot be derived compositionally from the literal meaning of its parts. For example, the English idiom *break a leg* is used to wish someone good luck, rather than being taken literally as an instruction to cause physical harm. Due to this unique nature, idioms can negatively impact the performance of models in various tasks, such as machine translation, word-sense disambiguation, and information retrieval (Korkontzelos et al., 2013; Isabelle et al., 2017).

Idiom corpora are essential for enhancing performance in numerous tasks, as they provide both idiomatic and non-idiomatic examples to help models better differentiate between literal and figurative meanings. Training models on a diverse and well-structured idiom corpus can reduce problems such as incorrect translations (Fadaee et al., 2018) or misinterpretation of idiomatic expressions (Adewumi et al., 2022). Moreover, idioms present a significant challenge for language learners, who often struggle with the non-literal meanings and cultural nuances embedded in these expressions (Cieślicka, 2015). Comprehensive idiom corpora can support the development of educational resources and tools designed to help learners master idiomatic usage more effectively. Consequently, both computers and humans require high-quality samples that exemplify idiom usage scenarios and patterns.

Traditional approaches to constructing idiom corpora, such as those relying on the annotation of natural text (Cook et al., 2008), face several challenges. These include unbalanced distributions of idiomatic versus non-idiomatic examples, a lack of diversity in surface forms, and issues related to data scarcity. While recent methods, such as obtaining idiomatic sentences from native speakers via gamified crowdsourcing platforms (Eryiğit et al., 2022), offer potential solutions, they still have notable limitations and continue to be time-consuming and costly, as they require the involvement of native speakers for effective execution. Due to the challenging nature of the data collection process, only a handful of studies have presented idiom corpora that include both idiomatic and non-idiomatic examples. These corpora are mostly limited to a few languages and a small set of idioms (see Table 1).

Recently, large language models (LLMs), such as GPT-3 (Brown et al., 2020), have shown their effectiveness as generators in few-shot (Wang et al., 2021) and zero-shot (Gao et al., 2023) settings, and have been utilized to generate training data for downstream tasks (Meng et al., 2022). In this article, we use GPT-4 to generate idiomatic in-

Proceedings of the 21st Workshop on Multiword Expressions (MWE 2025), pages 21–31
May 4, 2025 ©2025 Association for Computational Linguistics

Dataset	#Sentences	#Idioms	Language
VNC-Tokens* (Cook et al., 2008)	2,566	53	en
Open-MWE* (Hashimoto and Kawahara, 2009)	102,856	146	ja
Sporleder and Li (Sporleder and Li, 2009)	3,964	17	en
IDIX (Sporleder et al., 2010)	5,836	78	en
SemEval-2013 Task 5b (Korkontzelos et al., 2013)	4,350	65	en
PARSEME (Savary et al., 2015)	274,376	13,755	bg, cs, fr, de, he, it, lt, mt, el, pl, pt, ro, sl, es, sv, tr
MAGPIE (Haagsma et al., 2020)	56,622	2,007	en
EPIE (Saxena and Paul, 2020)	25,206	717	en
AStitchInLanguageModels	6,430	336	en, pt
ID10M$_{silver}$ (Tedeschi et al., 2022)	800	470	de, en, es, it
ID10M$_{gold}$ (Tedeschi et al., 2022)	262,781	10,118	de, en, es, fr, it, ja, nl, pl, pt, zh
SemEval-2022 Task 2 (Tayyar Madabushi et al., 2022)	8,683	50	en, gl, pt
Dodiom* (Eryiğit et al., 2022)	12,706	73	it, tr

Table 1: Overview of various idiom corpora, listing the number of sentences, idioms, and the languages they cover (based on ISO 639-1 language codes). Datasets used in this article are marked with an asterisk.

stances, providing a time and cost-efficient alternative to human-involved methods. We generate sentence examples containing idioms in English, Italian, Turkish, and Japanese using zero-shot and enhanced prompting settings. To assess the quality of the LLM-produced corpora against human-generated data, we fine-tune relatively smaller models (i.e., BERT variants) specifically for the task of idiomaticity detection. Models fine-tuned on synthetic data never reach the performance of those trained on human-generated data, likely due to LLMs' potential struggle to generate data instances that fully capture real-world scenarios. However, the results show that with further refinement in the reasoning process of LLMs for synthetic data generation and the usage of synthetic data in few-shot prompting settings, LLM-generated synthetic data could yield more competitive outcomes, highlighting potential for future development. Notably, task-specific models trained on synthetic data outperformed the large language model that generated it (in zero-shot setting) when tested on human datasets, demonstrating the effectiveness of leveraging large models for data generation and then training smaller models and offers a more efficient and scalable approach to model development while also indicating the potential for LLMs to perform better after fine-tuning.

We also investigate the effect of prompt engineering on dataset quality by comparing zero-shot and enhanced prompting through separate model training. Zero-shot prompting yields slightly higher quality data,[1] likely due to the enhanced prompt's complexity. Additionally, we train multilingual BERT models using the constructed data sets for all five languages (English, Italian, Japanese, Turkish). The results show minimal performance differences, suggesting that synthetic data can effectively train multilingual models without significant loss compared to monolingual models.

In summary, our main contributions can be listed as:

1. We construct synthetic idiom corpora for English, Japanese, Italian and Turkish using GPT-4.

2. We investigate the impact of synthetic datasets on the idiomaticity detection task.

3. We examine the impact of prompt style on creating synthetic idiom data.

4. We investigate the performance of different task-specific BERT models and GPT-4 on the idiomaticity detection task.

5. We investigate the effect of few-shot prompting on GPT-4's performance in the idiomaticity detection task.

[1]Here, quality refers to the data's ability to improve model performance in the idiomaticity detection task.

6. We investigate the impact of multilingual training on the idiomaticity detection task.

The constructed corpora, along with the code for synthetic data generation and training and testing models for idiomaticity detection, are available on GitHub.[2]

2 Background and Related Work

Idiom corpora are corpora that include sentences containing potentially idiomatic expressions (PIEs), where these expressions are used in both idiomatic and literal senses in different contexts. The process of constructing an idiom corpus generally involves three steps: (1) selecting a list of idioms from phrases identified in previous studies (Hashimoto and Kawahara, 2009; Tayyar Madabushi et al., 2021) or from dictionaries (Sporleder and Li, 2009; Haagsma et al., 2020), with optional filtering based on certain rules (Saxena and Paul, 2020), frequency (Sporleder et al., 2010), or expert judgment (Cook et al., 2008); (2) obtaining sentences that contain PIEs from existing corpora (Sporleder et al., 2010), the web (Tayyar Madabushi et al., 2022), or directly from native speakers (Eryiğit et al., 2022); and (3) labeling the sentences based on the usage sense, typically as idiomatic or literal, using native speakers or language experts (Tedeschi et al., 2022). In Table 1, we provide an overview of various idiom corpora, listing the number of sentences, idioms, and the languages they cover.

Synthetic data generation involves creating artificial datasets that mimic the statistical properties and patterns of real-world data. Recently, LLMs have emerged as powerful tools for generating synthetic data, leveraging their vast training on diverse textual data to produce high-quality, contextually relevant examples (Long et al., 2024). The general paradigms for synthetic data generation with LLMs typically involve prompt engineering, where carefully designed prompts guide the model to produce desired outputs, and iterative refinement, where generated data is evaluated and adjusted for quality and relevance. For instance, Li et al. (2023) utilizes LLMs to generate synthetic data for classification tasks, and analyzed the effect of task and instance subjectivity on model performance, finding a negative impact. Tang et al. (2023) demonstrates that directly utilizing LLMs for tasks like clinical text mining may result in poor performance and raise privacy issues related to patient information; however, creating high-quality synthetic labeled data with LLMs and subsequently fine-tuning a smaller model can substantially improve the performance of downstream tasks. Additionally, Heng et al. (2024) introduces a cost-efficient strategy to leverage LLMs with moderate NER capabilities for generating high-quality NER datasets, which significantly improves performance compared to traditional data generation methods.

3 Methodology

To construct the idiom corpora presented in this article, we select a list of PIEs identified in previous research that provides a diverse set of idiomatic expressions in different languages. Specifically, we choose the PIEs identified by Cook et al. (2008) for English, Hashimoto and Kawahara (2009) for Japanese, and Eryiğit et al. (2022) for Italian and Turkish.

For synthetic data generation, we prompt GPT-4 (specifically gpt-4-0125-preview) to generate a sentence containing an idiomatic or literal use of an identified PIE in two settings: zero-shot prompting and enhanced prompting (See Appendix A, Figure 1 and Figure 2). In both settings, the prompts are always given in the target language and the system prompt instructs the model to generate sentences as if it is proficient in the target language, using it in rich and creative ways. The model is specifically asked to retain the lemma of the idiom constituents, since syntactic operations for idioms are mainly restricted by the idiom's individual components and its overall idiomatic meaning (Cacciari and Tabossi, 2014). Additionally, it is prompted to avoid the use of human names, as our prior prompting trials indicate that including names results in poor-quality samples. In the enhanced prompting setting, the model is further instructed to avoid repeating previously generated sentences, and it is observed that explicitly encouraging creativity (e.g., prompting the model to be creative) sometimes results in similar sentence structures.

In the zero-shot setting, the model is introduced to a PIE and simply asked to generate sentences using it. In the enhanced setting, a two-stage data generation approach is applied using the chain-of-thought method (Wei et al., 2024). First, the model is presented with a PIE and its use cases, and then it is asked to generate use cases for another target PIE. In the second step, the model is

[2]github.com/itunlplab/idiom-corpus-llm

instructed to generate sentences based on those use cases, incorporating diverse grammatical structures, including declarative-interrogative forms, affirmative-negative constructions, variations in sentence length, and inserting additional words between the components of the idiom. This approach aims to ensure diversity in sentence structures within the generated corpus. Additionally, the model is encouraged once in a while to generate sentences "as-if it is a human" and to be "creative", to prevent it from simply paraphrasing previous answers. Illustrations of the zero-shot and enhanced prompting settings are provided in Figure 1 and Figure 2, respectively, which can be found in Appendix A.

For each PIE in the aforementioned corpora, we generate 200 sentences using GPT-4 through the OpenAI API, with each PIE appearing in both its idiomatic and literal senses, equally represented with 100 sentences for each sense. Of these, 60 sentences are generated using zero-shot prompting, while 40 are generated using enhanced prompting. The average cost of generating each sentence is approximately $0.004. The overall statistics for the generated datasets are summarized in Table 2.

Language	#Idioms	#Sentences
English	53	10,600
Japanese	47	9,400
Italian	37	7,400
Turkish	36	7,200

Table 2: An overview of the generated datasets, including the number of idioms used and the generated sentences for each language.

4 Experiments

To evaluate the quality of the synthetically generated datasets, we applied it to n-shot prompting of GPT-4 and fine-tuning smaller models specifically for the task of idiomaticity detection. Additionally, to examine the effects of different prompting techniques on data generation, we fine-tune separate models using examples obtained from zero-shot prompting and enhanced prompting, allowing for a comparison between these two approaches. Finally, we measure and compare the performance of multilingual models fine-tuned on idioms from multiple languages against monolingual models to assess the impact of multilingual idiom inclusion.

4.1 N-Shot Prompting

We evaluate GPT-4's performance in idiomaticity detection across various n-shot prompting settings, including zero-shot, one-shot, and few-shot scenarios, using both synthetic and human-generated data. In the zero-shot setting, GPT-4 is prompted to determine whether a given sentence contains a PIE used in a figurative or literal sense, with the expected output being 1 or 0, respectively. For the one-shot setting, GPT-4 is provided with two example sentences—one illustrating a figurative usage of a PIE and the other illustrating a literal usage. We conduct experiments where example sentences containing PIEs are either randomly selected or include the same PIE as the test sentence.

To investigate the impact of the number of sample sentences, we extend the experiments to include 3 and 5 synthetically generated examples for figurative and literal senses, all containing the same PIE as the test sentence. Additionally, we examine how the order of example presentation influences GPT-4's performance by presenting literal sentence examples before figurative ones.

Further experiments incorporate human-generated data into the prompts. Since some idioms in the English dataset exhibit only figurative or only literal meanings, missing examples are substituted with randomly selected entries from the dataset. This strategy is intended to simulate real-world scenarios more accurately by addressing gaps in the dataset.

4.2 Task-Specific Fine-tuning

To determine whether the generated datasets are sufficiently comprehensive and of comparable quality to human-produced data, we fine-tune various BERT variants such as mBERT (Devlin et al., 2019), XLM-RoBERTa (Conneau et al., 2020), DistilBERT (Sanh et al., 2020), and language-specific BERTS such as Japanese BERT,[3] Italian BERT (Schweter, 2020b), and BERTurk (Schweter, 2020a) on the task of idiomaticity detection using synthetically generated datasets. This task involves identifying whether the PIE in a given sentence is used figuratively or literally, and classifying the sentences accordingly. Classification is performed using a linear layer added on top of the models. This layer takes the hidden state of the [CLS] token as input and outputs a vector of size equal to the number of target classes. The models are fine-tuned

[3] github.com/cl-tohoku/bert-japanese

with a batch size of 8 and a learning rate of 5e-6 for 4 epochs. Experiments are repeated three times using different seed values (5, 42, 1773).

During the training phase, 80% of the synthetic datasets are used for training, and 20% for validation, maintaining the zero-shot to enhanced prompting ratio of 60% to 40% in both sets. For comparison, the same models are also trained on human-produced data, utilizing 60% of each dataset for training and 10% for validation. The relative sizes of the synthetic and human-produced datasets vary depending on the language. For English and Japanese, the sizes are highly unbalanced in favor of synthetic or human-produced data, respectively. In contrast, for Italian and Turkish, the synthetic and human-produced datasets are closer in size, but synthetic data remains slightly larger. In the test phase, 30% of the real-world datasets are employed to evaluate both types of models, ensuring a consistent comparison between those trained with synthetic and human-produced data. The test set sizes vary considerably, with Japanese having a much larger test set (15,239 examples) compared to English (807 examples), Italian (2,284 examples), and Turkish (2,084 examples).

In the English dataset, sentences labeled as "unknown"[4] are excluded from both the training and testing sets. In the Japanese dataset, to align with the other datasets, idioms containing over 900 samples were selected, resulting in a focus on 47 idioms for further analysis instead of using the original dataset, which consists of 146 idioms. All examples from the Italian and Turkish datasets are used directly without any filtering. For idioms in the human-generated datasets, if only one sentence represented the idiom, it is included in the training set. If there are two sentences, they are distributed between the training and validation sets. For idioms with at least three sentences, the sentences are distributed across the sets based on the above ratios, ensuring that at least one sentence appeared in each dataset.

4.3 Zero-Shot vs. Enhanced Prompting

To investigate the contributions of the two distinct prompting methods used for producing synthetic data, the previously mentioned models are trained separately on the data generated by each prompting approach (i.e., zero-shot and enhanced prompting) and tested with the human-generated data as in the earlier step. To ensure a fair comparison between the two prompting strategies and to address potential concerns related to data imbalance, we also conduct tests using 40 sample subsets for the zero-shot prompting (i.e., zero-shot filtered). Additionally, to investigate and compare the diversity of human-generated data and synthetic data constructed using zero-shot prompting and enhanced prompting, we apply the remote clique score (the average mean distance of a data instance to other instances) and the Chamfer distance score (the average minimum distance of a data instance to other instances).

4.4 Multilingual Idiomaticity Detection

To assess the impact of the training set on model performance in the idiomaticity detection task, we train models using synthetic data, combining all languages into a single multilingual training set. Specifically, we merge all available languages, allocating 80% of the data for training and 20% for validation. The trained multilingual models are then evaluated on human-generated test sets, following the same procedure as in previous steps.

5 Results

This section summarizes the findings from our experiments, which include comparing the performance of n-shot prompted GPT-4 and BERT variants fine-tuned on synthetic and human-generated data, analyzing the effects of different prompting methods, and evaluating the performance of multilingual models trained on synthetic datasets.

5.1 N-Shot Prompting

The performance results of GPT-4 for idiomaticity detection across multiple languages in different settings—zero-shot, few-shot with synthetic data, and few-shot with human-generated data—are presented in Table 3. GPT-4 performs the weakest in the zero-shot setting across all languages, with English showing the lowest performance (55.72%). However, performance improves significantly in the few-shot setting, with all languages exhibiting a notable increase in F1 scores. The use of human-generated data yields the highest performance for all languages, and the improvements are consistent across them. These results suggest that GPT-4 benefits significantly from few-shot prompting. Additionally, while human-generated examples lead to the best performance, results with synthetically generated examples are not far behind, in-

[4] In this study, an instance of a PIE that the judge could not classify based on the context were labeled as "unknown."

		EN		JP		IT		TR	
		Train	**Macro Avg. F1**	**Train**	**Macro Avg. F1**	**Train**	**Macro Avg. F1**	**Train**	**Macro Avg. F1**
GPT-4	**Zero-shot**	-	55.72	-	75.36	-	71.80	-	66.39
	Few-shot (w/ synthetic)	-	78.99	-	81.42	-	85.12	-	82.66
	Few-shot (w/ human-generated)	-	83.24	-	83.21	-	87.65	-	86.62
Task-specific models	**mBERT**	GPT-4	75.52±0.5	GPT-4	75.35±0.2	GPT-4	71.71±1.2	GPT-4	70.37±0.4
		VNC-Tokens	84.92±1.7	Open MWE	93.10±0.2	Dodiom	85.36±0.2	Dodiom	82.43±0.6
	XLM-Roberta	GPT-4	77.52±0.8	GPT-4	78.46±1.3	GPT-4	76.44±0.9	GPT-4	76.41±0.5
		VNC-Tokens	84.86±0.5	Open MWE	94.24±0.1	Dodiom	86.35±0.2	Dodiom	85.52±0.2
	DistilBERT	GPT-4	77.27±0.8	GPT-4	57.37±0.8	GPT-4	64.45±0.2	GPT-4	61.75±0.2
		VNC-Tokens	**89.02**±0.1	Open MWE	85.05±0.1	Dodiom	79.20±0.8	Dodiom	74.68±0.3
	Language-specific BERT	GPT-4	77.06±0.6	GPT-4	80.76±0.3	GPT-4	76.56±2.3	GPT-4	78.15±0.6
		VNC-Tokens	88.66±0.8	Open MWE	**94.36**±0.1	Dodiom	**89.22**±0.2	Dodiom	**88.81**±0.5

Table 3: A performance comparison of models trained on synthetically generated datasets, human-generated datasets, and GPT-4, tested using human-generated datasets, with standard errors also provided for task-specific models.

dicating that synthetic data can still be valuable for idiomaticity detection. Furthermore, the number of examples and the order of presentation (figurative-first vs. literal-first) also influence performance (Table 6).

5.2 Task-Specific Fine-tuning

The results of comparing models trained on synthetic data with those trained on human-generated data are presented in Table 3. While task-specific models trained with human-generated data outperform those trained with synthetic data consistently, overall, best results are obtained with DistilBERT in English (89.02%) and language-specific BERTs in Japanese (94.36%), Italian (89.22%) and Turkish (88.81%). Notably, the language-specific BERT model for English also achieve the near-best performances.

The average performance differences based on data source (synthetic vs. human-generated), favoring models trained on human-generated data, are 10 percentage points (pp) for English (ranging from 7 to 12), 19 pp for Japanese (ranging from 14 to 28), 13 pp for Italian (ranging from 10 to 15), and 11 pp for Turkish (ranging from 10 to 13). Additionally, the performance gap between the best-performing synthetically trained model and GPT-4 in zero-shot setting is 22 pp for English (55.72% vs. 77.52% with XLM-Roberta), 5 pp for Japanese (75.36% vs. 80.76% with Japanese BERT), 5 pp for Italian (71.80% vs. 76.56% with Italian BERT), and 12 pp for Turkish (66.39% vs. 78.15% with BERTurk). In each language, the top-performing task-specific models trained on synthetic data is outperformed by GPT-4 in few-shot setting with synthetic data.

The results indicate that, while synthetic data is less effective than human-generated data in helping models distinguish between idiomatic and literal meanings, training smaller task-specific models with synthetic data generated from LLMs is a more efficient approach compared to directly using the LLMs in zero-shot setting. Additionally, using synthetic data is more cost and time efficient than relying on human-generated data. For instance, we generate sentences at a cost of $0.004 each, while Haagsma et al. (2020) reports a cost of $0.04 per sentence using a crowdsourcing approach, making our method 10 times cheaper. Moreover, annotating 100,000 examples in Hashimoto and Kawahara (2009) takes 230 hours for two people, whereas using an LLM can achieve the same task in approximately 45 hours, providing a solution that is 5 times faster. This highlights the significant time and resource savings offered by synthetic data generation, especially given the lengthy and expensive process of human annotation.

5.3 Zero-Shot vs. Enhanced Prompting

To analyze the effect of different prompts used in dataset generation on data quality, the performances of models fine-tuned with samples generated by two distinct prompt types (i.e., zero-shot and enhanced prompting) is analyzed and presented in Table 4. Additionally, the averages

	EN		JP		IT		TR	
	Method	**Macro Avg. F1**	**Method**	**Macro Avg. F1**	**Method**	**Macro Avg. F1**	**Method**	**Macro Avg. F1**
mBERT	Zero-shot	74.31	Zero-shot	74.86	Zero-shot	65.68	Zero-shot	68.78
	Zero-shot filtered	75.04	Zero-shot filtered	74.12	Zero-shot filtered	68.92	Zero-shot filtered	69.48
	Enhanced	75.05	Enhanced	70.07	Enhanced	67.08	Enhanced	67.49
XLM-Roberta	Zero-shot	77.41	Zero-shot	80.46	Zero-shot	71.01	Zero-shot	75.14
	Zero-shot filtered	78.29	Zero-shot filtered	78.50	Zero-shot filtered	69.47	Zero-shot filtered	73.04
	Enhanced	77.97	Enhanced	77.69	Enhanced	72.02	Enhanced	73.62
DistilBERT	Zero-shot	77.29	Zero-shot	59.37	Zero-shot	62.30	Zero-shot	58.73
	Zero-shot filtered	76.57	Zero-shot filtered	57.58	Zero-shot filtered	61.12	Zero-shot filtered	59.67
	Enhanced	**79.19**	Enhanced	54.27	Enhanced	60.81	Enhanced	57.04
Language-specific BERT	Zero-shot	76.70	Zero-shot	80.69	Zero-shot	**77.31**	Zero-shot	77.16
	Zero-shot filtered	76.43	Zero-shot filtered	**80.95**	Zero-shot filtered	73.47	Zero-shot filtered	**77.77**
	Enhanced	76.90	Enhanced	76.86	Enhanced	73.71	Enhanced	77.54

Table 4: A performance comparison of models trained separately using data generated from different prompting settings and evaluated with human-generated datasets.

from three experiments, conducted on randomly selected subsets of 40 samples (referred to as zero-shot filtered) drawn from a total of 60, are provided. The enhanced prompt shows benefits only for English, achieving the highest score of 79.19% by fine-tuning DistilBERT with data from enhanced prompting. However, overall performance differences between the two prompt types are minimal. One possible explanation for the limited improvement from the enhanced prompt is the performance gap between GPT-4's capabilities in English and non-English languages (Ahuja et al., 2023). The sample size does not yield consistent results between the zero-shot and zero-shot filtered prompts; it decreases performance in some models while increasing it in others.

The diversity analysis results (Figure 3) indicate that data samples generated with enhanced prompting generally exhibit greater diversity than those generated by humans or with zero-shot prompting, except for English, where human-generated data demonstrates higher diversity. While the results highlight the effectiveness of enhanced prompting in generating more semantically diverse outputs, the observation that models trained with enhanced prompt-generated data are less successful than those trained with human-generated data suggests that idioms are often used with specific sentence structures in real-world scenarios, rather than with varied sentence structures.

	EN	JP	IT	TR
GPT-4 (zero-shot)	55.72	75.36	71.80	66.39
GPT-4 (few-shot w/ synthetic)	78.99	**81.42**	**85.12**	**82.66**
Monolingual best (w/ synthetic)	77.52	80.76	75.56	78.15
mBERT	77.99	77.12	72.36	71.98
XLM-Roberta	75.19	79.21	77.35	77.00
DistilBERT	77.78	61.15	65.28	64.05
Language-specific BERT	**79.31**	78.56	79.55	79.32

Table 5: A performance comparison of multilingual models trained with merged synthetic datasets from different languages. The results reflect macro average F1 scores. First three rows provide GPT-4 tested in zero-shot and few-shot setting, and monolingual best performances, respectively.

5.4 Multilingual Idiomaticity Detection

The multilingual idiomaticity detection experiments yield notable results when comparing various model architectures across English, Japanese, Italian, and Turkish (see Table 5). In particular, smaller multilingual task-specific models consistently outperform GPT-4 in the zero-shot setting. However, GPT-4 generally performs better when synthetic data is also provided during the test phase (i.e., in the few-shot setting). The only exception is in English, where English BERT achieves 79.31% compared to GPT-4's 78.99% in the few-shot setting. Comparing monolingual and multilingual task-specific models reveals that the best multilingual model generally outperforms the best monolingual model, except for Japanese. This performance disparity suggests that model size alone does not dictate effectiveness in the idiomaticity detection task. Instead, specialized architectures, even if smaller, or different prompting settings can better capture the necessary patterns for identifying idiomatic expressions across various languages.

6 Conclusion

In this article, we create synthetic idiom corpora in multiple languages using GPT-4 and evaluate the effectiveness of models trained on these corpora for the idiomaticity detection task. Additionally, we have analysed the impact of the prompts used during the example generation process on corpus quality and assessed the influence of synthetic data on the performance of multilingual models.

The results indicate that while synthetic data may not match the quality of human-generated data, it offers significant advantages in terms of cost and time efficiency. Furthermore, smaller task-specific models trained on the synthetic data generated by the LLM outperform the LLM itself on the same task in the zero-shot setting. However, the LLM surpasses these models when synthetic data is also provided during the test phase (i.e., in few-shot prompting setting), highlighting the potential of synthetic data to enhance LLM performance. In this setup, the LLM achieves results comparable to using human-generated data in few-shot prompting setting, with a difference of only 2 percentage points for Japanese and Italian and 4 percentage points for English and Turkish.

Our findings also reveal that more complex prompts during the synthetic data generation process do not consistently produce higher-quality examples. These complex prompts produce beneficial results only in English, likely because GPT-4 performs more effectively in English than in other languages across various tasks. Overall, while the LLM's performance in idiomaticity detection remains lower than that of task-specific models, as is the case in other natural language processing tasks, its generalization potential makes it a highly valuable resource.

Future work could focus on more sophisticated prompting methods, refining the reasoning process of the utilized LLM, and expanding the study to include additional languages and LLMs. Additionally, the generated data could be used for instruction-tuning of LLMs to explore potential improvements in their ability to handle idiomatic expressions across diverse languages. Overall, our findings highlight the pivotal role LLMs can play in generating idiom corpora as a cost and time-effective alternative to methods relying on human effort, as well as the effect of synthetic data in enhancing LLM performance on idiomaticity detection task.

Limitations

One notable limitation of the article is that synthetic data generation relied solely on GPT-4. Additionally, we constructed synthetic idiom corpora for English, Italian, Japanese, and Turkish, which limits our scope as these languages might not encompass the full spectrum of idiomatic usage found across all languages. Moreover, our data generation employed two distinct prompting techniques. While these prompts showed promise, further refinement in reasoning process of GPT-4 or exploration of more advanced prompt engineering could enhance data quality. Another consideration is that, given GPT-4's extensive training on a large and diverse corpus, there is potential for data leakage, where the model may have encountered datasets used. Such exposure could affect the diversity and authenticity of the generated samples. Furthermore, our evaluation setup exclusively utilized BERT variants for training task-specific models. However, fine-tuning or instruction-tuning a broader set of models could yield additional insights and highlight model-specific strengths.

Acknowledgments

This work received support from the CA21167 COST action UniDive, funded by COST (European Cooperation in Science and Technology).

References

Tosin Adewumi, Foteini Liwicki, and Marcus Liwicki. 2022. Vector representations of idioms in conversational systems. *Preprint*, arXiv:2205.03666.

Kabir Ahuja, Harshita Diddee, Rishav Hada, Millicent Ochieng, Krithika Ramesh, Prachi Jain, Akshay Nambi, Tanuja Ganu, Sameer Segal, Mohamed Ahmed, Kalika Bali, and Sunayana Sitaram. 2023. MEGA: Multilingual evaluation of generative AI. In *Proceedings of the 2023 Conference on Empirical Methods in Natural Language Processing*, pages 4232–4267, Singapore. Association for Computational Linguistics.

Tom B. Brown, Benjamin Mann, Nick Ryder, Melanie Subbiah, Jared Kaplan, Prafulla Dhariwal, Arvind Neelakantan, Pranav Shyam, Girish Sastry, Amanda Askell, Sandhini Agarwal, Ariel Herbert-Voss, Gretchen Krueger, Tom Henighan, Rewon Child, Aditya Ramesh, Daniel M. Ziegler, Jeffrey Wu, Clemens Winter, Christopher Hesse, Mark Chen, Eric Sigler, Mateusz Litwin, Scott Gray, Benjamin Chess, Jack Clark, Christopher Berner, Sam McCandlish, Alec Radford, Ilya Sutskever, and Dario Amodei. 2020. Language models are few-shot learners. In *Proceedings of the 34th International Conference on Neural Information Processing Systems*, NIPS'20, Red Hook, NY, USA. Curran Associates Inc.

Cristina Cacciari and Patrizia Tabossi. 2014. *Idioms*. Psychology Press.

Anna B. Cieślicka. 2015. Idiom acquisition and processing by second/foreign language learners. In *Bilingual Figurative Language Processing*, pages 208–244. Cambridge University Press.

Alexis Conneau, Kartikay Khandelwal, Naman Goyal, Vishrav Chaudhary, Guillaume Wenzek, Francisco Guzmán, Edouard Grave, Myle Ott, Luke Zettlemoyer, and Veselin Stoyanov. 2020. Unsupervised cross-lingual representation learning at scale. In *Proceedings of the 58th Annual Meeting of the Association for Computational Linguistics*, pages 8440–8451, Online. Association for Computational Linguistics.

Paul Cook, Afsaneh Fazly, and Suzanne Stevenson. 2008. The VNC-tokens dataset. *Towards a Shared Task for Multiword Expressions (MWE 2008)*, page 19.

Jacob Devlin, Ming-Wei Chang, Kenton Lee, and Kristina Toutanova. 2019. BERT: Pre-training of deep bidirectional transformers for language understanding. In *Proceedings of the 2019 Conference of the North American Chapter of the Association for Computational Linguistics: Human Language Technologies, Volume 1 (Long and Short Papers)*, pages 4171–4186, Minneapolis, Minnesota. Association for Computational Linguistics.

Gülşen Eryiğit, Ali Şentaş, and Johanna Monti. 2022. Gamified crowdsourcing for idiom corpora construction. *Natural Language Engineering*, 29(4):909–941.

Marzieh Fadaee, Arianna Bisazza, and Christof Monz. 2018. Examining the tip of the iceberg: A data set for idiom translation. In *Proceedings of the Eleventh International Conference on Language Resources and Evaluation (LREC 2018)*, Miyazaki, Japan. European Language Resources Association (ELRA).

Jiahui Gao, Renjie Pi, Yong Lin, Hang Xu, Jiacheng Ye, Zhiyong Wu, Weizhong Zhang, Xiaodan Liang, Zhenguo Li, and Lingpeng Kong. 2023. Self-guided noise-free data generation for efficient zero-shot learning. *Preprint*, arXiv:2205.12679.

Hessel Haagsma, Johan Bos, and Malvina Nissim. 2020. MAGPIE: A large corpus of potentially idiomatic expressions. In *Proceedings of the Twelfth Language Resources and Evaluation Conference*, pages 279–287, Marseille, France. European Language Resources Association.

Chikara Hashimoto and Daisuke Kawahara. 2009. Compilation of an idiom example database for supervised idiom identification. *Language Resources and Evaluation*, 43(4):355–384.

Yuzhao Heng, Chunyuan Deng, Yitong Li, Yue Yu, Yinghao Li, Rongzhi Zhang, and Chao Zhang. 2024. Proggen: Generating named entity recognition datasets step-by-step with self-reflexive large language models. In *Findings of the Association for Computational Linguistics ACL 2024*, page 15992–16030. Association for Computational Linguistics.

Pierre Isabelle, Colin Cherry, and George Foster. 2017. A challenge set approach to evaluating machine translation. In *Proceedings of the 2017 Conference on Empirical Methods in Natural Language Processing*, pages 2486–2496, Copenhagen, Denmark. Association for Computational Linguistics.

Ioannis Korkontzelos, Torsten Zesch, Fabio Massimo Zanzotto, and Chris Biemann. 2013. SemEval-2013 task 5: Evaluating phrasal semantics. In *Second Joint Conference on Lexical and Computational Semantics (*SEM), Volume 2: Proceedings of the Seventh International Workshop on Semantic Evaluation (SemEval 2013)*, pages 39–47, Atlanta, Georgia, USA. Association for Computational Linguistics.

Zhuoyan Li, Hangxiao Zhu, Zhuoran Lu, and Ming Yin. 2023. Synthetic data generation with large language models for text classification: Potential and limitations. In *Proceedings of the 2023 Conference on Empirical Methods in Natural Language Processing*, pages 10443–10461, Singapore. Association for Computational Linguistics.

Lin Long, Rui Wang, Ruixuan Xiao, Junbo Zhao, Xiao Ding, Gang Chen, and Haobo Wang. 2024. On LLMs-driven synthetic data generation, curation, and evaluation: A survey. In *Findings of the Association for Computational Linguistics ACL 2024*, page 11065–11082. Association for Computational Linguistics.

Yu Meng, Jiaxin Huang, Yu Zhang, and Jiawei Han. 2022. Generating training data with language models: Towards zero-shot language understanding. In *Advances in Neural Information Processing Systems*, volume 35, pages 462–477. Curran Associates, Inc.

Victor Sanh, Lysandre Debut, Julien Chaumond, and Thomas Wolf. 2020. DistilBERT, a distilled version of BERT: Smaller, faster, cheaper and lighter. *Preprint*, arXiv:1910.01108.

Agata Savary, Manfred Sailer, Yannick Parmentier, Michael Rosner, Victoria Rosén, Adam

Przepiórkowski, Cvetana Krstev, Veronika Vincze, Beata Wójtowicz, Gyri Smørdal Losnegaard, Carla Parra Escartín, Jakub Waszczuk, Mathieu Constant, Petya Osenova, and Federico Sangati. 2015. PARSEME – PARSing and Multiword Expressions within a European multilingual network. In *7th Language & Technology Conference: Human Language Technologies as a Challenge for Computer Science and Linguistics (LTC 2015)*, Poznań, Poland.

Prateek Saxena and Soma Paul. 2020. Epie dataset: A corpus for possible idiomatic expressions. In *Text, Speech, and Dialogue: 23rd International Conference, TSD 2020, Brno, Czech Republic, September 8–11, 2020, Proceedings*, page 87–94, Berlin, Heidelberg. Springer-Verlag.

Stefan Schweter. 2020a. BERTurk - BERT models for Turkish.

Stefan Schweter. 2020b. Italian BERT and ELECTRA models.

Caroline Sporleder and Linlin Li. 2009. Unsupervised recognition of literal and non-literal use of idiomatic expressions. In *Proceedings of the 12th Conference of the European Chapter of the ACL (EACL 2009)*, pages 754–762, Athens, Greece. Association for Computational Linguistics.

Caroline Sporleder, Linlin Li, Philip Gorinski, and Xaver Koch. 2010. Idioms in context: The IDIX corpus. In *Proceedings of the Seventh International Conference on Language Resources and Evaluation (LREC'10)*, Valletta, Malta. European Language Resources Association (ELRA).

Ruixiang Tang, Xiaotian Han, Xiaoqian Jiang, and Xia Hu. 2023. Does synthetic data generation of llms help clinical text mining? *Preprint*, arXiv:2303.04360.

Harish Tayyar Madabushi, Edward Gow-Smith, Marcos Garcia, Carolina Scarton, Marco Idiart, and Aline Villavicencio. 2022. SemEval-2022 task 2: Multilingual idiomaticity detection and sentence embedding. In *Proceedings of the 16th International Workshop on Semantic Evaluation (SemEval-2022)*, pages 107–121, Seattle, United States. Association for Computational Linguistics.

Harish Tayyar Madabushi, Edward Gow-Smith, Carolina Scarton, and Aline Villavicencio. 2021. AStitchInLanguageModels: Dataset and methods for the exploration of idiomaticity in pre-trained language models. In *Findings of the Association for Computational Linguistics: EMNLP 2021*, pages 3464–3477, Punta Cana, Dominican Republic. Association for Computational Linguistics.

Simone Tedeschi, Federico Martelli, and Roberto Navigli. 2022. Id10m: Idiom identification in 10 languages. In *Findings of the Association for Computational Linguistics: NAACL 2022*, page 2715–2726. Association for Computational Linguistics.

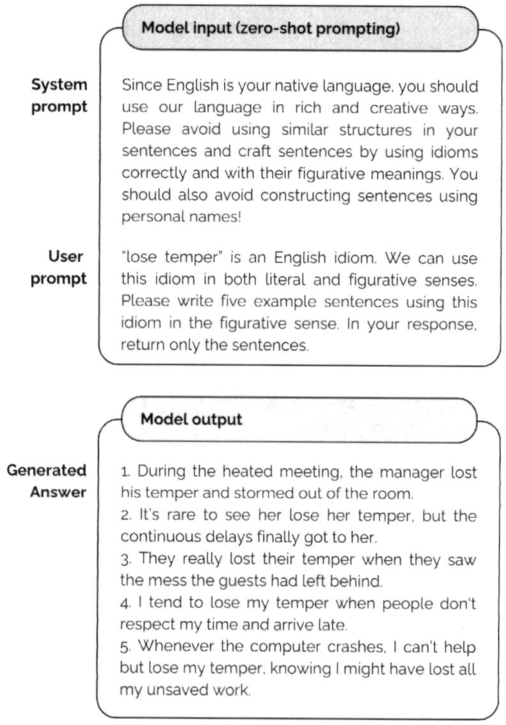

Figure 1: Illustration of a zero-shot prompting setup. The model input consists of a system prompt guiding idiomatic usage, followed by a user prompt requesting example sentences using an idiom in a figurative sense. The model output provides five example sentences following these instructions.

Zirui Wang, Adams Wei Yu, Orhan Firat, and Yuan Cao. 2021. Towards zero-label language learning. *Preprint*, arXiv:2109.09193.

Jason Wei, Xuezhi Wang, Dale Schuurmans, Maarten Bosma, Brian Ichter, Fei Xia, Ed H. Chi, Quoc V. Le, and Denny Zhou. 2024. Chain-of-thought prompting elicits reasoning in large language models. In *Proceedings of the 36th International Conference on Neural Information Processing Systems*, NIPS '22, Red Hook, NY, USA. Curran Associates Inc.

A Additional Figures

This appendix provides supplementary materials to enhance the understanding of the experimental setups and results presented in the main text. The figures and table included here illustrate key aspects of the data generation methods, evaluation settings, and diversity analysis.

Data Type	Setting	Same PIE?	# Examples	Order of Examples	Macro Avg. F1
Synthetic	Zero-shot	-	0	-	55.72
	One-shot	No	1	Figurative-first	51.16
		Yes	1	Figurative-first	65.57
	Few-shot	Yes	3	Figurative-first	74.96
		Yes	3	Literal-first	78.99
		Yes	5	Figurative-first	73.90
Human-generated	Few-shot	Yes	3	Literal-first	**83.24**

Table 6: Analysis of the effect of using synthetic or human-generated data, the number of examples, the order of examples, and whether the examples contain the same PIE as the test sentence in evaluating GPT-4 for English.

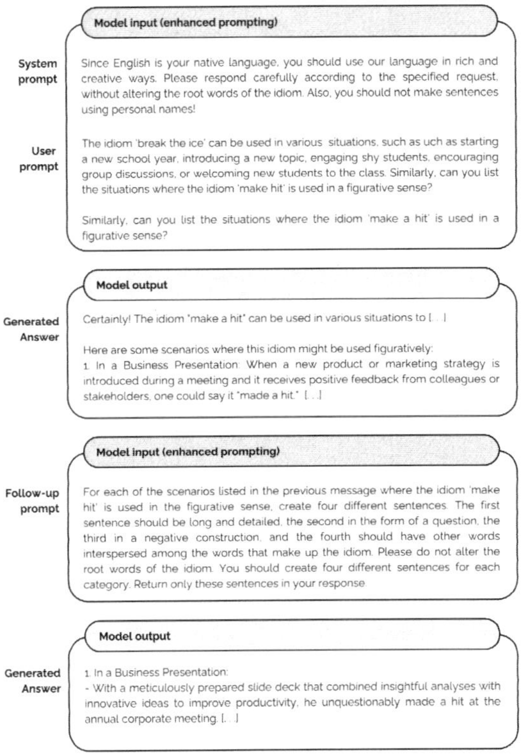

Figure 2: Illustration of an enhanced prompting setup. The model is instructed to explore an idiom in various scenarios, while following specific linguistic constraints. For each scenario, the model generates four unique sentences. Ellipsis ([...]) indicates omitted sections for brevity.

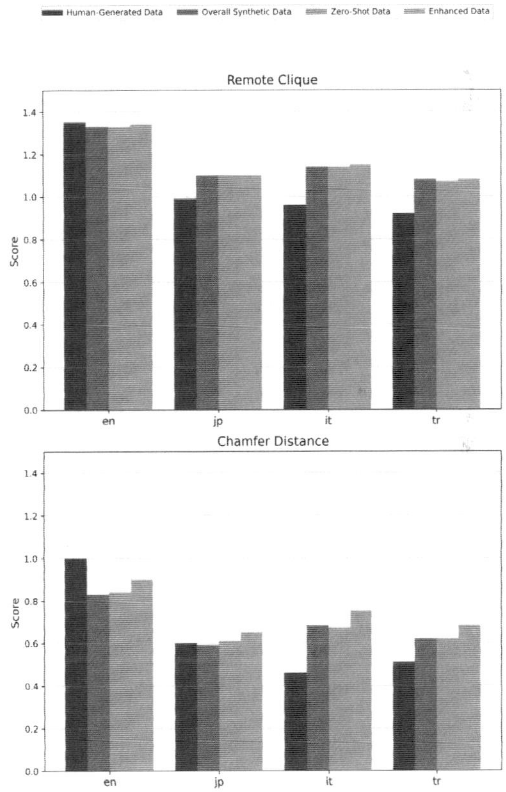

Figure 3: Comparison of the diversity between human-generated data and synthetic data produced using zero-shot and enhanced prompting, evaluated using remote clique score and Chamfer distance score. For both metrics, higher scores indicate greater diversity.

Gathering Compositionality Ratings of Ambiguous Noun-Adjective Multiword Expressions in Galician

Laura Castro and **Marcos Garcia**
Centro Singular de Investigación en Tecnoloxías Intelixentes (CiTIUS)
Universidade de Santiago de Compostela
{laura.castro,marcos.garcia.gonzalez}@usc.gal

Abstract

Multiword expressions pose numerous challenges to most NLP tasks, and so do their compositionality and semantic ambiguity. The need for resources that make it possible to explore such phenomena is rather pressing, even more so in the case of low-resource languages. In this paper, we present a dataset of noun-adjective compounds in Galician with compositionality scores at token level. These MWEs are ambiguous due to being potentially idiomatic expressions, as well as due to the ambiguity and productivity of their constituents. The dataset comprises 240 MWEs that amount to 322 senses, which are contextualized in two sets of sentences, manually created, and extracted from corpora, totaling 1,858 examples. For this dataset, we gathered human judgments on compositionality levels for compounds, heads, and modifiers. Furthermore, we obtained frequency, ambiguity, and productivity data for compounds and their constituents, and we explored potential correlations between mean compositionality scores and these three properties in terms of compounds, heads, and modifiers. This valuable resource helps evaluate language models on (non-)compositionality and ambiguity, key challenges in NLP, and is especially relevant for Galician, a low-resource variety lacking annotated datasets for such linguistic phenomena.

1 Introduction

Multiword expressions (MWE) are idiosyncratic word combinations that constitute both major challenges and interests in Natural Language Processing (Sag et al., 2002; Miletić and Walde, 2024). The reasons lie in their intricate nature, as MWEs can fall within a wide range of semantic compositionality, and both the expressions and their constituents may present different degrees of semantic ambiguity, among other challenging properties that complicate most NLP tasks (Constant et al., 2017). An example of the former is *dark horse*, which can be interpreted literally as a horse that is of a dark color or idiomatically as an *unexpected winner*, depending on the context. An example of the latter is *common sense*, which may be understood as the most frequent meaning of a word, expressions, etc., but can also be used to refer to a person's reasonable or good judgment, depending on the context.

In the last two decades, numerous datasets have been put forward to address the issues MWEs pose (Ramisch, 2023). Among them, we can find the dataset of English noun-compounds with compositionality ratings (Reddy et al., 2011), as well as its extensions for French and Portuguese (Cordeiro et al., 2019). For German, there exists a noun-noun compound dataset featuring compositionality ratings (Schulte im Walde et al., 2016b). Similarly, (Schulte im Walde, 2024) put forward a collection that comprises German compounds with compositionality ratings, where compound and constituent properties are also taken into account. Related datasets contain binary or three-way classification (literal/idiom/other) of MWEs and Potentially Idiomatic Expressions (PIE), such as the VNC-tokens dataset (Cook et al., 2008), comprising about 3,000 verb-noun combinations in English, or MAGPIE (Haagsma et al., 2020), featuring around 56k English PIEs in corpora-extracted sentences, also featuring the literal/idiomatic/other classification. Likewise, the SemEval-2022 Task 2 introduced binary classification datasets in English, Portuguese, and Galician (Tayyar Madabushi et al., 2022).

These datasets present highly valuable resources for NLP tasks. However, most of them are annotated at a type level (Reddy et al., 2011; Cordeiro et al., 2019). On the other hand, those that operate at a token level (Garcia et al., 2021) tend to comprise MWEs that convey the same meaning in all sentences compiled in the dataset. Therefore, such resources may not account for the wide variety of senses these idiosyncratic expressions can have.

Proceedings of the 21st Workshop on Multiword Expressions (MWE 2025), pages 32–40

This situation is only more dire in the case of language varieties with few annotated resources, like Galician, for which few such works exist despite being essential to explore if language models can adequately process MWEs (Dankers et al., 2022; Miletić and Walde, 2024; He et al., 2025).

We address such shortcomings by presenting a collection of noun-adjective compounds in Galician. Their ambiguity is two-fold, since the dataset contains 1) potentially idiomatic MWEs with different degrees of compositionality, and 2) MWEs whose constituents present different degrees of ambiguity and productivity. These expressions are disambiguated, and their senses are contextualized and preliminarily classified in terms of compositionality. Overall, the dataset comprises 240 noun-adjective MWEs, and 322 senses. Each sense is contextualized in two manually-written and four corpora-extracted sentences, which account for a total of 1,858 contextualizing sentences.[1]

As a key contribution of this paper, this resource provides a set of human ratings on semantic compositionality levels for the 322 senses, along with additional linguistic information. In this regard, we enrich the dataset with frequency, ambiguity, and productivity data extracted from corpora and lexical resources for compounds and their constituents, used to explore potential correlations between linguistic features of the dataset. This publicly available dataset constitutes a valuable resource for evaluating language models on compositionality prediction and sense disambiguation tasks, among others.[2]

2 Creation of the Dataset

The goal was to create a dataset of potentially idiomatic, ambiguous MWEs in Galician, contextualized in validated sentences used to rate the expressions' senses in terms of compositionality.

2.1 Multiword expressions and sentences

The Galician version of the Wikipedia, parsed with UDPipe (Straka, 2018), was used to extract noun-adjective compounds, which were ranked by number of occurrences. From them, a manual selection was carried out. The goal was to obtain MWEs with different degrees of frequency, compositionality, polysemy, and semantic ambiguity. For that matter, 240 compounds spanning different frequency ranges were selected. Then, for each of them, a manual definition of the potential senses the MWEs could take up depending on the context was carried out, totaling 322 senses. As a preliminary classification, senses were classified in terms of compositionality as *compositional*, *partial*, or *idiomatic*, depending on the transparency of their constituents or lack of thereof.

Thus, in those instances where the transparency of both constituents made it possible to infer the meaning of the compound as a whole, the expressions where classified as *compositional*. In cases where only the meaning of one of the constituents was transparent, expressions where ranked as *partial*. Lastly, when the meaning of the expressions could not be inferred from the semantics of their constituents, they were graded as *idiomatic*. Multiword expressions themselves were also classified in an identical manner, although a fourth label was used for those polysemic expressions whose different senses could take up more than one classification depending on the context. In these cases, expressions where classified as *Potentially Idiomatic Expressions* (PIE).

Compositional examples include *especie vexetal* ('plant species') and *enfermidade mental* ('mental illness'). Examples of partially idiomatic senses include *sentido común* ('common sense', meaning a person's 'sound judgment') and *tubo dixestivo* (which does not literally refer to a 'digestive tube', but to the 'digestive tract'). As for idiomatic expressions, the dataset includes *aire libre* (which does not literally refer to 'free air', but to the 'outdoors'), and *fillo predilecto* (which is not a 'favourite child', but a honorary title towns and cities give to remarkable citizens that were born within their jurisdiction). Potentially idiomatic MWEs include other noun-adjective compounds, such as *red line*, which can be used literally to talk about a line of a red color which is painted on a paper, for example, as well as idiomatically to talk about a personal *boundary* or limit that shall not be crossed.

Additionally, to contextualize the expressions comprised in the dataset, two sets of sentences were constructed. Firstly, a language expert created a set of two manually-written sentences per sense (644 in total). Secondly, the Wikipedia corpus and other textual resources were used to extract examples containing the MWEs, of which four were selected

[1] We build upon the expressions and sentences previously compiled in Castro et al. (2025), enriching them with additional information to enhance their scope and applicability in this work.

[2] The dataset can be found at: https://github.com/Castro-L/MWE_dataset_gl

	MWEs				Senses			Sentences	
	Comp.	**Part.**	**Idiom.**	**PIE**	**Comp.**	**Part.**	**Idiom.**	**Manual**	**Corpora**
Number	115	65	18	42	189	85	48	644	1,214
Total	**240**				**322**			**1,858**	

Table 1: Distribution and total number of multiword expressions, senses, and sentences contained in the dataset. The numbers for MWEs and senses correspond to the preliminary classification in Compositional, Partial, Idiomatic, and Potentially Idiomatic Expressions (PIEs).

per sense by the language expert (1,214 in total). The set of manual sentences was curated by two linguists that reviewed the expressions, senses, and examples. The set of extracted sentences was validated by five other linguists, who verified that at least the first of the sentences had the same meaning as one of the manually-written, curated examples. Table 1 summarizes the composition of the dataset, while Table 5 (Appendix C) contains a set of examples of multiword expressions and corpora-extracted sentences comprised in the dataset. A more detailed description of the creation process and the composition of the dataset can be found in Castro et al. (2025).

2.2 Annotation of compositionality levels

Once the dataset was completed, an annotation task was carried out to gather human judgments on the semantic compositionality of the expressions and their constituents.

2.2.1 Annotation task

The annotation task featured the total of 322 senses. To properly contextualize them, one of the two manually-written sentences was randomly selected for each sense. Given that such sentences had been curated, they allowed us to ensure that examples were not ambiguous, represented each sense correctly, and provided enough context for annotators to make meaningful judgments. Due to time and personnel constrains, only one of the two sentences could be annotated. The procedure and subtasks were inspired by other relevant works where compositionality scores were gathered for MWEs (Reddy et al., 2011; Schulte im Walde, 2024).

Instructions: To instruct annotators on how to carry out the task, guidelines were provided. The goal was set to *reflect on each expression and the elements they are made up of, in terms of how literal or not they may be, based on the example sentences*, and annotators were asked to answer the questions in strict order.

Compound: Firstly, annotators were asked to consider the expressions out of context. The aim was to prompt linguistic reflection on each compound as a whole, both in terms of semantics and compositionality levels.

Example sentence: Subsequently, annotators were asked to read an example sentence. Given the length of some examples, and the fact that certain expressions allow for other linguistic elements to appear in-between constituents, both elements were highlighted in bold for readability's sake.

Compositionality of the compound: Next, annotators had to consider the meaning of the compound within the example, and to provide a score for it. To further prompt linguistic reflection, questions were posed as follows: *In the sentence, and on a scale from 0 (not literal) to 5 (literal), is [MWE] literally a [noun] that is [adjective]?*

Compositionality of the constituents: Then, annotators had to consider how literal or not literal the head and the modifier were based on the example, and to provide a score for it: *In the sentence, and on a scale from 0 (not literal) to 5 (literal), how literal or not literal is [noun/adjective]?*

2.2.2 Annotation process

Two sets of annotations were obtained. One of them was completed by the main language expert. The second annotation was carried out by six external annotators, all of them native speakers of Galician with background in Linguistics. Both the expert and the annotators were given the same instructions, and an identical annotation task to complete. In the case of the external annotators, given its size, the task was equally and randomly divided into six annotation sheets, so that each annotator would rate the same number of instances, up to completing a full annotation. As a result, we put forward two sets of annotations, as well as the mean values of both sets, for compounds, heads, and modifiers of all MWEs and senses featured in the original dataset.

2.3 Results

Compositionality scores: Mean values were determined for the compounds, heads, and modifiers of the senses that had been preliminarily classified as *compositional*, *partial*, and *idiomatic*. Table 2 shows the mean compositionality scores of the MWEs and their constituents in each of the three classes. In general, the scores per class for the MWEs and the constituents follow the same tendencies as in similar datasets for other languages, only diverging in the compositionality score of the partially idiomatic compounds (1.87). A more detailed distribution of compositionality ratings per category can be found in the bloxplots in Appendix A.

Element	Idiom	Part	Comp
Compound	1.00	1.87	3.60
Head	1.25	2.57	3.88
Modifier	1.28	2.26	3.83

Table 2: Mean compositionality scores for compounds, heads, and modifiers belonging to senses classified as Idiomatic, Partial, and Compositional.

Similarly, annotation scores allowed us to obtain threshold values for the three categories. Thus, values ranging from 0 to 1.44 would be considered idiomatic; values ranging from 2.73 to 5 would be labeled as compositional, and in-between values would correspond to partially idiomatic compounds. Following such thresholds, 167 senses scored compositional values, while 155 were rated as non-compositional — from those, 93 senses were partially idiomatic, and 62 senses were considered idiomatic. In comparison with the preliminary classification, there are 100 senses that correspond to a different category. Of those hundred cases, 67% of instances obtained higher scores in human ratings than the threshold values of the preliminary category they had been given, thus indicating that the dataset may be more non-idiomatic than it was previously classified as.

Inter-annotator agreement: We determined 1) Krippendorff's α (Krippendorff, 2011) for the whole dataset using the scores provided in both sets of annotations, and 2) weighted Cohen's κ (Cohen, 1960) for the values of each annotator in their corresponding subsets. Krippendorff's α is 0.70 for compounds, 0.66 for heads, and 0.58 for modifiers. κ values for subsets range from 0.34 to 0.70. The complete inter-annotator agreement scores can be seen in Appendix B.

3 Frequency, ambiguity, and productivity

Following previous works on datasets of similar nature, frequency, ambiguity, and productivity data were obtained for compounds, heads, and modifiers of all senses, aimed at studying the relationships between these properties regarding their compositionality degrees (Schulte im Walde et al., 2016a; Schulte im Walde, 2024). For frequency and productivity, the original corpus of MWE extraction was used, while ambiguity data was extracted from Galnet (Gómez Guinovart, 2011).[3]

3.1 Frequency data

Regarding frequency, we enriched the dataset with the normalized frequencies of the compounds and their constituents: 1) **Compound frequency**, which represents the normalized frequency of each MWE within the original corpus; 2) **head frequency**, calculated using the total number of times it appears as a head in any noun-adjective compound, and 3) **modifier frequency**, computed also counting the total number of times it appears as a modifier in any noun-adjective compound within the corpus.

3.2 Ambiguity data

In this case, we have gathered: 1) **Head ambiguity**, where, for each syntactic head, the total number of synsets available in Galnet were extracted. In this case, we compiled two types of ambiguity data: 1.a) **overall head ambiguity** data, that represents the total number of synsets, regardless of its grammatical category, and 1.b) **category head ambiguity** data, where only those synsets corresponding to the *noun* category are accounted for. Besides, we obtained 2) **modifier ambiguity**, using the number of synsets available in Galnet for each modifier. As with heads, there are two types of data: 2.a) **overall modifier ambiguity** data, for the total number of synsets, and 2.b) **category modifier ambiguity** data, where only those synsets corresponding to the *adjective* category were taken into account.

3.3 Productivity data

Finally, we used the Wikipedia corpus to compile: 1) **Head productivity** data, where the total number of unique combinations within the extraction

[3]It is worth noting that Galnet is a relatively smaller lexical resource, containing approximately 36% of the synsets and 31% of the words found in the English WordNet (Guinovart et al., 2021).

	Frequency			Ambiguity				Productivity	
	Comp.	**Head**	**Modif.**	**Head-a**	**Modif-a**	**Head-c**	**Modif-c**	**Head**	**Modif.**
Comp.	0.063	0.081	0.136	-0.026	0.033	-0.022	0.023	0.082	0.143
Head	0.030	0.039	0.090	*-0.154*	0.141	*-0.152*	0.123	0.017	0.126
Modif.	0.103	0.093	0.130	0.085	-0.142	0.093	-0.138	0.105	0.083

Table 3: Spearman ρ correlations between the compositionality of the compounds, heads, and modifiers (rows) and frequency, ambiguity, and productivity (columns). Ambiguity includes overall (*-a*) and category-based (*-c*) results. Italics indicate p-values < 0.01, while underlining denotes p-values between ≥ 0.01 and 0.05. Results with p-values ≥ 0.05 remain unformatted.

corpus was determined for each head of the compounds present in the dataset. In this case, the normalized values are relative to the number of unique MWE combinations in the dataset; and 2) **modifier productivity**, where for each modifier in the dataset, the total number of unique combinations within the original corpus was determined. In the two cases, both raw and normalized values are provided.

3.4 Correlations

We computed Spearman's ρ correlation between the mean compositionality scores for compounds, heads, and modifiers and frequency data (compound, head, and modifier), ambiguity data (head and modifier, both overall and category-wise), and productivity data (head and modifier).

As it can be seen in Table 3, the correlations were overall weak, and mostly not significant. These results are in line with the findings of other related works, such as the German noun-noun compound dataset (Schulte im Walde et al., 2016b), where ρ between compositionality and productivity was -0.204 for heads and -0.023 for modifiers. Similarly, in a recent analysis of various datasets, Schulte im Walde (2024) found no correlations between compositionality scores and frequency, productivity, and ambiguity data across several English and German datasets, with the exception of the English NN-compounds dataset (Reddy et al., 2011), where moderate correlations were observed with frequency and productivity data. While our task was of a relative different nature, as ours operated at a token, not a type level, it is still worth noting that it follows the same general trend found in other works. However, since our dataset does account for the different senses MWEs can take up depending on the context, more exploration is needed, especially in relation to potential differences between monosemic and polysemic expressions.

4 Conclusions and Further work

In this work, we have introduced a dataset comprised of 240 noun-adjective MWEs in Galician that account for 322 senses, which present varying degrees of compositionality as well as semantic ambiguity. We have put forward human judgments on compositionality scores, which served to ascertain where MWEs fall within the spectrum of idiomaticity, and also provided frequency, ambiguity and productivity data. Using this information, we only found very weak and non-significant correlations with compositionality scores. The dataset, which comprises manually created sentences and examples extracted from corpora, fills a gap in annotated resources for Galician. The dataset will be freely released, except for the manually annotated sentences, which will be kept for evaluation purposes only to prevent data contamination in language models.

For future work, we aim to collect additional human ratings to strengthen the annotation of the dataset presented in this paper, ensuring greater reliability and consistency. Furthermore, we plan to apply the same methodology to construct similar datasets for other types of linguistic expressions, such as verb-object combinations. Additionally, it would be valuable to explore other linguistic properties and contextual cues that may influence human perception of semantic compositionality, providing deeper insights into the factors that shape meaning construction.

Limitations

Our dataset comprises a compilation of MWEs, senses, and contextualizing sentences. Additionally, it provides compositionality scores. They were the result of a meticulously crafted annotation task that contextualizes compounds in curated examples to ensure an adequate representation of senses. However, our main limitation is the number of human annotations obtained per sense. Our work was limited to seven annotators, which put forward two sets of ratings. Although insightful, the data provided could be greatly enriched by a higher number of ratings that fully represent the degrees of compositionality of the MWE senses. Additionally, Galnet made it possible to obtain four types of ambiguity data with which to explore the relationships between linguistic phenomena. However, it shall be pointed out that Galnet is a limited resource size-wise. Thus, further work is needed to gather more human judgments, as well as to further expand Galnet's number of synsets to allow for a finer representation of constituents' ambiguity.

Acknowledgments

This work was funded by MCIN/AEI/10.13039/501100011033 (grants with references PID 2021-128811OA-I00, and TED 2021-130295B-C33, the latter also funded by "European Union Next Generation EU/PRTR"), by the Galician Government ("Centro de investigación de Galicia" accreditation 2024-2027 ED431G-2023/04, and by the project with reference ED431F 2021/01) and the European Union (European Regional Development Fund - ERDF), and by a Ramón y Cajal grant (RYC2019-028473-I). This publication was also produced within the framework of the Nós Project, which is funded by the Spanish Ministry of Economic Affairs and Digital Transformation and by the Recovery, Transformation, and Resilience Plan, Funded by the European Union - NextGenerationEU (reference 2022/TL22/00215336), and by the Xunta de Galicia through the collaboration agreements signed in with the University of Santiago de Compostela.

References

Laura Castro, Anna Temerko, and Marcos Garcia. 2025. Compositionality and Ambiguity in Multiword Expressions: A Dataset for the Evaluation of Language Models in Galician. In *Progress in Artificial Intelligence*, volume 14969 of *Lecture Notes in Computer Science*, pages 228–240, Cham. Springer Nature Switzerland.

Jacob Cohen. 1960. A coefficient of agreement for nominal scales. *Educational and psychological measurement*, 20(1):37–46.

Mathieu Constant, Gülşen Eryiğit, Johanna Monti, Lonneke van der Plas, Carlos Ramisch, Michael Rosner, and Amalia Todirascu. 2017. Multiword expression processing: A survey. *Computational Linguistics*, 43(4):837–892.

Paul Cook, Afsaneh Fazly, and Suzanne Stevenson. 2008. The VNC-tokens dataset. In *Proceedings of the LREC Workshop Towards a Shared Task for Multiword Expressions (MWE 2008)*, pages 19–22.

Silvio Cordeiro, Aline Villavicencio, Marco Idiart, and Carlos Ramisch. 2019. Unsupervised compositionality prediction of nominal compounds. *Computational Linguistics*, 45(1):1–57.

Verna Dankers, Christopher Lucas, and Ivan Titov. 2022. Can transformer be too compositional? analysing idiom processing in neural machine translation. In *Proceedings of the 60th Annual Meeting of the Association for Computational Linguistics (Volume 1: Long Papers)*, pages 3608–3626, Dublin, Ireland. Association for Computational Linguistics.

Marcos Garcia, Tiago Kramer Vieira, Carolina Scarton, Marco Idiart, and Aline Villavicencio. 2021. Assessing the representations of idiomaticity in vector models with a noun compound dataset labeled at type and token levels. In *Proceedings of the 59th Annual Meeting of the Association for Computational Linguistics and the 11th International Joint Conference on Natural Language Processing (Volume 1: Long Papers)*, pages 2730–2741, Online. Association for Computational Linguistics.

Xavier Gómez Guinovart, Itziar Gonzalez-Dios, Antoni Oliver, and German Rigau. 2021. Multilingual Central Repository: a Cross-lingual Framework for Developing Wordnets. *arXiv preprint arXiv:2107.00333*.

Xavier Gómez Guinovart. 2011. Galnet: WordNet 3.0 do Galego. *Linguamática*, 3(1):61–67.

Hessel Haagsma, Johan Bos, and Malvina Nissim. 2020. MAGPIE: A large corpus of potentially idiomatic expressions. In *Proceedings of the Twelfth Language Resources and Evaluation Conference*, pages 279–287, Marseille, France. European Language Resources Association.

Wei He, Tiago Kramer Vieira, Marcos Garcia, Carolina Scarton, Marco Idiart, and Aline Villavicencio. 2025. Investigating Idiomaticity in Word Representations. *Computational Linguistics*.

Klaus Krippendorff. 2011. Computing Krippendorff's Alpha-Reliability. In *Departmental Paper (ASC)*, volume 43.

Filip Miletić and Sabine Schulte im Walde. 2024. Semantics of multiword expressions in transformer-based models: A survey. *Transactions of the Association for Computational Linguistics*, 12:593–612.

Carlos Ramisch. 2023. *Multiword expressions in computational linguistics: Down the rabbit hole and through the looking glass.* Aix Marseille Université.

Siva Reddy, Diana McCarthy, and Suresh Manandhar. 2011. An empirical study on compositionality in compound nouns. In *Proceedings of 5th International Joint Conference on Natural Language Processing*, pages 210–218, Chiang Mai, Thailand. Asian Federation of Natural Language Processing.

Ivan A. Sag, Timothy Baldwin, Francis Bond, Ann Copestake, and Dan Flickinger. 2002. Multiword expressions: A pain in the neck for nlp. In *Computational Linguistics and Intelligent Text Processing*, pages 1–15, Berlin, Heidelberg. Springer Berlin Heidelberg.

Sabine Schulte im Walde. 2024. Collecting and investigating features of compositionality ratings. In Voula Giouli and Verginica Barbu Mititelu, editors, *Multiword Expressions in Lexical Resources. Linguistic, Lexicographic and Computational Perspectives*, chapter 8, pages 269–308. Language Science Press.

Sabine Schulte im Walde, Anna Hätty, and Stefan Bott. 2016a. The role of modifier and head properties in predicting the compositionality of English and German noun-noun compounds: A vector-space perspective. In *Proceedings of the Fifth Joint Conference on Lexical and Computational Semantics*, pages 148–158, Berlin, Germany. Association for Computational Linguistics.

Sabine Schulte im Walde, Anna Hätty, Stefan Bott, and Nana Khvtisavrishvili. 2016b. GhoSt-NN: A representative gold standard of German noun-noun compounds. In *Proceedings of the Tenth International Conference on Language Resources and Evaluation (LREC'16)*, pages 2285–2292, Portorož, Slovenia. European Language Resources Association (ELRA).

Milan Straka. 2018. UDPipe 2.0 prototype at CoNLL 2018 UD shared task. In *Proceedings of the CoNLL 2018 Shared Task: Multilingual Parsing from Raw Text to Universal Dependencies*, pages 197–207, Brussels, Belgium. Association for Computational Linguistics.

Harish Tayyar Madabushi, Edward Gow-Smith, Marcos Garcia, Carolina Scarton, Marco Idiart, and Aline Villavicencio. 2022. SemEval-2022 task 2: Multilingual idiomaticity detection and sentence embedding. In *Proceedings of the 16th International Workshop on Semantic Evaluation (SemEval-2022)*, pages 107–121, Seattle, United States. Association for Computational Linguistics.

A Appendix: Distribution of compositionality scores

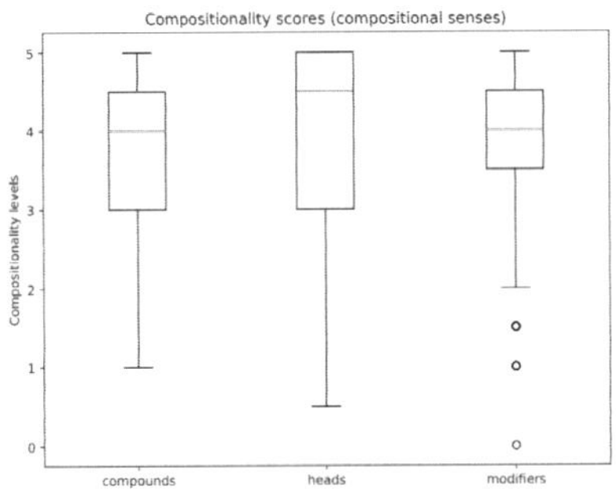

Figure 1: Scores for compounds, heads, and modifiers of expressions classified as compositional.

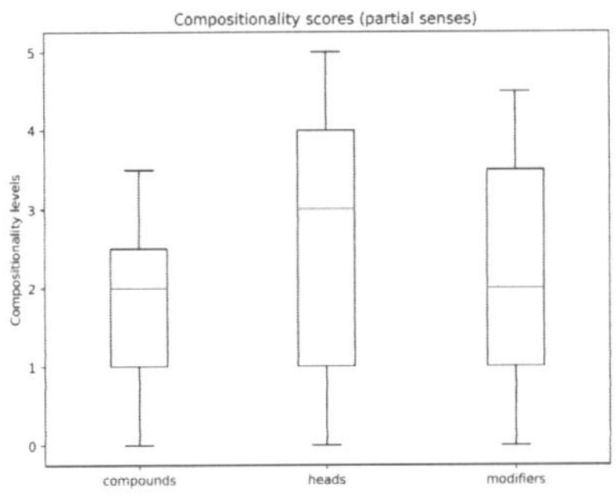

Figure 2: Scores for compounds, heads, and modifiers of expressions classified as partially idiomatic.

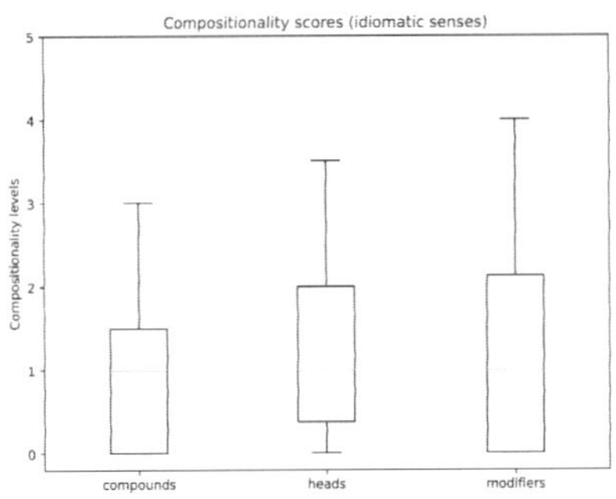

Figure 3: Scores for compounds, heads, and modifiers of expressions classified as idiomatic.

B Appendix: Inter-annotator agreement scores

Annot.	**Compound**	**Head**	**Modifier**
All (α)	0.705	0.663	0.584
Set-1 (κ)	0.549	0.518	0.489
Set-2 (κ)	0.520	0.565	0.434
Set-3 (κ)	0.473	0.463	0.345
Set-4 (κ)	0.528	0.526	0.525
Set-5 (κ)	0.640	0.708	0.540
Set-6 (κ)	0.556	0.558	0.577

Table 4: Agreement for compounds, heads, and modifiers per annotators' subsets. Top row are Krippendorff's α values for the whole dataset, while bottom rows refer to the weighted Cohen's κ of individual sets of MWEs.

C Appendix: Examples of multiword expressions and contextualizing sentences

Category	MWE	Galician Sentence	English Translation
Comp.	**bebida alcohólica** ('alcoholic drink')	A cervexa e todas as *bebidas alcohólicas* feitas a partir da fermentación tamén son produtos fúnguicos.	Beer and all *alcoholic drinks* made from fermentation are also fungal products.
	incendio forestal ('forest fire')	Este fenómeno aumenta considerablemente o perigo de *incendios forestais* nos outeiros e montañas.	This phenomenon considerably increases the risk of *forest fires* in hills and mountains.
	bandeira vermella ('red flag')	O 22 de setembro, a *bandeira vermella* reapareceu e pouco tempo despois a bandeira tricolor estoniana foi retirada.	On September 22nd, the *red flag* reappeared and shortly afterwards the Estonian tricolor flag was withdrawn.
Part.	**partido amigable** ('friendly game')	Por tal motivo a selección brasileira xoga os seus *partidos amigables* e clasificatorios en diferentes escenarios.	For this reason, the Brazilian national team plays its *friendly* and qualifying *matches* in different settings.
	paraíso fiscal ('fiscal paradise')	Moitos países teñen tratados fiscais bilaterais que evitan ao seus residentes pagar impostos dobres, pero poucos teñen tratados cos *paraísos fiscais*.	Many countries have bilateral tax treaties that prevent their residents from paying double taxes, but few have treaties with *tax havens*.
	bandeira vermella ('red flag')	Massa provocou unha *bandeira vermella* logo de chocar contra as barreiras na curva 3.	Massa caused a *red flag* after crashing into the barriers at Turn 3.
Idiom.	**sangue frío** ('cold blood')	A miña tía María recuperou o seu *sangue frío* e contestoulle con certa sequidade.	My aunt María regained *her composure* and answered him with certain dryness.
	vida útil ('useful life')	Aínda así, un uso prolongado do óxido nitroso pode acabar danando motor e acurtando a súa *vida útil*.	Even then, a prolonged use of nitrous oxide can end up damaging the engine and shortening its *service life*.
	bandeira vermella ('red flag')	Na lista de verificación de relacións emocionalmente abusivas, a manipulación é unha das *bandeiras vermellas* destacadas.	On the checklist of emotionally abusive relationships, manipulation is one of the prominent *red flags*.

Table 5: Examples of Compositional, Partial, and Idiomatic multiword expressions and corpora-extracted sentences contained in the dataset. Note that some of them, e.g., *bandeira vermella* are Potentially Idiomatic Expressions, with different compositionality scores depending on the context.

Survey on Lexical Resources Focused on Multiword Expressions for the Purposes of NLP

Verginica Barbu Mititelu
RACAI
Bucharest, Romania
vergi@racai.ro

Voula Giouli
Aristotle University of Thessaloniki
Greece
pgiouli@del.auth.gr

Gražina Korvel
Vilnius University
Vilnius, Lithuania
grazina.korvel@mif.vu.lt

Chaya Liebeskind
Jerusalem College of Technology
Jerusalem, Israel
liebchaya@gmail.com

Irina Lobzhanidze
Ilia State University
Tbilisi, Georgia
irina_lobzhanidze@iliauni.edu.ge

Rusudan Makhachashvili
B. Grinchenko Metropolitan Univ.
Kyiv, Ukraine
r.makhachashvili@kubg.edu.ua

Stella Markantonatou
ILSP and Archimedes Unit-RC ATHENA
Athens, Greece
marks@athenarc.gr

Alexandra Marković
Inst. for the Serbian Language SASA
Belgrade, Serbia
aleksandra.markovic@isj.sanu.ac.rs

Ivelina Stoyanova
Inst. for Bulgarian Language, BAS
Sofia, Bulgaria
iva@dcl.bas.bg

Abstract

Lexica of MWEs have always been a valuable resource for various NLP tasks. This paper presents the results of a comprehensive survey on multiword lexical resources that extends a previous one from 2016 to the present. We analyze a diverse set of lexica across multiple languages, reporting on aspects such as creation date, intended usage, languages covered and linguality type, content, acquisition method, accessibility, and linkage to other language resources. Our findings highlight trends in MWE lexicon development focusing on the representation level of languages. This survey aims to support future efforts in creating MWE lexica for NLP applications by identifying these gaps and opportunities.

1 Motivation

Multiword expressions (MWEs) pose a unique challenge in Natural Language Processing (NLP), primarily due to their semantic non-compositionality. This characteristic makes their automatic identification in text crucial for semantically driven downstream applications. Despite recent advances, including the advent of large (and small) language models, MWEs' inherent complexity and distributional properties continue to impede their effective processing. Lexical resources, that is, computational lexica dedicated to MWEs, are essential to address these challenges (Savary et al., 2019).

Our objective is to provide a comprehensive overview of the current landscape of MWE-related computational lexica that have been created for NLP purposes. The identification of relevant resources was meant to be as exhaustive as possible. Special emphasis was placed on the languages featured in the resources and their levels of representation in the NLP ecosystem. Thus, the survey aims to serve as a first step in highlighting the extent to which less-represented languages are included and supported in existing resources.

The paper is organized as follows. Section 2 presents previous surveys that focus on MWEs and outlines the new features offered by the current one. Section 3 discusses the sources and methodology we adopted to compile the list of resources with their relevant characteristics. The overview of the current landscape of MWE lexical resources is presented in Section 4, before concluding the paper by setting objectives for future work (Section 5).

2 Previous surveys

We are aware of four surveys heretofore focused on MWEs: Rosén et al. (2015) focused on the types of

Proceedings of the 21st Workshop on Multiword Expressions (MWE 2025), pages 41–57
May 4, 2025

MWEs that were more frequently annotated in treebanks at that time, namely named entities, phrasal verbs, and prepositional MWEs. Rosén et al. (2016) compared the way in which light verb constructions and verbal idioms were annotated in treebanks and proposed general guidelines for this. The survey by Mahajan et al. (2024) is focused on the methodologies and features required to implement MWE detection systems and is therefore of little relevance to our work.

Our survey builds on the one by Losnegaard et al. (2016) (henceforth, 'the PARSEME survey') that, in the framework of the PARSEME COST Action[1], provided a comprehensive overview of MWE resources, including lists, lexica (either dedicated to MWEs or including them alongside other lexical entries), and corpora such as treebanks available at that moment. The survey was based, on the one hand, on keyword querying of three language resource platforms: META-SHARE (Piperidis, 2012), ELRA[2] and SIGLEX-MWE[3]. On the other hand, the linguistic community was approached and asked to fill in a form about resources familiar to them.

General information about each resource was recorded, such as its name, a link to it, its type, contact information, the language(s) covered, its size, the maximum length of the contained MWEs, whether it includes non-contiguous expressions, its license and accessibility policies, as well as some more advanced information: relevant publications describing it, its special MWE features and the grammatical or lexical formalism (when applicable).

Our work extends the scope of the PARSEME survey by exploring and updating the state of MWE resources from 2016 to the end of 2024. Several resources published before 2016, either not included in the PARSEME survey or significantly updated after that, have also been added. Moreover, our survey expands the description of each lexical resource in terms of several criteria presented in Section 4.

3 Data collection

We aimed at a comprehensive collection of relevant data that would enable us to draw an accurate picture of the MWE resource landscape by cataloging MWE-related lexica and detailing their properties. To achieve this, we defined the criteria for resource inclusion, which focused on retaining only computational lexica, databases, and lists centered on MWEs while excluding corpora, terminological databases, and named entity lists, thus departing from the approach of Losnegaard et al. (2016), that considered both lexical resources and parsed corpora, i.e., treebanks, in their survey.

The sources for collecting information about MWE lexica include the following major repositories and databases:

1. *European Language Grid (ELG)*[4] (Rehm, 2023). This is the largest platform where language technologies and language resources alike, developed by public or private bodies, are cataloged and stored to increase their visibility among potential users and developers and to facilitate access to them. The catalog can be searched with keywords. To find the lexical resources of MWEs, we searched within the category *Lexical / Conceptual Resource* using the word 'expressions' and obtained 71 results. We examined their description to decide upon their inclusion in the dataset.
2. *ACL Anthology*[5] is an extensive repository of research publications from conferences in the field of computational linguistics. We retrieved all publications between 2016 and 2024 with their bibliographic description, including the title, keywords, and abstracts. We have automatically filtered the publications based on a pre-compiled list of 18 search terms (e.g., 'MWE', 'multiword expression', 'phraseme', etc.). A list of 1,251 publications was retrieved and was then checked by the authors.
3. *Europhras Conference Proceedings Repository*[6] provides lists of publications with relevant metadata. All publications after 2016 were checked. The resources retrieved overlapped with those from the ELG and ACL repositories.
4. *Phraseology and Multiword Expressions book series*[7] of Language Science Press was established in 2017. The series includes books and collections addressing topics related to theoretical, computational, and empirical approaches to multiword expressions, including lexical resources. Several resources were identified in these publications that provide a detailed description of the linguistic information and representation of MWEs.

[1] https://typo.uni-konstanz.de/parseme/
[2] https://www.elra.info/
[3] https://multiword.org/

[4] https://live.european-language-grid.eu/
[5] https://aclanthology.org/
[6] http://www.europhras.org/en/conferences
[7] https://langsci-press.org/catalog/series/pmwe

5. *Arxiv digital open access repository*[8] includes a wide range of scholarly articles in different areas. We have searched in the 'Computer science' category using the search terms list and identified several resources. While these mostly overlapped with previously identified resources, there were several new ones, mainly used in language processing applications.

In addition to the above, we asked community members working on MWEs for information on newly developed or updated resources not published in the examined repositories.

As noted, a systematic approach was adopted in this survey to identify and select resources related to MWEs. Inclusion criteria were defined to ensure that the reviewed resources fall within the scope of the survey and reflect the current state of MWE-related lexica that can be used in NLP tasks. The following inclusion criteria were applied: (i) date of creation, update, or publication of the resource, (ii) foreseen usage, (iii) type of lexicon (i.e., computational as opposed to lexica aimed at human users), and (iv) description of MWE entries. For comparison, only 45% of the monolingual and 66% of the multilingual resources in the PARSEME survey (Losnegaard et al., 2016, p. 2302–03) are classified as MWE lexica; the most significant proportion of the resources are lists of MWEs. In the present survey, we exclude lists unless they are supplied with linguistic information such as lemma, syntactic description, semantic properties, etc.

Summing up, the selected resources contain MWEs as entries, focusing on syntactic, semantic, and other information relevant to their structure, meaning, and usage. Resources that are freely available or have academic licenses were prioritized to support collaborative and accessible research. Finally, the survey focuses on collections supporting NLP tasks involving MWEs.

4 MWE lexical resources: overview

The result of this survey is a list of 66 resources (compared to 107 reported in the PARSEME survey) dedicated to MWEs or containing MWEs, alongside other words. The list records detailed information about each resource, such as publication date (or date of the last update), linguality (monolingual, bilingual, multilingual), resource type, acquisition method, licensing information, etc. These are extracted from the paper documenting the resource, from the resource website, or observed via manual resource inspection. The resources included in the survey are presented in Table 1 in the Appendix.

This section provides an overview of the lexical resources included in this survey along the following axes: (a) time span, (b) intended or foreseen usage of the resource, (c) linguality type (i.e., monolingual, bilingual, or multilingual lexicon) and language(s) covered, (d) types of MWEs included, (e) acquisition method, (f) accessibility and type of license, (g) representativeness, as well as (h) linking of MWE lexica to other resources (corpora or other lexica).

4.1 Time-span

The first inclusion criterion was the date of creation, update, or publication of the resources, focusing predominantly on lexical resources produced after 2016. Most identified resources are new; only three of them are enriched and updated. We also included several resources published before 2016 that were not included in the PARSEME survey. Figure 1 shows the number of resources reported in the PARSEME survey and our survey by year of publication. It can be seen that there was a peak in publishing resources in 2016, according to collective data from the PARSEME survey and ours. In the following years, a slower but steady trend is observed in the development of new MWE resources.[9] The distribution of resources by year of publication is plotted against relevant EU-funded initiatives for reference: META-NET Project[10], PARSEME COST Action[11], Horizon 2020 ELEXIS Project[12], UniDive COST Action[13].

4.2 Intended usage

The main inclusion criterion was intended or foreseen usage, as we were specifically interested in computational MWE lexica. However, we also identified lexical resources designed to serve both (downstream) NLP tasks and the needs and requirements of human users. The latter are less numerous

[8]https://arxiv.org/

[9]A possible explanation for the low numbers in 2021 is the limited number of conferences and forums for reporting research results due to the COVID-19 pandemic. The numbers for 2024 are expected to increase as publications from the second half of 2024 may not have been included in the examined repositories at the moment of our investigation.

[10]http://www.meta-net.eu/

[11]https://typo.uni-konstanz.de/parseme/

[12]https://elex.is/

[13]https://unidive.lisn.upsaclay.fr/

than the former: from the total of 66 resources, 52 (78%) are computational, 13 (19%) are both computational and for human users, and only one resource is non-computational. The PARSEME survey results report the same distribution: most resources are for NLP usage, and only a few are for human use.

Additionally, we evaluated the usage of the resources. Fifty resources were broadly designated as applicable for NLP purposes, with compositionality rating being the most prevalent NLP task (8 resources). Six resources are meant for human use. In the relevant documentation, the information about resource use was sometimes unclear (9) or absent (1).

4.3 Languages covered and linguality type

The linguality type of the resources refers to whether they are mono-, bi-, or multilingual. Of the selected 66 lexical resources, 51 (77.3%) are monolingual, 10 (15.2%) are bilingual, and 5 (7.5%) are multilingual. These lexica cover 37 languages (42 including varieties) in total. For comparison, the PARSEME survey included 14 bi- or multilingual resources (13% of the total resources count). The multilingual resources in the PARSEME survey are predominantly multilingual lists of MWEs or translational equivalents compiled from lexical-semantic networks (such as WordNet or BabelNet) with scarce or no linguistic description, and, as mentioned before, such resources are not included in the current survey.

More precisely, we identified monolingual lexica for 24 languages. Below, we list these languages, indicating in brackets the number of lexica available when more than one: Arabic (AR) (2 lexica), Bulgarian (BG) (2 lexica), Croatian (HR) (2 lexica), Czech (CZ) (5 lexica), Dutch (NL) (3 lexica), English (EN) (5 lexica), Estonian (ET) (2 lexica), Finnish (FI), French (FR), German (DE), Modern Greek (EL) (3 lexica), Hebrew (HE), Irish (GA), Italian (IT), Lithuanian (LT), Polish (PL) (2 lexica), Portuguese (PT) (2 lexica), Russian (RU) (2 lexica), Serbian (SR) (2 lexica), Slovenian (SL) (3 lexica), Spanish (ES) (3 lexica), Swedish (SV) (2), and Yiddish (YI). Notably, two lexica feature MWEs specific to two varieties of Spanish spoken in Chile (ES-CL) and Argentina (ES-AR). A minority language, Pomak, is represented by one MWE lexicon.

Another 10 lexica are bilingual, covering 12 languages (6 of which do not appear in monolingual resources) and 9 language pairs. Half of these are unidirectional from a source language to the target: Polish-English (PL-EN), English-French (EN-FR), English-Italian (EN-IT), English-Persian (EN-FA), Georgian-Modern Greek (KA-EL), Croatian-English (HR-EN); one resource is a bilingual dictionary that covers both directions, Basque-Spanish (EU-ES) and Spanish-Basque (ES-EU). One resource involves two languages, Bulgarian (BG) and Romanian (RO), linked using English (EN) as the pivot following the standard methodology for aligned wordnets. Finally, one resource involves two Indian language varieties, namely Hindi (HI) and Marathi (MR) – yet they are not aligned as translation dictionaries. Finally, 5 resources are multilingual, covering 10 languages in all (3 out of these languages appear neither in mono- nor in bilingual resources). The multilingual MWE resources vary only slightly in terms of the number of languages covered. One resource covers 5 languages, namely English (EN), German (DE), Italian (IT), Portuguese (PT), and Russian (RU), while another resource covers 4 languages, Japanese (JA), English (EN), Chinese (ZH) and Korean (KO). Two resources are trilingual; the first one includes English (EN), French (FR), and Portuguese (PT), and the second one includes English (EN), Chinese (ZH), and Japanese (JA). The final one includes one language as a source, Spanish (ES), with its varieties.

Our findings corroborate the observation by Losnegaard et al. (2016) that bilingual and multilingual MWE resources, including lexical ones, are rare. Despite years of research in this field, the scarcity of bilingual and multilingual MWE lexica remains a significant challenge. This limitation could impede research on MWE translation and cross-lingual NLP tasks.

4.4 Types of MWE lexica based on content

Both MWE-dedicated and MWE-aware lexica were identified. The former contains only MWEs of various types, such as verbal, nominal, or adverbial ones, as well as multiword named entities and terms. In contrast, general lexica that include MWEs alongside single-word entries are considered MWE-aware (or MWE-inclusive) lexica. They incorporate MWEs either as part of their macrostructure as independent entries or in their micro-structure as sub-entries under single-word main entries.

We also considered the type of MWEs in each

resource, whether all kinds of MWEs are included or are limited to some specific type(s) (nominal, verbal, compound phrases, idioms, collocations, or some combination of these types). Terminological resources were excluded from this survey based on the assumptions that (a) terms are not consistently selected according to solid criteria for idiosyncrasy and (b) no detailed linguistic descriptions of MWE-related phenomena are provided in pure terminological resources. However, we retained resources that either include terms alongside other types of MWEs (one resource) or handle multiword terms in a way that accounts for their idiosyncrasies.

We examined the MWE types that reference the morphosyntactic properties of the MWE and its function as part of speech (POS). While for 37.6% of the covered resources, all types of POS are declared to be included, for 29.4%, the POS is not specified. Of the remaining resources, those containing verbal MWEs are prevalent (17.7%), and two are limited to verb-noun structures. The resources of nominal MWEs account for 7.1% of the total count, with no additional restrictions.

4.5 Acquisition method

The acquisition method is also noteworthy. Most of the resources were reportedly developed either semi-automatically (26 resources or 39.9%) or fully automatically (8 resources or 12.1%). In contrast, 21 resources (31.8% – approximately one-third of the lexical resources in this survey) were developed manually. All these three development methods are mentioned by Losnegaard et al. (2016), but without offering any quantitative data. To a certain degree, the distribution reported for our survey is to be expected since many resources are compiled from pre-existing lexica or databases, which were processed at least partially automatically. However, a large proportion of the resources (over 70%) required at least some level of manual work, which shows the difficulty of providing reliable and accurate linguistic descriptions of MWEs automatically.

It is important to note that information on the acquisition method was not readily available for some resources, indicating a need for further investigations on reported works on the resource.

4.6 Accessibility

The availability of resources is crucial as it directly impacts their accessibility and potential for their (widespread) use. Resources, free or free for specific purposes, such as academic research, can foster greater collaboration and innovation within the community. Based on the information from the developers, we identified 49 (74%) resources that fall into these categories. Other resources are available for a fee (3 resources), which limits their accessibility. Additionally, for some resources, it remains unclear whether they are available at all (14 resources), further complicating their potential usage and integration into various downstream NLP tasks and applications. In the PARSEME survey, 95 resources (88% of the 107 resources) were found available, split almost even (46:49) between resources of unrestricted and restricted use, respectively.

Getting back to our survey, 21 resources (31.8%) are accessible through a dedicated link or platform, while 30 (45.5%) are available via specialized repositories, such as CLARIN, ELG, GitHub, LINDAT/CLARIAH.

4.7 Representativeness

Not all languages are equally represented in the language resource landscape. In this regard, we attempted to examine whether the level of language representation correlates with the number of MWE lexica available for that language. Hereon, we adopt the classification of languages presented by Maynard et al. (2022), the notion of Digital Language Equality (DLE) and the DLE metric defined by Gaspari et al. (2023). With respect to their overall state of technology support, we divide the languages into several categories: Good; Moderate; Fragmentary (higher); Fragmentary (lower); Weak or no support.[14]

According to Gaspari et al. (2023), DLE refers to the state where languages have the necessary technological support and situational context to thrive as living languages in the digital age. The DLE metric quantifies a language's digital readiness, its contribution to technology-enabled multilingualism, and its progress toward achieving DLE.

However, the ELE survey focused only on European languages and their level of representation

[14]Since the majority of European languages are of a fragmentary level of support, according to ELE reports (`https://european-language-equality.eu/deliverables/`), we split fragmentary level into two levels – fragmentary higher, which is closer to the moderate support level, and fragmentary lower, closer to the weak or no support level. For example, Finnish is very close to moderate level, Catalan would be on the very border between fragmentary higher and fragmentary lower, and all the other languages above this borderline would be fragmentary higher (Polish, Swedish, Dutch, Portuguese, Italian, and Finnish).

in the digital world, leaving out languages outside Europe. To fill this gap and account for languages other than those spoken in Europe, we used a metric defined by Joshi et al. (2020), who use somewhat different considerations for their measurements. Namely, they consider world languages and their role in language technologies. They suggest an existing correlation between language typology and the level of language resourcefulness. In short, they divide languages into six classes (0 to 5) according to the available resources and data. We align the six-point scale of Joshi et al. (2020) to the five-point ELE scale: merging level 0, which implies a total lack of resources, with level 1, and aligning them to Weak or no support; level 2 – Fragmentary (lower); level 3 – Fragmentary (higher); 4 – Moderate; 5 – Good).[15] In this way, we obtained data on the level of support for some of the languages which are not in the ELE survey: Chinese/Mandarin (Good/5), Japanese (Good/5), Arabic (Good/5), Russian (Moderate/4), Korean (Moderate/4), Hindi (Moderate/4), Persian (Moderate/4), Ukrainian (Fragmentary (higher)/3), Georgian (Fragmentary (higher)/3), Hebrew (Fragmentary (higher)/3), Marathi (Fragmentary (lower)/2), Yiddish (Weak or none/1). Pomak is not classified, but there are very limited resources for it, and we assume its level of support is 'Weak or none.' Although Spanish is generally classified as 'Moderate,' we have no sufficient information about the level of support for its variants, thus we classify them as 'Unknown.'

The overall distribution of languages in the reported resources with respect to their digital support is shown in Figure 2 (alternatively, the data are shown in Table 2 in the Appendix). Again, English is the best-represented language, appearing in nearly half of the language pairs as a source, target, or pivot language.

Figure 3 shows the distribution of resources with respect to the level of technical support of the languages involved (for bi- or multilingual resources, we assign the level of representation for the language at the lower or the lowest level of support) in the PARSEME survey and the new survey.

The data clearly shows that, while the community continues to develop MWE lexical resources for languages with good and moderate support, in recent years (since 2016), the focus has predominantly shifted toward compiling MWE lexica for lower-resourced languages (with fragmentary, weak, or no support). Furthermore, there has been extensive work on MWE lexica for non-European languages and language varieties, particularly varieties of Spanish.

Large corpora and rich embeddings remain scarce for low-resourced languages. This underscores the importance of reliable lexical data in facilitating the proper treatment of MWEs.

Moreover, the results show that resources for fragmentary lower-represented languages and fragmentary higher-represented languages alike are most linked to corpora or other data sources. In contrast, well- and moderately-represented languages tend to have lexical resources proportionally or equally linked to corpora and other data sources.

4.8 Linking of MWE lexica to other resources

Linking MWE lexica to corpora and other language resources would increase their applicability for various semantically oriented NLP tasks. Therefore, we further examined whether the identified lexica are linked to other language resources, such as corpora and other lexica (providing the name of the respective resource(s) where available). Of the lexical resources analyzed, only 22 (or 33.3%) are linked to a corpus, while the remaining 44 (66.7%) are not, as shown in Figure 4.

24.2% of the lexica covered in the survey are linked to other lexical resources (such as WordNet, BabelNet, or other computational dictionaries). As Figure 4 shows, a portion of the corpus-bound lexical resources is also linked to other lexical data sources.

Lexica linked to corpora are predominantly derived automatically (27.3%) or semiautomatically (50%), with only two cases (9.1%) of manually constructed lexica; in the remaining three cases, the method of compilation is unclear. No manually constructed MWE lexical resources are linked to other lexical data.

Overall, our analysis shows a deficiency in linking MWE resources to corpora and other lexical data. Corpora-linked MWE resources are predominantly automatically derived MWE lists with little

[15]There are some discrepancies in the alignment for two languages, namely for Irish (Weak or no support in ELE report and 2 in Joshi et al. (2020)) and Dutch (Fragmentary (higher) in ELE report and 4 in Joshi et al. (2020)). We decided to keep their ratings from the ELE report and acknowledge that the misalignment is small, only ±1 level. Also, Joshi et al. (2020) evaluates English at the same level as Spanish, German, and French, but we decided to keep the ratings from the ELE report. Full classification of languages by Joshi et al. (2020) is available here: `https://microsoft.github.io/linguisticdiversity/`.

or no linguistic description and no confirmed MWE status, which are not, as mentioned a few times, included in the present survey.

5 Conclusions and outlook for future research

We set out for this survey by examining several features of existing MWE resources. So, we described the macro-properties of computational lexica, such as linguality, availability, acquisition method, and linkage to external general lexica. In this section, we summarize and discuss our findings.

Regarding linguality, most lexica are either monolingual (e.g., Arabic, Portuguese, English) or bilingual (e.g., English-Spanish, Polish-English). The languages represented are predominantly European, with few exceptions, such as Arabic, Chinese, Japanese, Persian, Hebrew, and Korean. Less-resourced languages are underrepresented. The observation made by Losnegaard et al. (2016), namely that bilingual and multilingual MWE resources, including lexical ones, are hard to find, is still valid. English remains the best-represented language, appearing in nearly half of the language pairs as a source, target, or pivot language. The scarcity of bilingual and multilingual MWE lexica remains a significant challenge that could impede research and development of machine translation and other NLP-involved domains.

Most resources are MWE-dedicated, but some present both one-word and multi-word entries. MWE-dedicated resources are generally independent and not linked to general lexica. Resources tend to address the general language with few exceptions, such as lexica for specific purposes, i.e., expressions denoting sentiments. Again, a phenomenon of neglecting within-language diversity is observed as these (predominantly colloquial) language aspects have not been documented.

On the availability front, it is good news that most of the resources are included in comprehensive international catalogs or language repositories and are freely available, at least for research purposes. However, the description of the contents of the resources often lacks the detail and clarity required to understand precisely what type of information the resources offer.

Most of the resources were developed (semi-)automatically. However, the literature does not provide benchmarks or diagnostics for measuring the quality of resources, whether created automatically or manually.

The size of the resources varies, but generally, resources are not big; this might indicate the effort required to develop such resources. We chose not to include any information on the size of the resources since it is not uniformly documented or the size information is entirely missing.

Our survey has highlighted the role of EU-funded projects related to lexical resources, such as the COST actions PARSEME and UniDive, and Horizon-funded project ELEXIS. These initiatives, as well as the European Parliament resolution of 11 September 2018 on language equality in the digital age (2018/2028(INI))[16], have contributed significantly to the development of resources (see Figure 1). Related to this is the observation that more MWE resources have been developed recently for less-resourced languages rather than well-resourced ones. Although this might be due, among others, to the fact that well-resourced languages already possess MWE resources, one should consider that EU initiatives such as the ones listed above provide special encouragement for studying less-resourced languages and language varieties, in line with the EU priority to preserve multilinguality in Europe.

Our recommendations regarding the macroscopic properties of lexica are:
– Document the design and the contents of the resources thoroughly, clearly, and concisely.
– Make the resource freely available, at least for research purposes.
– Make the resource accessible through stable and friendly repositories.
– Ensure resource maintenance over time.
– Cover special usages of language, such as offensive speech.

In our future research, we will further explore the types of (linguistic) information about MWEs provided by these resources and the way in which it is described. We will further try to identify the best encoding practices.

6 Acknowledgments

This work received support from the CA21167 COST action UniDive, funded by COST (European Cooperation in Science and Technology). Also, part of this research was supported by Aristotle University of Thessaloniki (Grant ELKE-AUTH-

[16]https://eur-lex.europa.eu/legal-content/EN/TXT/?uri=CELEX%3A52018IP0332

13337) and the Ministry of Science, Republic of Serbia #GRANT 451-03-66/2024-03/200174.

References

Mohamed Al-Badrashiny. 2016. SAMER: A Semi-Automatically Created Lexical Resource for Arabic Verbal Multiword Expressions Tokens Paradigm and their Morphosyntactic Features. In *Proceedings of the 12th Workshop on Asian Language Resources (ALR12)*, pages 113–122.

Valentin Anders. 2022a. Chilenismos (deChile).

Valentin Anders. 2022b. Expressions (deChile).

Sandra Antunes and Amália Mendes. 2013. MWE in Portuguese: Proposal for a Typology for Annotation in Running Text. In *Proceedings of the 9th Workshop on Multiword Expressions*, pages 87–92, Atlanta, Georgia, USA. Association for Computational Linguistics.

Petra Barančíková and Václava Kettnerová. 2017. ParaDi: Dictionary of Paraphrases of Czech Complex Predicates with Light Verbs. In *Proceedings of the 13th Workshop on Multiword Expressions (MWE 2017)*, pages 1–10, Valencia, Spain. Association for Computational Linguistics.

Eduard Bejček. 2017. Czech Verbal MWEs. Charles University, Faculty of Mathematics and Physics, Institute of Formal and Applied Linguistics (UFAL).

Agnė Bielinskienė, Loïc Boizou, Ieva Bumbulienė, Jolanta Kovalevskaitė, Tomas Krilavičius, Justina Mandravickaitė, Erika Rimkutė, Jurgita Vaičenonienė, and Laura Vilkaitė-Lozdienė. 2022. The Database of Lithuanian multiword expressions. *https://arka.pastovu.vdu.lt/.*

Goranka Blagus Bartolec, Gorana Duplančić Rogošić, and Antonia Ordulj. 2024. INIKOL - Collocational Database for Learning Croatian as a Foreign Language. In *Proceedings of the 2024 CLASP Conference on Multimodality and Interaction in Language Learning*, pages 8–12, Gothenburg, Sweden. Association for Computational Linguistics.

Diana Bogantes, Eric Rodríguez, Alejandro Arauco, Alejandro Rodríguez, and Agata Savary. 2016. Towards Lexical Encoding of Multi-Word Expressions in Spanish Dialects. In *Proceedings of the Tenth International Conference on Language Resources and Evaluation (LREC'16)*, pages 2255–2261, Portorož, Slovenia. European Language Resources Association (ELRA).

Nyssa Z. Bulkes and Darren Tanner. 2017. "Going to town": Large-scale norming and statistical analysis of 870 American English idioms. *Behavior Research Methods*, 49(2):772–783.

Monika Czerepowicka and Agata Savary. 2015. SEJF -a Grammatical Lexicon of Polish Multi-Word Expressions. In *Proceedings of the Language Technology Conference 2015 (LTC 2015)*, page 5, Poznań, Poland.

Dutch Language Institute. 2016. Referentiebestand Belgisch-Nederlands. European Language Grid.

Samhaa R. El-Beltagy. 2016. NileULex: A Phrase and Word Level Sentiment Lexicon for Egyptian and Modern Standard Arabic. In *Proceedings of the Tenth International Conference on Language Resources and Evaluation (LREC'16)*, pages 2900–2905, Portorož, Slovenia. European Language Resources Association (ELRA).

ELRA. 2010. Terminology database of expressions.

ELRA. 2019. English-Persian database of idioms and expressions.

Ivana Filipović Petrović, Miguel López Otal, and Slobodan Beliga. 2024. Croatian Idioms Integration: Enhancing the LIdioms Multilingual Linked Idioms Dataset. In *Proceedings of the 2024 Joint International Conference on Computational Linguistics, Language Resources and Evaluation (LREC-COLING 2024)*, pages 4106–4112, Torino, Italia. ELRA and ICCL.

Beatriz Fisas. 2020. CollFrEn: Rich Bilingual English–French Collocation Resource. In *Proceedings of the Joint Workshop on Multiword Expressions and Electronic Lexicons*, pages 1–12.

Federico Gaspari, Annika Grützner-Zahn, Georg Rehm, Owen Gallagher, Maria Giagkou, Stelios Piperidis, and Andy Way. 2023. Digital language equality: Definition, metric, dashboard. In Georg Rehm and Andy Way, editors, *European Language Equality: A Strategic Agenda for Digital Language Equality*, pages 39–73. Springer International Publishing, Cham.

Voula Giouli. 2023. A model for representing the semantics of MWEs: From lexical semantics to the semantic annotation of complex predicates. *Frontiers in Artificial Intelligence*, 6.

Jette Hedegaard and Thomas Troelsgård. 2010. Dice in the Web: an Online Spanish Collocation Dictionary. In *Elexicography in the 21st century: new challenges, new applications. Proceedings of ELEX2009, Louvain-la-Neuve, 22-24 October 2009*, pages 369–374. Cahiers Du Cental 7. Louvain-la-Neuve, Presses Universitaires de Louvain.

Ferdy Hubers, Catia Cucchiarini, and Helmer Strik. 2020. Dedicated Language Resources for Interdisciplinary Research on Multiword Expressions: Best Thing since Sliced Bread. In *Proceedings of the Twelfth Language Resources and Evaluation Conference*, pages 4418–4425, Marseille, France. European Language Resources Association.

Institute of the Estonian Language. 2016. The Dictionary of Estonian Synonyms. European Language Grid.

Uxoa Iñurrieta, Itziar Aduriz, Arantza Díaz de Ilarraza, Gorka Labaka, and Kepa Sarasola. 2018. Konbitzul: an MWE-specific database for Spanish-Basque. In *Proceedings of the Eleventh International Conference on Language Resources and Evaluation (LREC 2018)*, Miyazaki, Japan. European Language Resources Association (ELRA).

Charles Jochim. 2018. SLIDE - a Sentiment Lexicon of Common Idioms. In *Proceedings of the Eleventh International Conference on Language Resources and Evaluation (LREC 2018)*.

Pratik Joshi, Sebastin Santy, Amar Budhiraja, Kalika Bali, and Monojit Choudhury. 2020. The state and fate of linguistic diversity and inclusion in the NLP world. In *Proceedings of the 58th Annual Meeting of the Association for Computational Linguistics*, pages 6282–6293, Online. Association for Computational Linguistics.

Kyoko Kanzaki. 2019. Towards linking synonymous expressions of compound verbs to Japanese WordNet. In *Proceedings of the 10th Global Wordnet Conference*, pages 185–190.

Maria Khokhlova. 2020. Collocations in Russian Lexicography and Russian Collocations Database. In *Proceedings of the Twelfth Language Resources and Evaluation Conference*, pages 3198–3206. European Language Resources Association.

Svetla Koeva, Ivelina Stoyanova, Maria Todorova, and Svetlozara Leseva. 2016. Semi-automatic compilation of the dictionary of Bulgarian multiword expressions. In *Proceedings of the Workshop on Lexicographic Resources for Human Language Technology*, pages 86–95.

Simon Krek, Apolonija Gantar, Cyprian Laskowski, Luka Krsnik, Iztok Kosem, Janez Brank, Kaja Dobrovoljc, Špela Arhar Holdt, Jaka Čibej, Marko Robnik-Šikonja, Bojan Klemenc, and Vojko Gorjanc. 2021. Multiword Expressions lexicon extracted from the Gigafida 2.1 corpus. *http://slovnica.ijs.si/*.

Cvetana Krstev, Ivan Obradović, Ranka Stanković, and Duško Vitas. 2013. An Approach to Efficient Processing of Multi-word Units. In Adam Przepiórkowski, Maciej Piasecki, Krzysztof Jassem, and Piotr Fuglewicz, editors, *Computational Linguistics*, volume 458, pages 109–129. Springer Berlin Heidelberg, Berlin, Heidelberg. Series Title: Studies in Computational Intelligence.

Murathan Kurfalı, Robert Östling, Johan Sjons, and Mats Wirén. 2020. A Multi-word Expression Dataset for Swedish. In *Proceedings of the Twelfth Language Resources and Evaluation Conference*, pages 4402–4409, Marseille, France. European Language Resources Association.

Svetlozara Leseva, Verginica Barbu Mititelu, and Ivelina Stoyanova. 2020. It Takes Two to Tango – Towards a Multilingual MWE Resource. In *Proceedings of the Fourth International Conference on Computational Linguistics in Bulgaria (CLIB 2020)*, pages 101–111, Sofia, Bulgaria. Department of Computational Linguistics, IBL – BAS.

Shuang Li, Jiangjie Chen, Siyu Yuan, Xinyi Wu, Hao Yang, Shimin Tao, and Yanghua Xiao. 2023. Translate Meanings, Not Just Words: IdiomKB's Role in Optimizing Idiomatic Translation with Language Models. *arXiv preprint*. ArXiv:2308.13961 [cs].

Chaya Liebeskind and Yaakov HaCohen-Kerner. 2016. A Lexical Resource of Hebrew Verb-Noun Multi-Word Expressions. In *Proceedings of the Tenth International Conference on Language Resources and Evaluation (LREC'16)*, pages 522–527, Portorož, Slovenia. European Language Resources Association (ELRA).

Chaya Liebeskind and Yaakov HaCohen-Kerner. 2018. Verbal Multi-Word Expressions in Yiddish. In *Natural Language Processing and Information Systems*, pages 205–216, Cham. Springer International Publishing.

Nikola Ljubešić, Kaja Dobrovoljc, Simon Krek, Marina Peršuric Antonic, and Darja Fišer. 2014. hrMWELex – a MWE lexicon of Croatian extracted from a parsed gigacorpus. In *9th Language Technologies Conference Information Society (IS 2014)*, pages 25–31.

Nikola Ljubešić, Kaja Dobrovoljc, and Darja Fišer. 2015. *MWELex – MWE Lexica of Croatian, Slovene and Serbian Extracted from Parsed Corpora. *Informatica*, 39(3).

Irina Lobzhanidze. 2019. Computational Model of the Modern Georgian Language and Search Patterns for an Online Dictionary of Idioms. In A. Silva, S. Staton, P. Sutton, and C. Umbach, editors, *Language, Logic, and Computation*, volume 11456 of *Lecture Notes in Computer Science*, pages 187–208. Springer.

Gyri Smørdal Losnegaard, Federico Sangati, Carla Parra Escartín, Agata Savary, Sascha Bargmann, and Johanna Monti. 2016. PARSEME survey on MWE resources. In *Proceedings of the Tenth International Conference on Language Resources and Evaluation (LREC'16)*, pages 2299–2306, Portorož, Slovenia. European Language Resources Association (ELRA).

Ujwala P. Mahajan, Ajay S. Patil, and Nita V. Patil. 2024. A survey of tools and techniques for multiword expression detection. *International Journal of Computer Applications*, 186(32):11–18.

Stella Markantonatou. 2019. IDION: A database for Modern Greek multiword expressions. In *Proceedings of the Joint Workshop on Multiword Expressions and WordNet (MWE-WN 2019)*, pages 130–134. Association for Computational Linguistics.

Stella Markantonatou, Nikolaos T. Kokkas, Panagiotis G. Krimpas, Ana O. Chirila, Dimitrios Karamatskos, Nicolaos Valeontisa, and George Pavlidis. 2024. Description of Pomak within IDION: Challenges in the representation of verb multiword expressions. In Voula Giouli and Verginica Barbu Mititelu, editors, *Multiword expressions in lexical resources: Linguistic, lexicographic, and computational perspectives*. Language Science Press.

Francesca Masini, M. Silvia Micheli, Andrea Zaninello, Sara Castagnoli, and Malvina Nissim. 2020. MWE_combinet_release_1.0. Associazione Italiana di Linguistica Computazionale.

Diana Maynard, Joanna Wright, Mark A. Greenwood, and Kalina Bontcheva. 2022. D1.11 Report on the English Language. Technical report, European Language Equality. `https://european-language-equality.eu/wp-content/uploads/2022/03/ELE___Deliverable_D1_11__Language_Report_English_.pdf`.

Marek Maziarz, Łukasz Grabowski, Tadeusz Piotrowski, Ewa Rudnicka, and Maciej Piasecki. 2023. Lexicalisation of Polish and English word combinations: an empirical study. *Poznan Studies in Contemporary Linguistics*, 59(2):381–406. Publisher: De Gruyter Mouton.

Diego Moussallem. 2018. LIdioms: A Multilingual Linked Idioms Data Set. In *Proceedings of the Eleventh International Conference on Language Resources and Evaluation (LREC 2018)*.

Zuzana Nevěřilová. 2018. Discovering Continuous Multi-word Expressions in Czech. *Computación y Sistemas*, 22(3).

Jan Odijk and Martin Kroon. 2024. A Canonical Form for Flexible Multiword Expressions. In *Proceedings of the 2024 Joint International Conference on Computational Linguistics, Language Resources and Evaluation (LREC-COLING 2024)*, pages 91–101, Torino, Italia. ELRA and ICCL.

Petya Osenova and Kiril Simov. 2024. Representation of multiword expressions in the Bulgarian integrated lexicon for language technology. In Voula Giouli and Verginica Barbu Mititelu, editors, *Multiword expressions in lexical resources: Linguistic, lexicographic, and computational perspectives*. Language Science Press.

Irene Pagliai. 2023. Bridging the Gap: Creation of a Lexicon of 150 Pairs of English and Italian Idioms Including Normed Variables for the Exploration of Idiomatic Ambiguity. *Journal of Open Humanities Data*, 9:16.

Pavel Pecina. 2008. Gold Standard Reference Data for Multiword Expression Extraction: Czech Dependency Bigrams from the Prague Dependency Treebank. Charles University, Faculty of Mathematics and Physics, Institute of Formal and Applied Linguistics (UFAL).

Stelios Piperidis. 2012. The META-SHARE language resources sharing infrastructure: Principles, challenges, solutions. In *Proceedings of the Eighth International Conference on Language Resources and Evaluation (LREC'12)*, pages 36–42, Istanbul, Turkey. European Language Resources Association (ELRA).

Dmitry Puzyrev, Artem Shelmanov, Alexander Panchenko, and Ekaterina Artemova. 2019. A Dataset for Noun Compositionality Detection for a Slavic Language. In *Proceedings of the 7th Workshop on Balto-Slavic Natural Language Processing*, pages 56–62, Florence, Italy. Association for Computational Linguistics.

Carlos Ramisch. 2016. How Naked is the Naked Truth? A Multilingual Lexicon of Nominal Compound Compositionality. In *Proceedings of the 54th Annual Meeting of the Association for Computational Linguistics (Volume 2: Short Papers)*, pages 156–161.

Siva Reddy, Diana McCarthy, and Suresh Manandhar. 2011. An Empirical Study on Compositionality in Compound Nouns. In *Proceedings of 5th International Joint Conference on Natural Language Processing*, pages 210–218, Chiang Mai, Thailand. Asian Federation of Natural Language Processing.

Georg Rehm. 2023. *European Language Grid: A Language Technology Platform for Multilingual Europe*. Cognitive Technologies. Springer. Cham.

Frankie Robertson. 2020. Filling the ___-s in Finnish MWE lexicons. In *Proceedings of the Joint Workshop on Multiword Expressions and Electronic Lexicons*, pages 13–21. Association for Computational Linguistics.

Barrios Rodriguez and Maria Auxiliadora. 2019. A Spanish E-dictionary of Collocations. In *Proceedings of the Fifth International Conference on Dependency Linguistics (Depling, SyntaxFest 2019)*, pages 160–167.

Adolfo Enrique Rodríguez et al. 2022. Lunfardo Dictionary. European Language Grid.

Victoria Rosén, Koenraad De Smedt, Gyri Smørdal Losnegaard, Eduard Bejček, Agata Savary, and Petya Osenova. 2016. MWEs in treebanks: From survey to guidelines. In *Proceedings of the Tenth International Conference on Language Resources and Evaluation (LREC'16)*, pages 2323–2330, Portorož, Slovenia. European Language Resources Association (ELRA).

V. Rosén, G. S. Losnegaard, K. De Smedt, E. Bejček, A. Savary, A. Przepiórkowski, P. Osenova, and V. Barbu Mititelu. 2015. A survey of multiword expressions in treebanks. In *Proceedings of the Fourteenth Workshop on Treebanks and Linguistic Theories (TLT14)*, pages 179—-193, Warsaw, Poland. Institute of Computer Science, Polish Academy of Sciences.

Agata Savary, Silvio Cordeiro, and Carlos Ramisch. 2019. Without lexicons, multiword expression identification will never fly: A position statement. In *Proceedings of the Joint Workshop on Multiword Expressions and WordNet (MWE-WN 2019)*, pages 79–91, Florence, Italy. Association for Computational Linguistics.

Agata Savary and Silvio Ricardo Cordeiro. 2017. Literal readings of multiword expressions: as scarce as hen's teeth. In *Proceedings of the 16th International Workshop on Treebanks and Linguistic Theories*, pages 64–72, Prague, Czech Republic.

Fran Ramovš Institute of the Slovenian Language ZRC Sazu. 2023. Terminological multiword expressions lexicon. *https://slovenscina.eu/*.

Sabine Schulte im Walde. 2024. Collecting and investigating features of compositionality ratings. In Voula Giouli and Verginica Barbu Mititelu, editors, *Multiword expressions in lexical resources: Linguistic, lexicographic, and computational perspectives*. Language Science Press.

Dhirendra Singh, Sudha Bhingardive, and Pushpak Bhattacharyya. 2016. Multiword Expressions Dataset for Indian Languages. In *Proceedings of the Tenth International Conference on Language Resources and Evaluation (LREC'16)*, pages 2331–2335, Portorož, Slovenia. European Language Resources Association (ELRA).

Amalia Todirascu. 2019. PolylexFLE : une base de données d'expressions polylexicales pour le FLE (PolylexFLE : a database of multiword expressions for French L2 language learning). In *Actes de la Conférence sur le Traitement Automatique des Langues Naturelles (TALN) PFIA 2019. Volume I : Articles longs*, pages 143–156. ATALA.

Elena Volodina, David Alfter, and Therese Lindström Tiedemann. 2024. Profiles for Swedish as a Second Language: Lexis, Grammar, Morphology. In *Proceedings of the Huminfra Conference (HiC 2024), Gothenburg, 10–11 January 2024*, pages 10–19.

Pavel Vondřička. 2019. Design of a Multiword Expressions Database. *The Prague Bulletin of Mathematical Linguistics*, 112(1):83–101.

Abigail Walsh, Teresa Lynn, and Jennifer Foster. 2019. Ilfhocail: A Lexicon of Irish MWEs. In *Proceedings of the Joint Workshop on Multiword Expressions and WordNet (MWE-WN 2019)*, pages 162–168, Florence, Italy. Association for Computational Linguistics.

Rodrigo Wilkens, Leonardo Zilio, Silvio Ricardo Cordeiro, Felipe Paula, Carlos Ramisch, Marco Idiart, and Aline Villavicencio. 2017. LexSubNC: A Dataset of Lexical Substitution for Nominal Compounds. In *Proceedings of the 12th International Conference on Computational Semantics (IWCS) — Short papers*.

Ziheng Zeng, Kellen Cheng, Srihari Nanniyur, Jianing Zhou, and Suma Bhat. 2023. IEKG: A Commonsense Knowledge Graph for Idiomatic Expressions. In *Proceedings of the 2023 Conference on Empirical Methods in Natural Language Processing*, pages 14243–14264, Singapore. Association for Computational Linguistics.

Asta Õim. 2000. *Fraseoloogiasõnaraamat*, 2-ne, täiendatud ja parandatud trükk edition. Eesti keele sihtasutus, Tallinn.

Appendix

Table 1: List of resources included in the survey with basic reference information. Method: M – manual processing; S/A – semi-automatic; A – automatic.

Lexicon	Link	Reference	Langs	Method	Access
LEMUR	→	(Vondřička, 2019)	CZ	S/A	unclear
NileULex	→	(El-Beltagy, 2016)	AR	S/A	free
LEX-MWE-PT: Word Combination in Portuguese	→	(Antunes and Mendes, 2013)	PT	other-unclear	paid
Lexicalisation of Polish and English word combinations	→	(Maziarz et al., 2023)	PL, EN	M	free
The Database of Lithuanian MWEs	→	(Bielinskienė et al., 2022)	LT	S/A	free
srMWELex v0.5 – Serbian lexicon of MWEs	→	(Ljubešić et al., 2015)	SR	A	free
hrMWELex – Croatian lexicon of MWEs	→	(Ljubešić et al., 2014)	HR	A	free
slMWELex – Slovene lexicon of MWEs	→	(Ljubešić et al., 2015)	SL	A	free
Srp_DELAC	→	(Krstev et al., 2013)	SR	M	academic
Expressions (deChile)	→	(Anders, 2022b)	ES	M	free
Czech MWEs	→	(Nevěřilová, 2018)	CZ	M	free
Dictionary of Estonian Phraseology	→	(Õim, 2000)	ET	M	unclear
Terminological MWE lexicon	→	(Sazu, 2023)	SL	M	free
Terminology database of expressions	→	(ELRA, 2010)	EN, FR	M	paid
Idioms of Chile [Chilenismos]	→	(Anders, 2022a)	ES-CL	M	free
Lunfardo Dictionary	→	(Rodríguez et al., 2022)	ES-AR	M	free
Dictionary of Estonian Synonyms	→	(Institute of the Estonian Language, 2016)	ET	M	unclear
ilFhocail	→	(Walsh et al., 2019)	GA	M	unclear
Referentiebestand Belgisch-Nederlands	→	(Dutch Language Institute, 2016)	NL	M	free
Czech Dependency Bigrams from the Prague Dependency Treebank	→	(Pecina, 2008)	CZ	M	free
Konbitzul	→	(Iñurrieta et al., 2018)	EU, ES	M	free
English-Persian database of idioms and expressions	→	(ELRA, 2019)	EN, FA	S/A	paid
ParaDi 2.0 dataset	→	(Barančíková and Ketnerová, 2017)	CZ	M	free
MWE lexicon extracted from the Gigafida 2.1 corpus	→	(Krek et al., 2021)	SL	S/A	unclear
Czech Verbal MWEs	→	(Bejček, 2017)	CZ	S/A	free
Bulgarian MWE dictionary	→	(Koeva et al., 2016)	BG	unclear	unclear
ConceptNet-el	→	(Giouli, 2023)	EL	M	free
CollFrEn: Rich Bilingual English–French Collocation Resource	→	(Fisas, 2020)	EN, FR	A	free
FinnMWE: a lexicon of Finnish MWEs	→	(Robertson, 2020)	FI	A	free
Russian Collocations Database	→	(Khokhlova, 2020)	RU	A	free
Diretes (DIccionario RETicular de ESpañol)	→	(Rodriguez and Auxiliadora, 2019)	ES	unclear	unclear
IDION: A database for Modern Greek MWEs		(Markantonatou, 2019)	EL	unclear	free
PolylexFLE	→	(Todirascu, 2019)	FR	unclear	unclear

Japanese compound verb lexicon	→	(Kanzaki, 2019)	JA, EN, ZH, KO	other-unclear	free
Sentiment Lexicon of IDiomatic Expressions (SLIDE)	→	(Jochim, 2018)	EN	S/A	free
LIDIOMS: A Multilingual Linked Idioms Data Set	→	(Moussallem, 2018)	EN, DE, IT, PT, RU	S/A	free
LexSubNC: A Dataset of Lexical Substitution for Nominal Compounds	→	(Wilkens et al., 2017)	PT	S/A	unclear
SAMER: A Semi-Automatically Created Lexical Resource for Arabic Verbal MWEs	→	(Al-Badrashiny, 2016)	AR	S/A	unclear
Multilingual Lexicon of Nominal Compound Compositionality	→	(Ramisch, 2016)	EN, FR, PT	S/A	free
Lexical Resource of Hebrew Verb-Noun MWEs	→	(Liebeskind and HaCohen-Kerner, 2016)	HE	M	free
MWEs in Spanish Dialects	→	(Bogantes et al., 2016)	ES, dialects: ES-CO, ES-CR, ES-MEX, ES-PE	S/A	unclear
MWEs Dataset for Indian Languages	→	(Singh et al., 2016)	HI, MR	S/A	free
Noun Compound Senses (NCS) dataset	→	(Reddy et al., 2011)	EN	S/A	free
MWE Dataset for Swedish	→	(Kurfalı et al., 2020)	SV	S/A	free
Noun Compound Dataset for Russian	→	(Puzyrev et al., 2019)	RU	S/A	free
Diccionario de Colocaciones del Español (DiCE)	→	(Hedegaard and Troelsgård, 2010)	ES	S/A	free
Polish verbal MWEs	→	(Savary and Cordeiro, 2017)	PL	A	free
Dutch idiomatic expressions		(Hubers et al., 2020)	NL	A	free
MWE_combinet_release_1.0	→	(Masini et al., 2020)	IT	S/A	free
Grammatical Dictionary of Polish MWEs	→	(Czerepowicka and Savary, 2015)	PL	S/A	free
Dictionary of idioms for Georgian	→	(Lobzhanidze, 2019)	KA, EL	S/A	free
IDION POMAK	→	(Markantonatou et al., 2024)	POMAK	M	free
DUCAME	→	(Odijk and Kroon, 2024)	NL	unclear	unclear
MWE dictionary for Bulgarian and Romanian		(Leseva et al., 2020)	BG, RO	S/A	free
Feature-NN	→	(Schulte im Walde, 2024)	DE	S/A	free
Compound Noun Compositionality Dataset	→	(Reddy et al., 2011)	EN	M	free
MWE-CEFR Profiles	→	(Volodina et al., 2024)	SV	S/A	free
Bulgarian Integrated Lexicon	TBA	(Osenova and Simov, 2024)	BG		
MWEs in FrameNet-EL	TBA		EL		
Verbal MWEs in Yiddish	→	(Liebeskind and HaCohen-Kerner, 2018)	YI	M	free
IdiomKB	→	(Li et al., 2023)	EN, ZH, JA	S/A	free
870 English idioms: norming and statistical analysis	→	(Bulkes and Tanner, 2017)	EN	M	free
Collocational Database for Learning Croatian as a Foreign Language		(Blagus Bartolec et al., 2024)	HR, EN	other-unclear	free

Normed lexicon of English and Italian idioms	→	(Pagliai, 2023)	EN, IT	unclear	free for specific uses
Croatian dictionary of idioms	→	(Filipović Petrović et al., 2024)	HR	S/A	free
IEKG: A Commonsense Knowledge Graph for Idiomatic Expressions	→	(Zeng et al., 2023)	EN	S/A	free

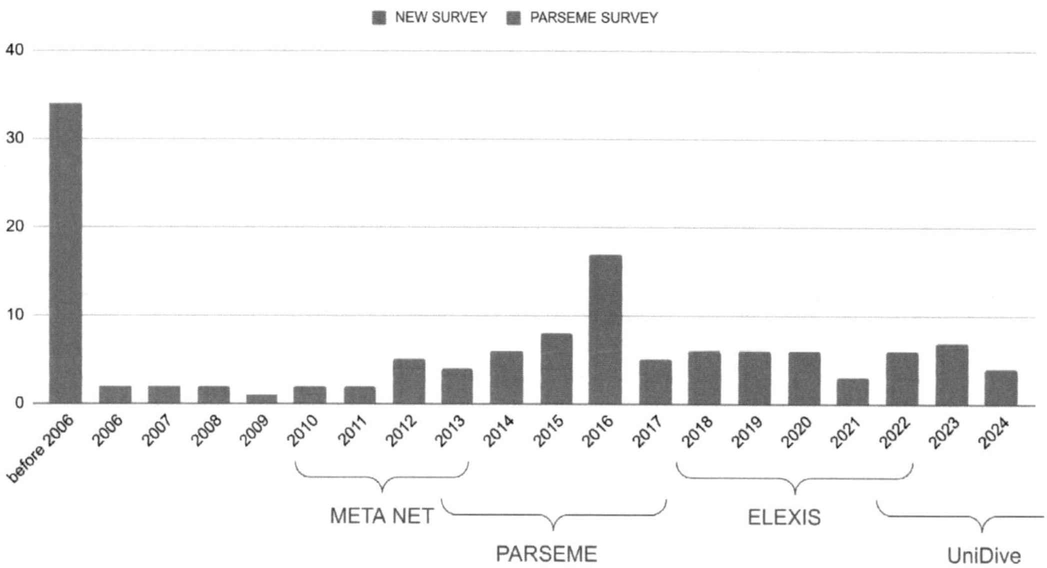

Figure 1: Distribution of resources by year of publication

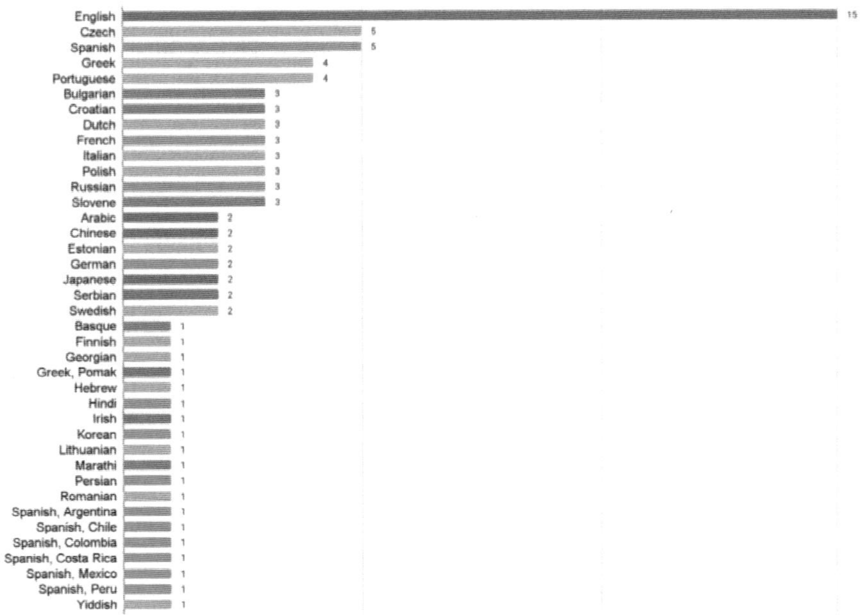

Figure 2: Distribution of different languages and the number of MWE resources they are involved in. The color shows the level of technical support: blue – Good; green – Moderate; orange – Fragmentary (higher); purple – Fragmentary (lower); red – Weak or none; gray – Unknown.

Table 2: Distribution of different languages with their level of technical support (according to ELE report and Joshi et al. (2020)) and the number of MWE resources they are involved in. *Resources whose evaluation is not present in ELE report and is extracted from Joshi et al. (2020). **Pomak is not classified but there are very limited resources on it, thus we assume its support to be 'Weak or none.'

Language	**Support (ELE report)**	**# resources**	**Language**	**Support (ELE report)**	**# resources**
English	GOOD	15	Basque	FRAGM (LOWER)	1
Czech	FRAGM (HIGHER)	5	Finnish	FRAGM (HIGHER)	1
Spanish	MODERATE	5	Georgian	FRAGM (HIGHER)/3*	1
Greek	FRAGM (HIGHER)	4	Pomak	WEAK OR NONE**	1
Portuguese	FRAGM (HIGHER)	4	Hebrew	FRAGM (HIGHER)/3*	1
Bulgarian	FRAGM (LOWER)	3	Hindi	MODERATE/4*	1
Croatian	FRAGM (LOWER)	3	Irish	WEAK OR NONE	1
Dutch	FRAGM (HIGHER)	3	Korean	MODERATE/4*	1
French	MODERATE	3	Lithuanian	FRAGM (HIGHER)	1
Italian	FRAGM (HIGHER)	3	Marathi	FRAGM (LOWER)/2*	1
Polish	FRAGM (HIGHER)	3	Persian	MODERATE/4*	1
Russian	MODERATE/4*	3	Romanian	FRAGM (HIGHER)	1
Slovene	FRAGM (LOWER)	3	Spanish, Argentina	UNKNOWN	1
Arabic	GOOD/5*	2	Spanish, Chile	UNKNOWN	1
Chinese (ZH)	GOOD/5*	2	Spanish, Colombia	UNKNOWN	1
Estonian	FRAGM (HIGHER)	2	Spanish, Costa Rica	UNKNOWN	1
German	MODERATE	2	Spanish, Mexico	UNKNOWN	1
Japanese	GOOD/5*	2	Spanish, Peru	UNKNOWN	1
Serbian	WEAK OR NONE	2	Yiddish	WEAK OR NONE/1*	1
Swedish	FRAGM (HIGHER)	2			

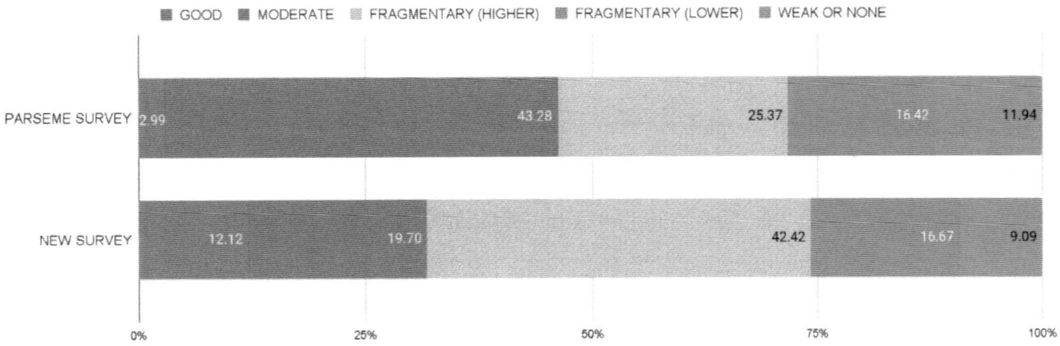

Figure 3: Distribution of resources according to level of technical support

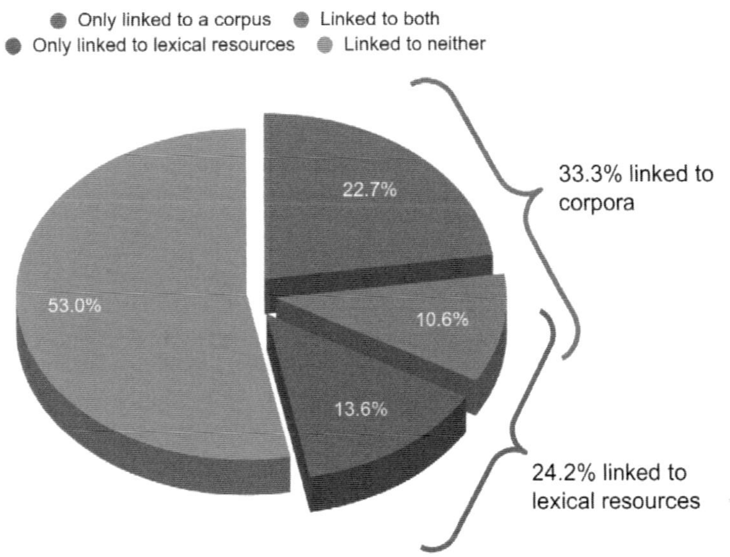

Figure 4: Distribution of resources according to their links to corpora and/or other lexical resources

A European Portuguese corpus annotated for verbal idioms

David Antunes
HLT, INESC ID Lisboa
david.f.l.antunes@inesc-id.pt

Jorge Baptista
HLT, INESC ID Lisboa
FCHS, Univ. Algarve
jbaptis@ualg.pt

Nuno J. Mamede
HLT, INESC ID Lisboa
IST, Univ. Lisboa
nuno.mamede@tecnico.ulisboa.pt

Abstract

This paper presents the construction of VIDiom-PT, a *corpus* in European Portuguese annotated for verbal idioms (e.g. '*O Rui* ***bateu a bota***' (lit. "Rui hit the boot") "Rui died"). This linguistic resource aims to support the development of systems capable of processing such constructions in this language variety. To assist in the annotation effort, two tools were built. The first allows for the detection of possible instances of verbal idioms in texts, while the second provides a graphical interface for annotating them. This effort culminated in the annotation of a total of 5,178 instances of 747 different verbal idioms in more than 200,000 sentences in European Portuguese. A highly reliable inter-annotator agreement was achieved, using Krippendorff's alpha for nominal data (0.869) with 5% of the data independently annotated by 3 experts. Part of the annotated corpus is also made publicly available.

1 Introduction

This paper addresses *verbal idioms* (or *idiomatic expressions*), with a focus on European Portuguese (PT). These are a special type of *multiword expression* (MWE) where the main verb and one or more of its arguments are frozen together (Gross, 1982; Baptista et al., 2004), that is, they have unpredictable distributional and syntactic constraints. Furthermore, the overall meaning of these expressions often cannot be derived from the meaning that each element presents when used separately; in other words, the meaning of these constructions is *non-compositional* (Constant et al., 2017; Galvão, 2019). The example '*A Ana* ***atirou*** *o projeto* ***às urtigas***' (lit. "Ana threw the project at the nettles") "Ana abandoned the project" showcases how the conventionalized meaning conveyed by these expressions cannot be directly deduced from its constituents.

Several aspects make analyzing and automatically processing these expressions a challenging task, notably, the unpredictability of distributional constraints; the limited possibility of inflection of frozen complements; the syntactic structure they often exhibit, allowing for insertions and permutations of constituents; and the non-compositionality of these expressions; in addition, their frequency in texts is usually very low.

Although one might assume that the frequency of MWEs in spoken dialogue or written text is low enough to disregard their unique characteristics during text analysis, their estimated number in a native speaker's lexicon is surprisingly significant. Estimates range from being of the same order of magnitude as the number of single-word verbs (Jackendoff, 1997); to several times the number of simple, distributional verbs: for example, (Gross, 1996) presents a French lexicon of 20,340 frozen sentences, which contrasts with that of 13,225 simple, distributionally free, verbs.

Considering all of this, it is clear that to achieve a good performance in the syntactic and semantic analysis of natural language texts, one cannot overlook the existence of these constructions, as they contain essential information to understand the content of a given text. Moreover, studies have shown how properly identifying MWE can lead to better parser performance (Hogan et al., 2007; Constant et al., 2017) as it reduces parsing errors.

A great amount of work has been developed to integrate the analysis of verbal idioms into NLP systems (de Uzeda Garrão and Dias, 2001; Salton et al., 2014; Peng and Feldman, 2017; Zeng and Bhat, 2021). As posited by Savary et al. (2019), several natural language processing (NLP) systems address MWEs by resorting to a lexicon. This is also the case for the system used in this paper (self-reference), which also adopts a lexicon-based approach, in this case, a lexicon of verbal idioms. In this system, this lexicon takes the form of a *lexicon-grammar*, that is, a matrix database, where lines correspond to the lexical entries (the verbal

Proceedings of the 21st Workshop on Multiword Expressions (MWE 2025), pages 58–66
May 4, 2025 ©2025 Association for Computational Linguistics

idioms) and columns encode their structural, distributional, semantic, and transformational properties. At the time of writing, the lexicon-grammar of verbal idioms of European Portuguese contains 2,714 lexical entries and 106 columns describing their individual properties.

It is based on this lexicon-grammar and the linguistic constraints described therein that the system identifies instances of verbal idioms, through the extraction of a relation called `FIXED`, linking the frozen elements of the verbal idiom (e.g., '***meter** a **mão na massa***' (lit. "to put the hand in the dough") "to work actively on something" which is represented by `FIXED_C1P2(meter,mão,na,massa)`).

In order to assess the ability of such systems at identifying natural occurrences of verbal idioms, it is essential to have access to written texts (*corpora*) annotated with this phenomenon. Recently, the PARSEME project (Savary et al., 2017)[1], an initiative developed by a European research network focused on the role of MWE in parsing, produced a multilingual 5-million-word annotated *corpus*. This includes a Brazilian Portuguese partition, which served as the basis for a MWE identification shared task (Ramisch et al., 2018). For verbal idioms specifically, the second edition of this shared task (Ramisch et al., 2018) found that around 20% of the annotated MWE (1,130 out of 5,536) corresponded to verbal idioms (tagged as 'VID').

It is important to note that no equivalent corpus in the European variety had been included in any edition of this shared task, and that, while the two varieties are quite similar and intercomprehensible most of the time, a previous comparison experiment (Baptista, 2008) has shown that they only share a reduced number of equivalent verbal idioms (around *10%*). It was, therefore, essential to create a new corpus for European Portuguese, since, to the best of our knowledge, no such resource, if it exists, has been made publicly available until now.

2 Related Work

The annotation of idioms in English corpora has seen a significant amount of work. One can find important resources like the '*High Fixed Corpus*' and '*Low Fixed Corpus*' presented in Salton et al. (2014). This project aimed to advance the machine translation of verbal idioms employing a substitution method and using 3 dictionaries: a dictionary of idioms in the source language; a dictionary of idioms in the target language; and a bilingual dictionary with a correspondence between idioms of the two languages. To test their system, they chose to translate between English and Brazilian-Portuguese and built two test *corpora*: the '*High Fixed Corpus*' and '*Low Fixed Corpus*'. The first *corpus* features 17 different idioms of the type *Verb + noun*, while the second one features 11 different idioms of the same type. These *corpora* contain 10 sentences featuring each different idiom which were extracted from the web.

In more recent years, there are works like Haagsma et al. (2020), which focuses on the automatic identification of potential idiomatic expressions based on existing dictionaries of idioms. Potential instances of such constructions are extracted from the *British National Corpus* (BNC), through a parsing-based method that considers the lemmata and the dependency relations. They are then manually annotated using graphical interfaces built for that purpose. The sense of these idioms is classified, mainly as being literal or non-literal. Haagsma et al. (2020) culminated in the *MAGPIE* corpus which features 56,622 annotated phrases with 1,756 different idiom types annotated as being literal or not.

Adewumi et al. (2021) performed a similar task with two main differences: the extraction of potential idiomatic expressions was performed manually, which reduces the likelihood of false-positives and false-negatives, but massively increases the amount of time and effort required for this task; the annotation of idioms considered a broader set of senses such as 'irony' and 'euphemism'. This project achieved a corpus with 1,197 cases of idioms totaling over 20,100 samples/sentences.

When it comes to other languages, Hashimoto and Kawahara (2008) is a good example of a similar approach to verbal idiom annotation. First, they use a dependency parser for Japanese and a dictionary of Japanese idioms to detect examples of these expressions in the Japanese Web corpus (Kawahara and Kurohashi, 2006). Then, human annotators classify the expressions as idiomatic or literal, which resulted in a corpus spanning 146 ambiguous idioms across 102,846 sentences.

Recently, for German, Ehren et al. (2024) presented another effort towards the annotation of verbal idioms. Based on an electronic dictionary of German idioms (featuring roughly 30,000 verbal idioms), candidate instances of relevant expressions are fetched from the Parallel Meaning Bank (PMB),

[1] `https://typo.uni-konstanz.de/parseme/` (last access: March 28, 2025)

using the same extraction method described in Haagsma et al. (2020). Potential idiomatic expressions are marked as one of 5 categories: idiomatic, probably idiomatic, probably literal, literal or both, which poses an interesting variation from the rest of the works here discussed, as it addresses the lack of context that is made available to the annotator. The resulting collection features 1,945 annotated verbal idioms across 5,821 sampled sentences.

For the target language of this article, European Portuguese, the amount of work addressing verbal idioms is scarce. However, the MWE research topic in general has seen the construction of resources, namely, a lexical database of MWEs of Portuguese in the scope of project *COMBINA-PT* (Antunes et al., 2006; Mendes et al., 2006). The expressions were automatically extracted through the analysis of a balanced 50 million word written corpus sampled from the Reference Corpus of Contemporary Portuguese (in Portuguese, *Corpus de Referência do Português Contemporâneo*). This information was then statistically interpreted with lexical association measures and validated by hand. The phenomena were broadly classified as 5 types of MWE: (i) groups forming a lexical category, (ii) groups forming a phrase (e.g., nominal or adverbial phrase), (iii) groups that constitute a verbal phrase (the group of which verbal idioms are a part of), (iv) groups that specify named entities, and (v) cases that require further attention as they are doubtful expressions (includes some verbal idioms).

Lastly, one can find works like LIDIOMS (Moussallem et al., 2018) which consists of a multilingual dataset of idioms (in general) containing five languages: English, German, Italian, Portuguese, and Russian. The data was crawled and integrated from 4 online data sources. The idioms had to be manually filtered by experts, so that only the non-compositional constructions (corresponding to roughly half of the crawled expressions) were considered. Moreover, all idioms were evaluated by two native speakers and one linguist (per language) in order to ensure the quality of the data. The LIDIOMS dataset provides linking between idioms across languages by using English as a pivot language since all the target translations are in English. This means multilingual translation makes use of inference and multiple bilingual patterns, where English definitions are used as a bridge. This dataset presents a total of 13,889 annotated samples which model 815 different concepts with 488 translations (where 115 are indirect translations).

3 The Corpus

3.1 Corpus Description

The corpus comprises a total of 178 documents selected from two sources: 127 texts are transcriptions from sessions of the Portuguese Parliament, spanning May 2004 to March 2005 and March 2018 to September 2018, and the remaining 51 documents were obtained from the *CETEMPúblico* corpus (Santos and Rocha, 2001)[2]. Table 1 provides a breakdown of the documents from both sources, detailing the total number of documents and sentences.

Source	Portuguese Parliament	CETEMPúblico
# Documents	127	51
# Sentences	101,600	101,725
# Words	3,024,005	2,886,279

Table 1: Description of the documents that make up the *corpus*.

Although the number of documents from each source differs significantly, the number of sentences and words in each subset is remarkably similar. In practice, this means that both sources are considered equally.

3.2 Corpus Annotation

The partition of the annotated corpus corresponding to the texts of *CETEMPúblico* is publicly available[3]. However, due to licensing restrictions, we are unable to release the documents from the Portuguese Parliament at this time. The resource is in the format of a set of TXT files, with one file for each original source document (these documents are also made available). In each file, there is a set of two consecutive lines for each annotated instance of a verbal idiom, presenting the `FIXED` dependency that corresponds to the expression as well as a sentence in which the expression is found (the frozen elements of the construction are not explicitly delimited in the original sentence).

[2] https://www.linguateca.pt/CETEMPublico/

[3] https://portulanclarin.net/repository/search/?q=VIDiom-PT

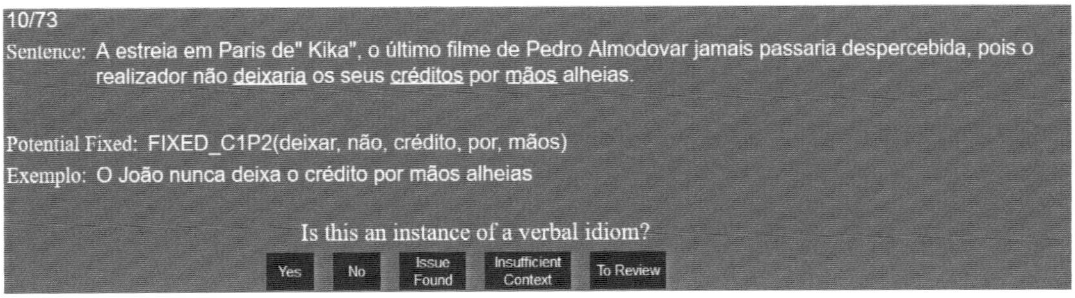

Figure 1: General appearance of the annotation tool.

As an example, this is the content corresponding to an annotation of the verbal idiom '***bater na tecla***' (lit. "to hit the key") "to dwell on":

Verbal Idiom: `FIXED_CP1(bater,em,tecla)`
Is present in sentence: 'Mas tem carácter obrigatório : a oposição também está a bater na mesma tecla.'

3.2.1 Annotation Tools

For the purpose of reducing the amount of human resources as well as the time necessary to perform the annotation of the existing verbal idioms in the corpus, we developed two programs to support human annotators: the first is responsible for detecting possible instances of idiomatic expressions, while the second consists of a graphical interface where annotators are presented with the findings of the first program, allowing them to decide whether each case is a proper verbal idiom or not.

Detection of Potential Verbal Idioms

This program skims through the textual content while looking for possible instances of verbal idioms in each sentence and then compiles its findings in a well-formatted file. A sentence is considered to contain a potential verbal idiom if all (lemmatized) lexical elements that define an idiomatic expression (the main verb and frozen complements) are present. Furthermore, following a heuristic derived from Manning and Schütze (1999), the maximum distance between consecutive elements of the expression in the analyzed sentence should not exceed five tokens. For example, for the verbal idiom '*meter a mão na massa*' (lit. "to put the hand in the dough") "to work actively on something", previously mentioned, the tool retrieves sentences where the inflected forms associated with the lexical elements (lemmas) 'meter', 'mão' and 'massa' are present, in any order, with no more than 5 tokens between each element.

This tool leverages the lexicon-grammar of verbal idioms integrated into the NLP system as a source of information, identifying relevant expressions and, in particular, their frozen elements. Consequently, the program exclusively searches for verbal idioms documented in the lexicon-grammar. While this resource does not encompass the entirety of idiomatic constructions in the language, it includes a comprehensive and systematically described set of 2,714 verbal idioms, covering the most frequently used expressions.

Annotation Interface

The annotation interface (Figure 1) makes it possible for the annotators to mark which of the potential verbal idioms detected by the previous tool are indeed instances of the target idiom. Once the annotators identify themselves, they can annotate their assigned documents, one by one.

For each document, the interface displays a dedicated screen for every detected potential idiomatic expression. Each screen presents the user with a structured set of informational components: the sentence from the corpus where the potential verbal idiom appears, with its frozen elements underlined; the `FIXED` dependency that identifies the verbal idiom; and the corresponding example from the lexicon-grammar matrix for that idiom.

Additionally, at the bottom of the screen, five buttons enable the annotator to classify the instance as a valid instance of a verbal idiom or not, as well as to report any detected issues.

3.2.2 Annotation Process

The annotation of documents in the *corpus* was performed by three annotators with expertise in European Portuguese verbal idioms, using the annotation tools described in Section 3.2.1 and following the guidelines outlined in Appendix A.

A subset of the *corpus*, consisting of 7 documents, randomly selected, and representing roughly 5% of the potential verbal idioms detected, was annotated by all annotators. This step aimed to measure inter-annotator agreement and evaluate the effectiveness of the annotation guidelines. Given the nature of the task, Krippendorff's alpha for nominal data (Krippendorff, 2008) was employed as the agreement metric. This produced a K-alpha of 0.869, indicating a reliable classification among the annotators. After completing this task, the annotators collaboratively resolved discrepancies to produce a consensual annotation, thereby creating a golden collection.

Annotator	A	B	C
Precision in Golden Collection	0.914	0.963	0.979
Recall in Golden Collection	0.933	0.948	0.948
F1-score in Golden Collection	0.923	0.956	0.963
Inter-Annotator Agreement		0.869	

Table 2: Performance of each annotator when compared to the golden collection, as well as inter-annotator agreement. The annotators are denoted as 'A', 'B', and 'C' to maintain anonymity.

Table 2 details the Precision and Recall of each annotator in comparison to the consensual annotation, as well as the overall inter-annotator agreement. As shown in this table, the performance of all annotators in comparison to the golden collection is similar. The discussion between the three annotators to reach a consensual annotation highlighted the complexity of verbal idioms, as determining the idiomaticity of an expression proved challenging with limited context. However, most discrepancies in the annotation were attributed to annotator oversight. For instance, in the sentence 'Vedou toda a placa central com rede pintada de verde, **tapou** alguns dos **buracos** existentes no pavimento...' 'He covered the entire central board with a green-painted mesh and covered some of the existing holes in the pavement...', where the potential verbal idiom ***'tapar buracos'*** (lit. "to cover holes") "to temporarily mend a situation" was detected, one annotator incorrectly marked it as an idiomatic expression. A more careful analysis reveals that the sentence conveys the literal meaning. This example underscores the influence of human error on the annotation process, which must be considered when interpreting the results. The discussion towards a consensual annotation also exposed some limitations in the NLP system, leading to necessary compromises in the annotation guidelines, which are presented in the next section.

Limitations of the annotation process

Two main issues were identified. Firstly, many verbal idioms have not yet been included in the lexicon-grammar matrix, but they share key components with already defined expressions, while conveying a different meaning. This means these constructions will be identified as potential idiomatic expressions. For instance, the (not yet included) idiom ***'falar com língua bífide'*** (lit. "to speak with a forked tongue") "to speak deceptively" was mistakenly identified as a potential instance of the (already defined) verbal idiom ***'falar** a **língua** de alguém'* (lit. "talking someone's language") "to agree with someone"; e.g. '...um dia viria a **falar** com **língua** bífide, afirmando no discurso científico o que negava no poético.' '...one day, he would come to speak deceptively, affirming in scientific discourse what he denied in poetic language.'. Secondly, many other verbal idioms are not yet defined in the lexicon-grammar at all. As a result, they are not detected as potential verbal idioms, thus it is impossible to annotate them.

Compromises in the annotation guidelines

Several pragmatic solutions were devised to address the issues outlined above. First, expressions not yet described in the lexicon-grammar but identified as potential verbal idioms—due to shared frozen elements with existing idiomatic expressions—were provisionally annotated as instances of those already defined. Subsequently, these expressions were incorporated into the lexicon-grammar, and their annotations were refined to reflect the appropriate verbal idioms.

Secondly, when multiple, already defined, expressions that share key components are detected as potential idioms within the same sentence, all are marked as instances of verbal idioms. After the document at hand is fully annotated, the annotator must look back on these situations so that, for each, only one expression is annotated. For example, the expressions (1) *'bater à porta de alguém'* (lit. "to knock on someone's door") "to approach someone (for help) *or* (some problem) to affect someone"; (2) *'bater à porta errada'* (lit. "to knock on the wrong door") "to seek help, information, or support from the wrong person or source"; and (3) *'bater à porta certa'* (lit. "to knock on the right door") "same as (2), but from the right person or source"; these 3 verbal idioms were all detected as potential idiomatic expressions in the sentence '...o desencanto e o insucesso, que **batem à porta** de milhares de jovens e adolescentes...' '...the disenchantment and failure that affect thousands of young people and teenagers...'. Initially, all were marked as being idiomatic, but in the end, this case was reviewed and it was marked as an instance of the first verbal idiom.

Thirdly, sentences where the annotator cannot determine whether the meaning is idiomatic or literal due to a lack of context are marked as non-idiomatic. For example, in the sentence 'Vai integralmente ao fundo!' ('lit. It goes completely to the bottom!'), the potential expression *'ir ao fundo'* (lit. "to go to the bottom") "to go under", can have an idiomatic meaning (e.g., if the subject is 'projeto' 'project') or a literal one (e.g., if the subject is 'barco' 'boat').

With an inter-annotator agreement of 0.869 (surpassing the 0.8 threshold for satisfactory reliability[4]), it was reasonable to assume a consistent performance among annotators in the annotation task. This enabled an optimized workflow for the remaining 171 documents, which were evenly and randomly split among the annotators, with each document being assigned to a single annotator.

4 Results

Table 3 presents a detailed breakdown of the detected potential verbal idioms, along with those annotated in documents from both sources.

It is noteworthy that the documents from the Portuguese Parliament exhibit a substantially higher number of potential verbal idioms compared to the other document source. While the presence of potential verbal idioms does not directly reflect the frequency of valid idiomatic instances, in this case, the number of annotated verbal idioms is also significantly greater in the parliamentary documents.

Taking this analysis further, we observe that the verbal idioms annotated in the documents from this source exhibit considerably less variation, with a total of 377 distinct expressions, compared to the 606 different constructions identified in the *CETEMPúblico* documents (resulting in an overall count of 747 distinct verbal idioms). This suggests that the higher number of verbal idioms in the first source is primarily driven by the repetition of the same, likely context-specific, constructions. This hypothesis is reinforced by expressions such as *'esgotar o tempo'* (lit. "to deplete the time") "to run out of time" and *'usar da palavra'* (lit. "to use of the word") "to speak", which appear frequently in the Portuguese Parliament documents, with 275 and 128 instances, respectively, whereas in the other source, they occur only three times each.

Source	Portuguese Parliament	CETEMPúblico
# Potential Expressions	5,824	4,797
# Annotated Expressions	2,981	2,197
% Potential Annotated	51.18%	45.80%
# Diff Idioms Annotated	377	606

Table 3: Annotations of the *corpus* across sources of documents.

It is important to highlight that approximately 50% of the detected potential verbal idioms correspond to actual idiomatic expressions. This finding suggests that the criteria established for identifying potential verbal idioms are sufficiently stringent to prevent an excessive number of non-idiomatic constructions from being captured.

When it comes to the number of frozen elements in the annotated verbal idioms, Table 4 shows that the shorter and, in a sense, simpler expressions are more common than larger ones.

Lastly, it is noteworthy that the lexicon-grammar matrix describes a total of 2,714 different verbal idioms, of which only 747 were actually found in the documents analyzed. This makes evident how rare some of these idiomatic constructions really are, as well as the relevance of building and maintaining lexicons of such MWE. Considering that recent trends in NLP consist of training models on

[4] https://www.k-alpha.org/methodological-notes

# Frozen Elements	Example	Count
2	**'tirar partido'** "to benefit from"	3419
3	**'vir a público'** "to go public"	1478
4	**'não se fazer esperar'** "to not take long"	244
5	**'não fazer mal a mosca'** "to be harmless"	37

Table 4: Number of instances of verbal idioms based on the number of frozen elements present (including the main verb).

existing data/texts, the sparse distribution of verbal idioms in *corpora* may raise concerns regarding the overall efficacy of these approaches instead of lexicon-based methods (Savary et al., 2019).

Table 5 shows the overall number of annotations of the 10 most frequent verbal idioms in both *corpora* combined.

Verbal Idiom	Count
FIXED_C1(valer,pena)	358
FIXED_CAN(chamar,atenção)	335
FIXED_C1(esgotar,tempo)	278
FIXED_C1PN(pedir,desculpa)	264
FIXED_C1PN(dizer,respeito)	248
FIXED_CADV(ir,longe)	226
FIXED_CP1(chegar,a,fim)	224
FIXED_C1PN(abrir,porta)	146
FIXED_CP1(usar,de,palavra)	131
FIXED_C1(seguir,caminho)	121

Table 5: Number of instances of the most frequent verbal idioms annotated in both *corpora* combined. Number of different FIXED dependencies: 747; Total number of annotations: 5,178.

5 Conclusion

This paper introduced VIDiom-PT, a *corpus* of European Portuguese annotated for verbal idioms which is made publicly available. We outlined the selection criteria for source texts, the lexicon-grammar framework adopted for the linguistic description of verbal idioms, the annotation process—including guidelines—and the development of two annotation tools, culminating in a fully annotated dataset. The paper discusses several issues involved in the annotation process, mostly the challenge of distinguishing idiomatic (i.e., non-compositional) from literal meanings, a central issue in idiom annotation. The resulting corpus comprises 5,178 annotated instances covering 747 distinct verbal idioms. The annotation process was validated through an inter-annotator agreement assessment, yielding a Krippendorff's alpha of 0.869 based on independent annotations of 5% of the data by three specialists, indicating a high level of reliability. A golden standard was established based on the consensus annotation of this data subset.

We anticipate that VIDiom-PT will serve as a valuable resource for advancing research in various NLP tasks involving verbal idioms in European Portuguese, including idiom identification, meaning extraction, and machine translation.

Acknowledgments

This work was funded by Portuguese national funds through the Fundação para a Ciência e a Tecnologia (Reference: UIDB/50021/2020, DOI: 10.54499/UIDB/50021/2020) and by the European Commission (Project: iRead4Skills, Reference: 1010094837, Program: HORIZON-CL2-2022-TRANSFORMATIONS-01-07, DOI: 10.3030/101094837).

References

Tosin P Adewumi, Roshanak Vadoodi, Aparajita Tripathy, Konstantina Nikolaidou, Foteini Liwicki, and Marcus Liwicki. 2021. Potential Idiomatic Expression (PIE)-English: Corpus for Classes of Idioms. *arXiv preprint arXiv:2105.03280.*

Sandra Antunes, Maria Fernanda Bacelar do Nascimento, João Miguel Casteleiro, Amália Mendes, Luísa Pereira, and Tiago Sá. 2006. A Lexical Database of Portuguese Multiword Expressions. In *Computational Processing of the Portuguese Language*, pages 238–243, Berlin, Heidelberg. Springer Berlin Heidelberg.

Jorge Baptista. 2008. Structuring of cross-linguistic database of frozen sentences. In Carmen González Royo and Pedro Mogorròn Huerta, editors, *Estudios y análisis de fraseología contrastiva: lexicografía y traducción*, pages 37–46. Universidade de Alicante, Alicante.

Jorge Baptista, Anabela Correia, and Graça Fernandes. 2004. Frozen Sentences of Portuguese: Formal

Descriptions for NLP. In *Workshop on Multiword Expressions: Integrating Processing*, pages 72–79, Barcelona, Spain. International Conference of the European Chapter of the Association for Computational Linguistics, ACL.

Mathieu Constant, Gülşen Eryiğit, Johanna Monti, Lonneke van der Plas, Carlos Ramisch, Michael Rosner, and Amalia Todirascu. 2017. Multiword expression processing: A Survey. *Computational Linguistics*, 43(4):837–892.

Milena de Uzeda Garrão and Maria Carmelita P Dias. 2001. Um estudo de expressões cristalizadas do tipo V+ SN e sua inclusão em um tradutor automático bilíngüe (português/inglês). *Cadernos de Tradução*, 2(8):165–182.

Rafael Ehren, Kilian Evang, and Laura Kallmeyer. 2024. To Leave No Stone Unturned: Annotating Verbal Idioms in the Parallel Meaning Bank. In *Proceedings of the Joint Workshop on Multiword Expressions and Universal Dependencies (MWE-UD)@ LREC-COLING 2024*, pages 115–124.

Ana Galvão. 2019. Processing Frozen Sentences in Portuguese - Automatic Rule and Example Generation from a Lexicon-Grammar. Master's thesis, Universidade de Lisboa, Instituto Superior Técnico.

Maurice Gross. 1982. Une classification des phrases « figées » du français. *Revue québécoise de linguistique*, 11(2):151–185.

Maurice Gross. 1996. Lexicon-grammar. In Keith Brown and Jim Miller, editors, *Concise Encyclopedia of Syntactic Theories*, pages 244–259. Pergamon, Cambridge.

Hessel Haagsma, Johan Bos, and Malvina Nissim. 2020. MAGPIE: A Large Corpus of Potentially Idiomatic Expressions. In *12th Language Resources and Evaluation Conference: LREC 2020*, pages 279–287. European Language Resources Association (ELRA).

Chikara Hashimoto and Daisuke Kawahara. 2008. Construction of an Idiom Corpus and its Application to Idiom Identification based on WSD Incorporating Idiom-specific Features. In *Proceedings of the 2008 Conference on Empirical Methods in Natural Language Processing*, pages 992–1001.

Deirdre Hogan, Conor Cafferkey, Aoife Cahill, and Josef van Genabith. 2007. Exploiting multi-word units in history-based probabilistic generation. In *Proceedings of the 2007 Joint Conference on Empirical Methods in Natural Language Processing and Computational Natural Language Learning (EMNLP-CoNLL)*, pages 267–276, Prague, Czech Republic. Association for Computational Linguistics.

Ray Jackendoff. 1997. *The Architecture of the Language Faculty*. MIT Press.

Daisuke Kawahara and Sadao Kurohashi. 2006. Case Frame Compilation from the Web Using High-Performance Computing. In *LREC*, pages 1344–1347.

Klaus Krippendorff. 2008. Systematic and Random Disagreement and the Reliability of Nominal Data. *Communication Methods and Measures*, 2(4):323–338.

Christopher D. Manning and Hinrich Schütze. 1999. *Foundations of Statistical Natural Language Processing*. The MIT Press.

Amália Mendes, Sandra Antunes, Maria Fernanda Bacelar do Nascimento, João Miguel Casteleiro, Luísa Pereira, and Tiago Sá. 2006. COMBINA-PT: A Large Corpus-extracted and Hand-checked Lexical Database of Portuguese Multiword Expressions. In *Proceedings of the V International Conference on Language Resources and Evaluation-LREC2006*. European Language Resources Association.

Diego Moussallem, Mohamed Ahmed Sherif, Diego Esteves, Marcos Zampieri, and Axel-Cyrille Ngonga Ngomo. 2018. LIDIOMS: A Multilingual Linked Idioms Data Set. *arXiv preprint arXiv:1802.08148*.

Jing Peng and Anna Feldman. 2017. Automatic Idiom Recognition with Word Embeddings. In *Information Management and Big Data: Second Annual International Symposium, SIMBig 2015, Cusco, Peru, September 2-4, 2015, and Third Annual International Symposium, SIMBig 2016, Cusco, Peru, September 1-3, 2016, Revised Selected Papers 2*, pages 17–29. Springer.

Carlos Ramisch, Renata Ramisch, Leonardo Zilio, Aline Villavicencio, and Silvio Cordeiro. 2018. A Corpus Study of Verbal Multiword Expressions in Brazilian Portuguese. In *Computational Processing of the Portuguese Language*, pages 24–34, Cham. Springer International Publishing.

Giancarlo Salton, Robert J Ross, and John D Kelleher. 2014. Evaluation of a Substitution Method for Idiom Transformation in Statistical Machine Translation. In *10th Workshop on Multiword Expressions (MWE 2014)*. Technological University Dublin.

Diana Santos and Paulo Rocha. 2001. Evaluating CETEMPúblico, a free resource for Portuguese. In *Proceedings of the 39th annual meeting of the association for computational linguistics*, pages 450–457.

Agata Savary, Silvio Ricardo Cordeiro, and Carlos Ramisch. 2019. Without Lexicons, Multiword Expression Identification Will Never Fly: A Position Statement. In *Joint Workshop on Multiword Expressions and WordNet (MWE-WN 2019)*, pages 79–91. Association for Computational Linguistics.

Agata Savary, Carlos Ramisch, Silvio Cordeiro, Federico Sangati, Veronika Vincze, Behrang QasemiZadeh, Marie Candito, Fabienne Cap, Voula Giouli, Ivelina Stoyanova, and Antoine Doucet. 2017. The

PARSEME shared task on automatic identification of verbal multiword expressions. In *Proceedings of the 13th Workshop on Multiword Expressions (MWE 2017)*, pages 31–47, Valencia, Spain. Association for Computational Linguistics.

Ziheng Zeng and Suma Bhat. 2021. Idiomatic Expression Identification Using Semantic Compatibility. *Transactions of the Association for Computational Linguistics*, 9:1546–1562.

A Annotation Guidelines

Annotation Process

The annotation tool will display a sentence, highlighting words that potentially form a verbal idiom. The *targeted words* can be separated by up to 5 tokens (words or punctuation). For example:

- **Sentence** 'A estreia em Paris de "Kika", o último filme de Pedro Almodovar jamais passaria despercebida, pois o realizador não deixaria os seus créditos por mãos alheias' 'The premiere of "Kika", the latest film by Pedro Almodóvar, in Paris would never go unnoticed, as the director would not let his reputation be handled by others'.
- **Potential Fixed Expression**: `FIXED_C1PN(deixar, não, crédito, por, mãos, alheias);`
- **Example of Use** 'O João nunca deixa o crédito por mão alheias' 'João never lets his reputation be handled by others'.

Task

The tool asks: *Is this an instance of a verbal idiom?*. You have two buttons to select from: *Yes* or *No*.

When to Select *Yes*: Select *Yes* if the underlined words in the sentence are part of a verbal idiom, even if it does *not exactly match* the provided potential `FIXED` or the example. For instance, if the underlined expression forms a different verbal idiom that partially overlaps with the targeted expression in the potential `FIXED`, answer *Yes*.

When to Select *No*: Select *No* if the underlined words in the sentence are being *used literally*, or the expression does not function as an idiomatic expression. For example: 'O Pedro foi mais longe do que o João no trajeto indicado' 'Pedro went farther than João on the indicated route'.

Reporting Issues

If you encounter any technical issues, click the *Issue Found* button. Use this option *before* selecting *Yes* or *No* so the tool does not proceed to the next sentence. Examples of Issues: the sentence has no text; no words were underlined; the underlined words are unrelated to the potential `FIXED` expression or the example; words are incorrectly or only partially underlined.

Insufficient Context

Select the *Insufficient Context* button if the provided sentence lacks sufficient context to determine whether it includes a verbal idiom or not. The tool will mark it as *No* and proceed to the next sentence.

To Review

Click the *To Review* button if the provided sentence may contain a verbal idiom, but the annotator is uncertain about the intended meaning of the expression used. The tool will mark it as *Yes* and proceed to the next sentence.

MultiCoPIE: A Multilingual Corpus of Potentially Idiomatic Expressions for Cross-lingual PIE Disambiguation

Uliana Sentsova[1], Debora Ciminari[2], Josef van Genabith[1,3], Cristina España-Bonet [3,4]

[1]Saarland University, [2]University of Bologna,
[3]DFKI GmbH, Saarland Informatics Campus,
[4]Barcelona Supercomputing Center (BSC-CNS)

uliana.sentsova@uni-saarland.de, debora.ciminari@studio.unibo.it,
{josef.van_genabith, cristinae}@dfki.de

Abstract

Language models are able to handle compositionality and, to some extent, non-compositional phenomena such as semantic idiosyncrasy, a feature most prominent in the case of idioms. This work introduces the MultiCoPIE corpus that includes potentially idiomatic expressions in Catalan, Italian, and Russian, extending the language coverage of PIE corpus data. The new corpus provides additional linguistic features of idioms, such as their semantic compositionality, part-of-speech of idiom head as well as their corresponding idiomatic expressions in English. With this new resource at hand, we first fine-tune an XLM-RoBERTa model to classify figurative and literal usage of potentially idiomatic expressions in English. We then study cross-lingual transfer to the languages represented in the MultiCoPIE corpus, evaluating the model's ability to generalize an idiom-related task to languages not seen during fine-tuning. We show the effect of 'cross-lingual lexical overlap': the performance of the model, fine-tuned on English idiomatic expressions and tested on the MultiCoPIE languages, increases significantly when classifying 'shared idioms'—idiomatic expressions that have direct counterparts in English with similar form and meaning. While this observation raises questions about the generalizability of cross-lingual learning, the results from experiments on PIEs demonstrate strong evidence of effective cross-lingual transfer, even when accounting for idioms similar across languages.

1 Introduction

High-level language understanding is reflected in the ability to combine meaning units into larger units; this process is known as composition. Natural language often departs from the principle of simple compositionality, as in the case of multiword expressions, or MWEs, commonly described as combinations of words that exhibit a certain degree of lexical, morphological, syntactic and/or semantic idiosyncrasy (Sag et al., 2002; Baldwin and Kim, 2010). A particular category of MWEs are idioms: this category stands out through its idiosyncratic semantics, i.e. the meaning of idiomatic MWEs cannot be obtained by compositionally interpreting their components (Fazly et al., 2009).

In this work, we focus on a subset of MWEs, namely, idiomatic expressions with literal-idiomatic ambiguity (Savary et al., 2018), or expressions that can be used in a literal or figurative sense, such as *blow the whistle* or *black sheep*. Idiomatic expressions with this property can be referred to as 'potentially idiomatic expressions', or PIEs, a term introduced by Haagsma et al., 2020. This term is often used in the context of PIE disambiguation — a task that typically consists of classifying specific idiom occurrences as 'literal' or 'figurative', based on the surrounding context.

In this paper, we present MultiCoPIE, a multilingual corpus of idiomatic expressions with literal and figurative occurrences in Catalan, Italian, and Russian.[1] We fine-tune a masked language model well suited for classification—XLM-RoBERTa (Conneau et al., 2019)—for the PIE disambiguation task on available English data and investigate cross-lingual transfer to the three languages in MultiCoPIE, comparing the cross-lingual model to a baseline, fine-tuned monolingually on the MultiCoPIEdata. We also measure whether the model's performance is affected by the size of provided context.

The cross-lingual experiment allows us to measure whether a classifier fine-tuned for the PIE disambiguation task on English data generalizes to idiomatic expressions in the MultiCoPIE languages, as these PIEs have not been seen by the classifier at the fine-tuning stage. However, it is important to

[1]The MultiCoPIE corpus is publicly available at https://github.com/at-uliana/multicopie

Proceedings of the 21st Workshop on Multiword Expressions (MWE 2025), pages 67–81
May 4, 2025 ©2025 Association for Computational Linguistics

consider that certain idiomatic expressions in the `MultiCoPIE` languages have idiomatic equivalents in English, i.e. cross-lingual pairs of idiomatic expressions with direct lexico-syntactic correspondence and similar semantics (Baldwin and Kim, 2010), such as the Italian idiom *rompere il ghiaccio* (lit. 'to break the ice'), the Catalan idiom *trencar el gel* (lit. 'to break the ice'), and the corresponding English idiom *break the ice*. Since contextualized models produce similar embeddings for words with similar semantics across languages, it becomes difficult to properly interpret the classifier's performance on these cross-lingual idiom pairs and identify whether the model truly evaluates the idiomatic expression in a language outside of the fine-tuning set. To this end, we compare the performance of the classifier on two groups: idiomatic expressions in the `MultiCoPIE` languages that have direct equivalents in English and idiomatic expressions without such equivalents.

2 Related Work

PIE Corpora for English The MAGPIE corpus (Haagsma et al., 2020), a sense-annotated corpus of potentially idiomatic expressions, remains one of the most comprehensive corpora on potentially idiomatic expressions in English. It provides 56,622 annotated instances of idiomatic and literal use of 1,756 idioms extracted from the The British National Corpus (BNC Consortium, 2007) as well as the Parallel Meaning Bank (Abzianidze et al., 2017). The IDIX corpus (Sporleder et al., 2010), also primarily based on the BNC corpus, contains 6k occurrences of 78 English verbal MWEs with a fine-grained annotation of PIE usage with six labels. The EPIE corpus (Saxena and Paul, 2020) is a dataset of 25k instances of 717 idioms, labeled by an automatic system. Adewumi et al. (2022) present the PIE corpus that comprises a collection of 20k instances of 1,200 idioms categorized into 10 classes, such as such as euphemisms, oxymorons, metaphors, literal occurrences and more.

Multilingual and Non-English PIE Corpora A pivotal role in advancing the field of multiword expressions plays the PARSEME project, an international research community that provides MWE-related tools and resources (Savary et al., 2015). The PARSEME corpus (Savary et al., 2023), a multilingual corpus annotated with MWEs[2], covers 26 languages and multiple MWE categories, such as light verb constructions, verbal idioms, and more. Savary et al. (2019) use the PARSEME data to identify idiomatic, literal and coincidental[3] occurrences of verbal MWEs in Basque, German, Greek, Polish and Portuguese; they also provide a formal definition of literal occurrences. The SemEval-2022 Task 2a corpus was released as the dataset for the SemEval-2022 task on Multilingual Idiomaticity Detection and Sentence Embedding (Tayyar Madabushi et al., 2022). The corpus contains multiword expressions in English, Portuguese and Galician and is based on the Noun Compound Senses dataset by Garcia et al. (2021b) as well as on the dataset by Tayyar Madabushi et al. (2021). The ID10M corpus by Tedeschi et al. (2022) provides a token-level annotated dataset of PIEs for 10 languages. PIE corpora also exist for Indian languages (Agrawal et al., 2018), German (Fritzinger et al., 2010; Ehren et al., 2020), Swedish (Kurfalı et al., 2020), Russian (Aharodnik et al., 2018), Persian (Sarlak et al., 2023), Arabic (Hadj Mohamed et al., 2024) and Japanese (Hashimoto and Kawahara, 2008).

Idiomaticity Processing in Transformer Models Shwartz and Dagan (2019) show that BERT (Devlin et al., 2019) outperforms other contextualized models in tasks related to lexical composition. The probing tasks by Tan and Jiang (2021) similarly suggests that BERT is able to encode the idiomatic meaning of PIEs and separates the literal and idiomatic usages of PIEs with high precision. A word-level probing experiment by Nedumpozhimana and Kelleher (2021) shows that BERT recognizes idioms by focusing both on the idiomatic expressions themselves and on the surrounding context. Dankers et al. (2022) use analysis of attention patterns to investigate idiom processing in pre-trained models for the task of translation; their finding gives evidence that idioms are treated differently by the encoder in comparison to literal instances.

Tian et al. (2023) demonstrate that models such as BERT, multilingual BERT (mBERT) (Devlin et al., 2019) and DistilBERT (Sanh et al., 2020) display different attention patterns when representing tokens within idioms. Liu and Lareau (2024)

[2]https://parsemefr.lis-lab.fr/parseme-st-guidelines/1.3/

[3]In simplified terms, a coincidental occurrence of an idiomatic expression does not preserve the syntactic dependencies between the components of its canonical form. To illustrate with an example from MAGPIE, the sentence *Britain is the world leader in deaths caused by heart disease* constitutes a coincidental occurrence of the idiom *by heart*.

employ CamemBERT (Martin et al., 2020), the pre-trained BERT-derived model for French, for a de-masking task and show that the model makes better predictions for tokens within idioms, as compared to tokens within simple lexemes. Despite the evidence that transformer-based pre-trained language models are able to distinguish between idiomatic and literal contexts with high accuracy, multiple studies highlight that transformer-based models struggle to represent phrase meanings in a nuanced way (Nandakumar et al., 2019; Yu and Ettinger, 2020; Garcia et al., 2021a).

PIE Disambiguation with Transfomer-Based Models Hashempour and Villavicencio (2020) leverage the Idiom Principle[4] and use Context2Vec (Melamud et al., 2016) and BERT to classify literal and figurative senses of English idioms in the VNC-tokens dataset (Cook et al., 2008), with BERT-based model achieving the mean F-score of 0.71. Kurfalı and Östling (2020) utilize contextual embeddings by BERT and mBERT, for supervised and unsupervised PIE classification tasks in English and German, achieving the F-score of 0.93 on the Semeval5b dataset (Korkontzelos et al., 2013), 0.90 on the VNC-tokens dataset (Cook et al., 2008), and 0.94 on the German data (Horbach et al., 2016) in the supervised setting. The study by Zeng and Bhat (2021) proposes a novel architecture that uses contextualized and static word embeddings to detect PIE occurrences based on their semantic compatibility with context. In SemEval-2022, Tayyar Madabushi et al. (2022) introduced the Multilingual Idiomaticity Detection and Sentence Embedding task, with Subtask A dedicated to binary classification of literal and figurative idiom usage. The majority of contributions are based on the transformer architecture, including pre-trained multilingual models (Chu et al., 2022; Hauer et al., 2022; Yamaguchi et al., 2022). In contrast to fine-tuning experiments performed jointly in several languages, Fakharian and Cook (2021) take a different approach: in addition to monolingual experiments, researchers explore cross-lingual transfer for English and Russian by fine-tuning several models from the BERT family for binary classification of PIEs; the fine-tuned mBERT achieves 72.4% accuracy in the English-to-Russian experiment and 80.1% accuracy in the Russian-to-English experiment.

[4]The Idiom Principle states that preconstructed phrases such as multiword expressions are stored and retrieved by language users as a single unit (Sinclair, 1991).

3 Corpus Creation

3.1 Candidate Selection

We manually create `MultiCoPIE`, a multilingual corpus of potentially idiomatic expressions, for three languages: Catalan, Italian, and Russian. The corpus encompasses potentially idiomatic expressions that can be understood figuratively or literally, depending on the surrounding context.

Idiomatic expressions do not constitute a homogeneous set of language items and are notoriously difficult to define precisely (Grant, 2004). The boundaries separating idiomatic expressions and other classes of multiword expressions are often blurred (Nunberg et al., 1994; Baldwin and Kim, 2010; Fazly et al., 2009). In this work, we use the following definition of idioms: an idiom is a conventionalized multiword expression that is semantically idiosyncratic, i.e. the meaning of an idiom cannot be derived by combining the meanings of its components. An idiom can be fully non-compositional when none of the components contribute to the meaning of the idiom (such as *spill the beans* or *break the ice*), or partially compositional when some components contribute to the meaning but not others (for instance, *green with envy*, *box clever*). For `MultiCoPIE`, we favor fully non-compositional idioms but include partially compositional expressions as well.

The selection of idiomatic expressions depends on resources available for the language. For Italian, we compile a list of idioms by consulting online dictionaries, such as Il Nuovo De Mauro[5] and Dizionario dei Modi di Dire Hoepli.[6] For Catalan, we select frequent idioms from online resources.[7,8,9] For Russian, we manually extract relevant idiomatic expressions from the Russian Wiktionary[10] as well as from online lexicographic resources.[11] For all languages, we select syntactically diverse idiomatic expressions, with verbal idioms constituting the majority for all `MultiCoPIE` languages.

It is important to consider that idiomatic expressions display great variability in how often they are used in a figurative and literal sense. In ad-

[5]`https://dizionario.internazionale.it/`
[6]`https://dizionari.corriere.it/dizionario-modi-di-dire`
[7]`https://rodamots.cat/tema/frases-fetes/`
[8]`https://visca.com/apac/dites/`
[9]`https://pccd.dites.cat/`
[10]`https://ru.wiktionary.org/wiki/`
[11]`https://phraseology.academic.ru/`

Language	Idioms	Instances	Sentences	Tokens	Figurative Instances	Literal Instances
Catalan	123	2733	8.1k	200k	2221 (81.3%)	512 (18.7%)
Italian	111	2245	6.7k	129k	1887 (84.1%)	358 (15.9%)
Russian	145	2902	8.9k	140k	1734 (59.8%)	1168 (40.2%)

Table 1: Statistics on our new corpus `MultiCoPIE`.

dition to truly ambiguous idioms (*dig deep*, *cold feet*, *hold water*) that allow straightforward literal interpretation and are equally frequent in their literal and figurative sense, comprehensive corpora such as MAGPIE (Haagsma et al., 2020) include idiomatic expressions where literal interpretation is unlikely or implausible (*armed to the teeth*, *food for thought*, *play for keeps*, *throw caution to the wind*), at least not without disrupting the idiom's internal dependency structure. The MAGPIE authors point out that truly ambiguous idioms are rare, with 58.94% of idiom types in MAGPIE occurring only in their idiomatic sense (Haagsma et al., 2020). With this in mind, we add idioms where literal interpretation is less likely. We believe that inclusion of less ambiguous idiomatic expressions could provide valuable information for models learning about non-compositional semantics.

We annotate each selected candidate idiom with two additional features: syntactic category and semantic compositionality. Details on the annotation process are provided in Appendix A.

Cross-Lingual Lexical Overlap As mentioned earlier, the `MultiCoPIE` corpus contains idiomatic expressions that have idiomatic equivalents in English with similar form and meaning. In this study, we refer to these cross-language idiom pairs as 'shared idioms'. We find a considerable amount of such shared idioms and annotate them in `MultiCoPIE`, for instance, the Italian idiom *piangere sul latte versato* that literally translates as 'to cry over spilled milk' —a corresponding idiom in English with the same semantics. We also annotate idioms that have a close lexical (but not identical) correspondence, such as the Italian idiom *mettere nero su bianco* (lit. 'to put black on white') which broadly corresponds to the English idiom *to be (down) in black and white* and its variation *in black and white*.

3.2 Extraction of Instances

To extract literal and figurative instances of selected idioms, we use the Open Super-large Crawled Aggregated coRpus (OSCAR), a multilingual corpus of documents created by filtering Common Crawl (Ortiz Suárez et al., 2019; Abadji et al., 2021). We download and pre-process OSCAR versions 22.01 (Catalan) and 23.01 (Italian and Russian). We split the documents at paragraph level, eliminate duplicate paragraphs and normalize the texts using Moses scripts (Koehn et al., 2007).

For all languages, we locate idiom occurrences in OSCAR, not necessarily in the dictionary form, and extract the instance with the idiom and the context required by a human to disambiguate it. We use broad-coverage string-matching search patterns to ensure that a diverse set of instances is extracted, including lexical variations in idiomatic expressions. We collect instances where the idiom sense can be easily resolved within one or two sentences, excluding cases of word play and instances without sufficient context. Each target instance typically consists of one sentence with two surrounding sentences. All extracted instances are labeled as `figurative` or `literal` by a native speaker.

We aim at maintaining a balanced distribution of `figurative` versus `literal` labels, rather than reflecting their frequency in corpora such as OSCAR, which is challenging to estimate precisely. As mentioned in Section 3.1, PIE corpora typically tend to have more figurative than literal instances; `MultiCoPIE` is not an exception. Due to this imbalance, we include some literal instances from additional sources such as recent online newspapers and books.

The selection of literal instances generally aligns with the study by Savary et al. (2019) which provides a semantically and syntactically motivated definition of what constitutes a literal occurrence of a MWE. As such, we only collect instances where the target idiomatic expression preserves the same internal dependency structure as its canonical form and disregard coincidental occurrences.

Similar to Tayyar Madabushi et al. (2022), we include occurrences of idioms when encountering them as part of named entities (for instance, *the movie "The Devil's Advocate"*), annotating them with the `literal` label. These instances

	Zero-shot		One-shot		Random	
	w/o context	with context	w/o context	with context	w/o context	with context
`majority-class` **accuracy**	.77 ± .02	.77 ± .02	.73 ± .03	.73 ± .03	.76 ± .01	.76 ± .01
`majority-class` **F1-score**	.87 ± .02	.87 ± .02	.84 ± .02	.84 ± .02	.87 ± .00	.87 ± .00
Accuracy	.86 ± .02	.86 ± .02	.86 ± .02	.86 ± .01	**.93 ± .01**	.92 ± .01
F1-score	.91 ± .02	.91 ± .02	.91 ± .01	.91 ± .01	**.95 ± .01**	**.95 ± .01**
Precision	.92 ± .02	.92 ± .03	.92 ± .01	.90 ± .03	**.96 ± .01**	**.96 ± .01**
Recall	.89 ± .03	.90 ± .04	.90 ± .03	.92 ± .03	**.95 ± .01**	.94 ± .01

Table 2: Performance scores (mean and standard deviation) averaged over 10 runs after fine-tuning XLM-RoBERTa on the English data. The first two rows report the majority class baseline F1 and accuracy scores. The best overall performance scores are highlighted in **bold**.

proved to be useful for idiom-related tasks, as shown by Tedeschi and Navigli (2022) who leverage named entity recognition for idiomaticity detection. In addition, we separately mark cases of idioms occurring within a metaphor and label them as `figurative`; however, we find only a few such cases.

3.3 Token-Level Annotation

In each collected instance, we annotate the lexicalized components of idioms, i.e. components that are always present in variations of an idiomatic expression (Savary et al., 2018). We additionally annotate other idiomatic expressions that appear in the instances. We do not annotate expressions where the idiomaticity is statistical (collocations) or pragmatic (formulaic expressions such as *Thank God*) as well as other types of figurative language, such as metaphors, proverbs, or sarcasm.

Table 1 shows the `MultiCoPIE` statistics.

4 Monolingual PIE Classification

4.1 English Data

To fine-tune our idiom disambiguation classifier, we use monolingual English data comprised of MAGPIE and the English subset of the SemEval-2022 Task 2a dataset. Both corpora were manually annotated by native speakers and include not only the target sentences containing idioms but also the surrounding context. While MAGPIE serves as a backbone of our training data due to its size, the SemEval-2022 Task 2a corpus provides additional idiom types as well as interesting cases when an idiom functions as part of a named entity. From the SemEval dataset, we exclude less idiomatic items, such as *law firm* and *application form*; for the selected 75 idioms, we keep all the instances. From MAGPIE, we select 1513 phrase-level idioms, excluding clauses and dependent clauses. We exclude instances with the inter-annotator agreement lower than 75% and use one preceding and one following sentence as context. The combined dataset consists of 37.9k instances of 1582 idiom types; 75.9% of the instances are labeled as `figurative`.

4.2 Problem Setting

As a base for our classifier, we use the HuggingFace `xlm-roberta-base` implementation (Wolf et al., 2020) of the multilingual XLM-RoBERTa model (Conneau et al., 2019) and fine-tune it for the binary PIE disambiguation task in English with the dataset described in Section 4.1. We fine-tune the model in three settings: zero-shot, one-shot, and random. In the zero-shot setting, the model is tested on idioms that were not present in the training set, reflecting its ability to generalize to unseen cases. In the one-shot setting, the model is exposed to one instance of each idiom during fine-tuning. The random setting is not type-aware and the test instances are selected randomly. For the zero-shot and one-shot settings, 15% of idioms (240 idioms) were allocated for validation and another 15% for testing. For the random setting, the sizes of the validation and test sets were predefined to approximately match those of the other two settings. This ensures a fair comparison across all settings. As a result, in each setting, the models were fine-tuned on 26k instances, with approximately 5.9k instances each in the validation and test sets. Appendix B (Table 7) provides a detailed description of the data splits.

In each setting, the models are fine-tuned either with context or without context: in the 'without context' setting, we use only the sentence containing the idiomatic expression, while in the 'with context' setting, we additionally include the surrounding context (± one sentence).

4.3 Model Selection and Fine-Tuning

The binary classification head on top of the pretrained XLM-RoBERTa consists of a dense linear layer with 768 input and output features, followed by a dropout layer with the dropout rate of 0.1. We perform a grid search to determine the most appropriate values for the learning rate and batch size (see Appendix B). For each setting, we fine-tune 10 models with the best parameters. Table 2 provides the classification results on English averaged over 10 models. Results are compared to the `majority-class` baseline that always considers the majority class (`figurative`) as output label.

4.4 Analysis

Table 2 summarizes the results of the PIE classification task in three settings (zero-shot, one-shot, and random), with and without context. All models outperform the `majority-class` baseline. While the zero-shot and one-shot settings perform similarly, with an average F1-score of 0.91 and 86% accuracy, models trained in the random setting achieve a significant improvement, showing an increase of 0.04 F1 points and 7% accuracy over the other settings. This notable performance gain in the random setting can be explained by the distribution of idiom types in the training and test sets. Although the models in each setting are fine-tuned on a comparable number of instances, the random setting's training set includes a substantially higher number of instances of idioms that also appear in the test set.

Regarding the 'with context' and 'without context' classification, none of the settings shows notable differences in performance when surrounding sentences are included. Our finding corroborates the conclusion by Knietaite et al. (2024) who show that in PIE disambiguation, sentence-level models outperform models fine-tuned on paragraph-wide context. The authors hypothesize that surrounding sentences do not provide relevant clues for PIE disambiguation and may distract the model.

5 Cross-Lingual Lexical Overlap and Transfer

To explore cross-lingual transfer, we use models fine-tuned for the PIE disambiguation task on the English data and evaluate them on the `MultiCoPIE` languages, which have not been observed during fine-tuning. We employ two baselines: the `majority-class` baseline and the `xlm-r-multicopie` baseline. The `majority-class` assigns the `figurative` label (majority class) to all observations, reflecting label distribution in the `MultiCoPIE` for each language. For the `xlm-r-multicopie` baseline, we fine-tune an XLM-RoBERTa classifier on the `MultiCoPIE` data, separately for each language. We fine-tune 10 models in a zero-shot setting, selecting 70% of the idioms for the training set, 15% for validation and 15% for testing. Table 4 shows training, validation and test set sizes for each language. The hyperparameters used are those identified through grid search for the monolingual English classifier (see Section 4.3).

5.1 Analysis of Classification Results

When evaluated on the `MultiCoPIE` data, the zero-shot and one-shot models show comparable performance, while the models fine-tuned in the random setting have slightly lower scores. We choose the one-shot setting to demonstrate the results of the cross-lingual transfer; the results of the zero-shot and random models are reported in the Appendix C (Tables 8 and 10). Table 3 summarizes the results of the one-shot English classifier, evaluated on `MultiCoPIE` with and without context.

The classifier, fine-tuned on English data, consistently outperforms the majority class baseline across all three languages in both the 'without context' and 'with context' settings, as evidenced by improvements in accuracy and F1-scores. When compared to the `xlm-r-multicopie` baseline, the largest gains are observed for Catalan, where the classifier achieves an average F1-score of 0.94 in both context settings, reflecting an increase of 0.05 points and 0.04 points over the baseline. In terms of accuracy, the classifier reaches 91% ('without context') and 90% ('with context'), representing an 8% and 7% improvement over the baseline, respectively. For Italian, the classifier achieves an average F1-score of 0.92, representing an increase of 0.02 points over the baseline in both settings. It also attains an average accuracy of 87%, corresponding to a relative improvement of 4% ('without context') and 3% ('with context') over the baseline. In contrast, for Russian, the classifier does not surpass the baseline, achieving average F1-scores of 0.89 ('without context') and 0.88 ('with context'), compared to the baseline's 0.91 in both settings. Similarly, the classifier's accuracy for Russian — 87% ('without context') and 85% ('with context')— falls short of the baseline's 89% accuracy.

	w/o context			with context		
	CA	IT	RU	CA	IT	RU
`majority-class` **accuracy**	$.81 \pm .00$	$.84 \pm .00$	$.60 \pm .00$	$.81 \pm .00$	$.84 \pm .00$	$.60 \pm .00$
`majority-class` **F1-score**	$.90 \pm .00$	$.91 \pm .00$	$.75 \pm .00$	$.90 \pm .00$	$.91 \pm .00$	$.75 \pm .00$
`xlm-r-multicopie` **accuracy**	$.83 \pm .09$	$.83 \pm .04$	$\mathbf{.89 \pm .02}$	$.83 \pm .06$	$.84 \pm .04$	$\mathbf{.89 \pm .02}$
`xlm-r-multicopie` **F1-score**	$.89 \pm .06$	$.90 \pm .02$	$\mathbf{.91 \pm .01}$	$.90 \pm .04$	$.90 \pm .02$	$\mathbf{.91 \pm .01}$
Accuracy	$\mathbf{.91 \pm .01}$	$\mathbf{.87 \pm .01}$	$.87 \pm .01$	$\mathbf{.90 \pm .01}$	$\mathbf{.87 \pm .02}$	$.85 \pm .02$
F1-score	$\mathbf{.94 \pm .00}$	$\mathbf{.92 \pm .01}$	$.89 \pm .01$	$\mathbf{.94 \pm .01}$	$\mathbf{.92 \pm .01}$	$.88 \pm .02$
Precision	$.95 \pm .01$	$.94 \pm .01$	$.89 \pm .03$	$.93 \pm .02$	$.93 \pm .01$	$.88 \pm .04$
Recall	$.94 \pm .01$	$.90 \pm .02$	$.90 \pm .02$	$.95 \pm .03$	$.92 \pm .04$	$.88 \pm .06$

Table 3: Performance scores (mean and standard deviation) averaged over 10 runs, obtained by fine-tuning XLM-RoBERTa on the English training set (see Section 4.3) and evaluating on the `MultiCoPIE` languages. The first two rows report the majority class baseline F1 and accuracy scores. The following two rows show the results of XLM-RoBERTa models fine-tuned monolingually on `MultiCoPIE`, also averaged over 10 runs. The best performance scores for each language and context setting are highlighted in **bold**.

		Idioms	Instances
CA	**training**	85	1900 ± 167
	validation	19	412 ± 108
	test	19	421 ± 113
IT	**training**	77	1556 ± 13
	validation	17	341 ± 7
	test	17	385 ± 51
RU	**training**	101	2028 ± 44
	validation	22	451 ± 40
	test	22	423 ± 47

Table 4: Sizes of the `MultiCoPIE` data splits used for fine-tuning XLM-RoBERTa models, which serve as monolingual baselines for each language in the cross-lingual transfer experiment.

	shared and seen		not shared or not seen	
	Acc.	F1	Acc.	F1
CA *	$.95 \pm .01$	$.97 \pm .01$	$.90 \pm .01$	$.94 \pm .00$
IT *	$.95 \pm .01$	$.97 \pm .01$	$.86 \pm .01$	$.92 \pm .01$
RU *	$.89 \pm .02$	$.91 \pm .02$	$.87 \pm .01$	$.89 \pm .01$

Table 5: Accuracy and F1 scores (mean and standard deviation) for idioms whose English equivalent are present ('shared and seen') or absent ('not shared or not seen') in the training set. The rows marked with an asterisk (*) indicate statistically significant results (p-value < 0.05).

Similar to the testing on English data, the 'without context' classification yields rather mixed results compared to the 'with context' classification, improving certain performance metrics while negatively impacting others.

The performance of the classifier, fine-tuned on English and evaluated on the `MultiCoPIE` languages, can be interpreted through two key factors. First, the XLM-RoBERTa model was pre-trained on a multilingual corpus with an uneven distribution of language data, which may favor high-resource languages (Conneau et al., 2019). For instance, the pre-training corpus contains 23,408 million tokens for Russian, significantly more than the 4,983 million tokens for Italian and 1,752 million tokens for Catalan. This disparity in data availability could contribute to the stronger `xlm-r-multicopie` baseline performance on Russian. Second, the effectiveness of cross-lingual transfer is known to be influenced by linguistic similarity between the source and target languages (Lauscher et al., 2020). This may explain why the model performs better when transferring from English to Catalan and Italian —languages that share closer typological and lexical ties with English— compared to Russian, which exhibits greater morphological complexity and distinct syntactic features.

5.2 Cross-Lingual Lexical Overlap

In addition to the cross-lingual transfer, we measure the effect of cross-lingual lexical overlap between idioms in the English training set and the `MultiCoPIE` corpus.

To estimate the effect of shared idioms on the PIE classifier, we separate the `MultiCoPIE` data into two groups:

(1) 'shared and seen': `MultiCoPIE` idioms that have an equivalent in English with similar form and meaning, and the English equivalent was present in the training set during fine-tuning (see Section 3.1);

(2) 'not shared or not seen': `MultiCoPIE` idioms

without an English equivalent, or when the English equivalent was not present during fine-tuning.

We evaluate the classifier's performance in the 'without context' setting on the two groups of idioms, calculating accuracy and F1-scores for each of the 10 fine-tuned models. To determine whether the average performance differs significantly between the two groups, we conduct a one-way analysis of variance (ANOVA) on the performance scores. Table 5 summarizes the average performance by group and language, while Table 11 in Appendix C provides detailed ANOVA statistics. Across all languages, both accuracy and F1-score show a remarkable improvement for 'shared' idioms. The ANOVA test confirms that the classifier's performance improves significantly when evaluating a non-English idiom that corresponds to a seen English expression with similar form and meaning. Importantly, when cross-lingual lexical overlap is absent (as in 'not shared or not seen' group), the classifier outperforms the majority baseline for all languages and surpasses the `xlm-r-multicopie` baseline for Italian and Catalan. This suggests that the metrics for the 'not shared or not seen' group provide a more accurate assessment of the model's cross-lingual learning and generalization capabilities.

6 Conclusions and Future Work

In this paper, we introduce a new corpus, `MultiCoPIE` , extending language coverage of PIE data. We then evaluate the performance of a classifier fine-tuned on idiom disambiguation in monolingual (English) and cross-lingual settings (Catalan, Italian, Russian).

In the monolingual setting, our classifier outperforms the majority baselines in the zero-shot, one-shot, and random settings. In the cross-lingual experiment, our classifier, fine-tuned on English data only, surpasses the majority baseline for all languages in `MultiCoPIE`. It also outperforms XLM-RoBERTa models fine-tuned monolingually on the `MultiCoPIE` data for Italian and Catalan, while showing slightly lower performance on Russian. This indicates that, when leveraging pre-trained models like XLM-RoBERTa, less-resourced languages may benefit substantially from cross-lingual transfer, often outperforming fine-tuning on small monolingual datasets. In contrast, high-resource languages such as Russian may achieve better results when fine-tuned on even modest amounts of monolingual data, given their richer representation in the pre-training corpus.

We also demonstrate that the cross-lingual model shows an increase in performance when classifying `MultiCoPIE` idioms that have an English equivalent with similar form and meaning present in the English training set during fine-tuning. This finding supports the idea that a PIE classifier, fine-tuned on one language, can benefit from the lexical overlap between cross-lingual idiom pairs during evaluation on unseen languages, which may result in overly optimistic performance scores. This finding may be especially relevant for closely related languages that share a large amount of idiomatic expressions.

While this result highlights limitations in cross-lingual learning and cautions against overestimating cross-lingual generalization, the experiment on PIE disambiguation clearly demonstrates the presence of cross-lingual transfer, even after accounting for cross-lingual overlap between languages.

Limitations

There are a few limitations to consider when interpreting the results. Although comprehensive, the datasets in English, Italian and Catalan are biased toward idiomatic instances. Future research could address these limitations by selecting balanced data for fine-tuning as well as for monolingual and cross-lingual testing. Another constraint is the availability of only one annotator per language when creating and annotating `MultiCoPIE`.

Currently, only limited conclusions can be made about the cross-lingual generalization in the PIE task due to presence of only Indo-European languages in the cross-lingual transfer experiments; expanding this work to include non-Indo-European languages could provide more comprehensive insights and it is planned as future work. Also, a broader range of classification approaches and classifiers should be considered.

Acknowledgements

This work has been funded by the *Deutsche Forschungsgemeinschaft* (DFG, German Research Foundation) – SFB 1102 Information Density and Linguistic Encoding.

References

Julien Abadji, Pedro Javier Ortiz Suárez, Laurent Romary, and Benoît Sagot. 2021. Ungoliant: An optimized pipeline for the generation of a very large-scale multilingual web corpus. In *Proceedings of the Workshop on Challenges in the Management of Large Corpora (CMLC-9) 2021. Limerick, 12 July 2021 (Online-Event)*, pages 1–9, Mannheim. Leibniz-Institut für Deutsche Sprache.

Lasha Abzianidze, Johannes Bjerva, Kilian Evang, Hessel Haagsma, Rik van Noord, Pierre Ludmann, Duc-Duy Nguyen, and Johan Bos. 2017. The Parallel Meaning Bank: Towards a multilingual corpus of translations annotated with compositional meaning representations. In *Proceedings of the 15th Conference of the European Chapter of the Association for Computational Linguistics: Volume 2, Short Papers*, pages 242–247, Valencia, Spain. Association for Computational Linguistics.

Tosin Adewumi, Roshanak Vadoodi, Aparajita Tripathy, Konstantina Nikolaido, Foteini Liwicki, and Marcus Liwicki. 2022. Potential idiomatic expression (PIE)-English: Corpus for classes of idioms. In *Proceedings of the Thirteenth Language Resources and Evaluation Conference*, pages 689–696, Marseille, France. European Language Resources Association.

Ruchit Agrawal, Vighnesh Chenthil Kumar, Vigneshwaran Muralidharan, and Dipti Sharma. 2018. No more beating about the bush : A step towards idiom handling for Indian language NLP. In *Proceedings of the Eleventh International Conference on Language Resources and Evaluation (LREC 2018)*, Miyazaki, Japan. European Language Resources Association (ELRA).

Katsiaryna Aharodnik, Anna Feldman, and Jing Peng. 2018. Designing a russian idiom-annotated corpus. In *International Conference on Language Resources and Evaluation.*

Timothy Baldwin and Su Nam Kim. 2010. Multiword expressions. In *Handbook of Natural Language Processing.*

BNC Consortium. 2007. The british national corpus, XML edition. Distributed by Oxford University Computing Services on behalf of the BNC Consortium. URL: http://www.natcorp.ox.ac.uk/.

Zheng Chu, Ziqing Yang, Yiming Cui, Zhigang Chen, and Ming Liu. 2022. HIT at SemEval-2022 task 2: Pre-trained language model for idioms detection. In *Proceedings of the 16th International Workshop on Semantic Evaluation (SemEval-2022)*, pages 221–227, Seattle, United States. Association for Computational Linguistics.

Alexis Conneau, Kartikay Khandelwal, Naman Goyal, Vishrav Chaudhary, Guillaume Wenzek, Francisco Guzmán, Edouard Grave, Myle Ott, Luke Zettlemoyer, and Veselin Stoyanov. 2019. Unsupervised cross-lingual representation learning at scale. *CoRR*, abs/1911.02116.

Paul Cook, Afsaneh Fazly, and Suzanne Stevenson. 2008. The vnc-tokens dataset.

Verna Dankers, Christopher Lucas, and Ivan Titov. 2022. Can transformer be too compositional? analysing idiom processing in neural machine translation. In *Proceedings of the 60th Annual Meeting of the Association for Computational Linguistics (Volume 1: Long Papers)*, pages 3608–3626, Dublin, Ireland. Association for Computational Linguistics.

Jacob Devlin, Ming-Wei Chang, Kenton Lee, and Kristina Toutanova. 2019. BERT: Pre-training of deep bidirectional transformers for language understanding. In *Proceedings of the 2019 Conference of the North American Chapter of the Association for Computational Linguistics: Human Language Technologies, Volume 1 (Long and Short Papers)*, pages 4171–4186, Minneapolis, Minnesota. Association for Computational Linguistics.

Rafael Ehren, Timm Lichte, Laura Kallmeyer, and Jakub Waszczuk. 2020. Supervised disambiguation of German verbal idioms with a BiLSTM architecture. In *Proceedings of the Second Workshop on Figurative Language Processing*, pages 211–220, Online. Association for Computational Linguistics.

Samin Fakharian and Paul Cook. 2021. Contextualized embeddings encode monolingual and cross-lingual knowledge of idiomaticity. In *Proceedings of the 17th Workshop on Multiword Expressions (MWE 2021)*, pages 23–32, Online. Association for Computational Linguistics.

Afsaneh Fazly, Paul Cook, and Suzanne Stevenson. 2009. Unsupervised type and token identification of idiomatic expressions. *Computational Linguistics*, 35(1):61–103.

Fabienne Fritzinger, Marion Weller, and Ulrich Heid. 2010. A survey of idiomatic preposition-noun-verb triples on token level. In *Proceedings of the Seventh International Conference on Language Resources and Evaluation (LREC'10)*, Valletta, Malta. European Language Resources Association (ELRA).

Marcos Garcia, Tiago Kramer Vieira, Carolina Scarton, Marco Idiart, and Aline Villavicencio. 2021a. Assessing the representations of idiomaticity in vector models with a noun compound dataset labeled at type and token levels. In *Proceedings of the 59th Annual Meeting of the Association for Computational Linguistics and the 11th International Joint Conference on Natural Language Processing (Volume 1: Long Papers)*, pages 2730–2741, Online. Association for Computational Linguistics.

Marcos Garcia, Tiago Kramer Vieira, Carolina Scarton, Marco Idiart, and Aline Villavicencio. 2021b. Probing for idiomaticity in vector space models. In *Proceedings of the 16th Conference of the European Chapter of the Association for Computational Linguistics: Main Volume*, pages 3551–3564, Online. Association for Computational Linguistics.

Lynn Grant. 2004. Criteria for re-defining idioms: Are we barking up the wrong tree? *Applied Linguistics - APPL LINGUIST*, 25:38–61.

Hessel Haagsma, Johan Bos, and Malvina Nissim. 2020. MAGPIE: A large corpus of potentially idiomatic expressions. In *Proceedings of the Twelfth Language Resources and Evaluation Conference*, pages 279–287, Marseille, France. European Language Resources Association.

Najet Hadj Mohamed, Agata Savary, Cherifa Ben Khelil, Jean-Yves Antoine, Iskandar Keskes, and Lamia Hadrich-Belguith. 2024. Lexicons gain the upper hand in Arabic MWE identification. In *Proceedings of the Joint Workshop on Multiword Expressions and Universal Dependencies (MWE-UD) @ LREC-COLING 2024*, pages 88–97, Torino, Italia. ELRA and ICCL.

Reyhaneh Hashempour and Aline Villavicencio. 2020. Leveraging contextual embeddings and idiom principle for detecting idiomaticity in potentially idiomatic expressions. In *Proceedings of the Workshop on the Cognitive Aspects of the Lexicon*, pages 72–80, Online. Association for Computational Linguistics.

Chikara Hashimoto and Daisuke Kawahara. 2008. Construction of an idiom corpus and its application to idiom identification based on WSD incorporating idiom-specific features. In *Proceedings of the 2008 Conference on Empirical Methods in Natural Language Processing*, pages 992–1001, Honolulu, Hawaii. Association for Computational Linguistics.

Bradley Hauer, Seeratpal Jaura, Talgat Omarov, and Grzegorz Kondrak. 2022. UAlberta at SemEval 2022 task 2: Leveraging glosses and translations for multilingual idiomaticity detection. In *Proceedings of the 16th International Workshop on Semantic Evaluation (SemEval-2022)*, pages 145–150, Seattle, United States. Association for Computational Linguistics.

Andrea Horbach, Andrea Hensler, Sabine Krome, Jakob Prange, Werner Scholze-Stubenrecht, Diana Steffen, Stefan Thater, Christian Wellner, and Manfred Pinkal. 2016. A corpus of literal and idiomatic uses of German infinitive-verb compounds. In *Proceedings of the Tenth International Conference on Language Resources and Evaluation (LREC'16)*, pages 836–841, Portorož, Slovenia. European Language Resources Association (ELRA).

Agne Knietaite, Adam Allsebrook, Anton Minkov, Adam Tomaszewski, Norbert Slinko, Richard Johnson, Thomas Pickard, Dylan Phelps, and Aline Villavicencio. 2024. Is less more? quality, quantity and context in idiom processing with natural language models. *Preprint*, arXiv:2405.08497.

Philipp Koehn, Hieu Hoang, Alexandra Birch, Chris Callison-Burch, Marcello Federico, Nicola Bertoldi, Brooke Cowan, Wade Shen, Christine Moran, Richard Zens, Chris Dyer, Ondřej Bojar, Alexandra Constantin, and Evan Herbst. 2007. Moses: Open source toolkit for statistical machine translation. In *Proceedings of the 45th Annual Meeting of the Association for Computational Linguistics Companion Volume Proceedings of the Demo and Poster Sessions*, pages 177–180, Prague, Czech Republic. Association for Computational Linguistics.

Ioannis Korkontzelos, Torsten Zesch, Fabio Massimo Zanzotto, and Chris Biemann. 2013. SemEval-2013 task 5: Evaluating phrasal semantics. In *Second Joint Conference on Lexical and Computational Semantics (*SEM), Volume 2: Proceedings of the Seventh International Workshop on Semantic Evaluation (SemEval 2013)*, pages 39–47, Atlanta, Georgia, USA. Association for Computational Linguistics.

Murathan Kurfalı and Robert Östling. 2020. Disambiguation of potentially idiomatic expressions with contextual embeddings. In *Proceedings of the Joint Workshop on Multiword Expressions and Electronic Lexicons*, pages 85–94, online. Association for Computational Linguistics.

Murathan Kurfalı, Robert Östling, Johan Sjons, and Mats Wirén. 2020. A multi-word expression dataset for Swedish. In *Proceedings of the Twelfth Language Resources and Evaluation Conference*, pages 4402–4409, Marseille, France. European Language Resources Association.

Anne Lauscher, Vinit Ravishankar, Ivan Vulić, and Goran Glavaš. 2020. From zero to hero: On the limitations of zero-shot language transfer with multilingual Transformers. In *Proceedings of the 2020 Conference on Empirical Methods in Natural Language Processing (EMNLP)*, pages 4483–4499, Online. Association for Computational Linguistics.

Li Liu and Francois Lareau. 2024. Assessing BERT's sensitivity to idiomaticity. In *Proceedings of the Joint Workshop on Multiword Expressions and Universal Dependencies (MWE-UD) @ LREC-COLING 2024*, pages 14–23, Torino, Italia. ELRA and ICCL.

Louis Martin, Benjamin Muller, Pedro Javier Ortiz Suárez, Yoann Dupont, Laurent Romary, Éric de la Clergerie, Djamé Seddah, and Benoît Sagot. 2020. Camembert: a tasty french language model. In *Proceedings of the 58th Annual Meeting of the Association for Computational Linguistics*. Association for Computational Linguistics.

Oren Melamud, Jacob Goldberger, and Ido Dagan. 2016. context2vec: Learning generic context embedding with bidirectional LSTM. In *Proceedings of the 20th SIGNLL Conference on Computational Natural Language Learning*, pages 51–61, Berlin, Germany. Association for Computational Linguistics.

Navnita Nandakumar, Timothy Baldwin, and Bahar Salehi. 2019. How well do embedding models capture non-compositionality? a view from multiword expressions. In *Proceedings of the 3rd Workshop on Evaluating Vector Space Representations for NLP*, pages 27–34, Minneapolis, USA. Association for Computational Linguistics.

Vasudevan Nedumpozhimana and John Kelleher. 2021. Finding BERT's idiomatic key. In *Proceedings of the 17th Workshop on Multiword Expressions (MWE 2021)*, pages 57–62, Online. Association for Computational Linguistics.

Geoffrey Nunberg, Ivan A. Sag, and Thomas Wasow. 1994. Idioms. *Language*, 70(3):491–538.

Pedro Javier Ortiz Suárez, Benoît Sagot, and Laurent Romary. 2019. Asynchronous pipelines for processing huge corpora on medium to low resource infrastructures. In *Proceedings of the Workshop on Challenges in the Management of Large Corpora (CMLC-7) 2019. Cardiff, 22nd July 2019*, pages 9–16, Mannheim, Germany. Leibniz-Institut für Deutsche Sprache.

Carlos Ramisch. 2023. *Multiword expressions in computational linguistics*. Habilitation à diriger des recherches, Aix Marseille Université (AMU).

Ivan A. Sag, Timothy Baldwin, Francis Bond, Ann A. Copestake, and Dan Flickinger. 2002. Multiword expressions: A pain in the neck for nlp. In *Conference on Intelligent Text Processing and Computational Linguistics*.

Victor Sanh, Lysandre Debut, Julien Chaumond, and Thomas Wolf. 2020. Distilbert, a distilled version of bert: smaller, faster, cheaper and lighter. *Preprint*, arXiv:1910.01108.

Mahtab Sarlak, Yalda Yarandi, and Mehrnoush Shamsfard. 2023. Predicting compositionality of verbal multiword expressions in Persian. In *Proceedings of the 19th Workshop on Multiword Expressions (MWE 2023)*, pages 14–23, Dubrovnik, Croatia. Association for Computational Linguistics.

Agata Savary, Cherifa Ben Khelil, Carlos Ramisch, Voula Giouli, Verginica Barbu Mititelu, Najet Hadj Mohamed, Cvetana Krstev, Chaya Liebeskind, Hongzhi Xu, Sara Stymne, Tunga Güngör, Thomas Pickard, Bruno Guillaume, Eduard Bejček, Archna Bhatia, Marie Candito, Polona Gantar, Uxoa Iñurrieta, Albert Gatt, Jolanta Kovalevskaite, Timm Lichte, Nikola Ljubešić, Johanna Monti, Carla Parra Escartín, Mehrnoush Shamsfard, Ivelina Stoyanova, Veronika Vincze, and Abigail Walsh. 2023. PARSEME corpus release 1.3. In *Proceedings of the 19th Workshop on Multiword Expressions (MWE 2023)*, pages 24–35, Dubrovnik, Croatia. Association for Computational Linguistics.

Agata Savary, Marie Candito, Verginica Barbu Mititelu, Eduard Bejček, Fabienne Cap, Slavomír Čéplö, Silvio Ricardo Cordeiro, Gülşen Cebiroğlu Eryiğit, Voula Giouli, Maarten van Gompel, Yaakov Hacohen-Kerner, Jolanta Kovalevskaitė, Simon Krek, Chaya Liebeskind, Johanna Monti, Carla Parra Escartín, Lonneke van Der Plas, Behrang Qasemizadeh, Carlos Ramisch, Federico Sangati, Ivelina Stoyanova, and Veronika Vincze. 2018. PARSEME multilingual corpus of verbal multiword expressions. In *Multiword expressions at length and in depth: Extended papers from the MWE 2017 workshop*.

Agata Savary, Silvio Cordeiro, Timm Lichte, Carlos Ramisch, Uxoa Iñurrieta, and Voula Giouli. 2019. Literal occurrences of multiword expressions: Rare birds that cause a stir. 112:5–54.

Agata Savary, Manfred Sailer, Yannick Parmentier, Michael Rosner, Victoria Rosén, Adam Przepiórkowski, Cvetana Krstev, Veronika Vincze, Beata Wójtowicz, Gyri Smørdal Losnegaard, Carla Parra Escartín, Jakub Waszczuk, Mathieu Constant, Petya Osenova, and Federico Sangati. 2015. PARSEME – PARSing and Multiword Expressions within a European multilingual network. In *7th Language & Technology Conference: Human Language Technologies as a Challenge for Computer Science and Linguistics (LTC 2015)*, Poznań, Poland.

Prateek Saxena and Soma Paul. 2020. Epie dataset: A corpus for possible idiomatic expressions. In *Text, Speech, and Dialogue: 23rd International Conference, TSD 2020, Brno, Czech Republic, September 8–11, 2020, Proceedings*, page 87–94, Berlin, Heidelberg. Springer-Verlag.

Vered Shwartz and Ido Dagan. 2019. Still a pain in the neck: Evaluating text representations on lexical composition. *Transactions of the Association for Computational Linguistics*, 7:403–419.

J. Sinclair. 1991. *Corpus, Concordance, Collocation*. Describing English language. Oxford University Press.

Caroline Sporleder, Linlin Li, Philip Gorinski, and Xaver Koch. 2010. Idioms in context: The IDIX corpus. In *Proceedings of the Seventh International Conference on Language Resources and Evaluation (LREC'10)*, Valletta, Malta. European Language Resources Association (ELRA).

Minghuan Tan and Jing Jiang. 2021. Does BERT understand idioms? a probing-based empirical study of BERT encodings of idioms. In *Proceedings of the International Conference on Recent Advances in Natural Language Processing (RANLP 2021)*, pages 1397–1407, Held Online. INCOMA Ltd.

Harish Tayyar Madabushi, Edward Gow-Smith, Marcos Garcia, Carolina Scarton, Marco Idiart, and Aline Villavicencio. 2022. SemEval-2022 task 2: Multilingual idiomaticity detection and sentence embedding. In *Proceedings of the 16th International Workshop on Semantic Evaluation (SemEval-2022)*, pages 107–121, Seattle, United States. Association for Computational Linguistics.

Harish Tayyar Madabushi, Edward Gow-Smith, Carolina Scarton, and Aline Villavicencio. 2021. AStitchInLanguageModels: Dataset and methods for the exploration of idiomaticity in pre-trained language models. In *Findings of the Association for Computational Linguistics: EMNLP 2021*, pages 3464–3477, Punta Cana, Dominican Republic. Association for Computational Linguistics.

Simone Tedeschi, Federico Martelli, and Roberto Navigli. 2022. ID10M: Idiom identification in 10 languages. In *Findings of the Association for Computational Linguistics: NAACL 2022*, pages 2715–2726, Seattle, United States. Association for Computational Linguistics.

Simone Tedeschi and Roberto Navigli. 2022. NER4ID at SemEval-2022 task 2: Named entity recognition for idiomaticity detection. In *Proceedings of the 16th International Workshop on Semantic Evaluation (SemEval-2022)*, pages 204–210, Seattle, United States. Association for Computational Linguistics.

Ye Tian, Isobel James, and Hye Son. 2023. How are idioms processed inside transformer language models? In *Proceedings of the 12th Joint Conference on Lexical and Computational Semantics (*SEM 2023)*, pages 174–179, Toronto, Canada. Association for Computational Linguistics.

Thomas Wolf, Lysandre Debut, Victor Sanh, Julien Chaumond, Clement Delangue, Anthony Moi, Pierric Cistac, Tim Rault, Remi Louf, Morgan Funtowicz, Joe Davison, Sam Shleifer, Patrick von Platen, Clara Ma, Yacine Jernite, Julien Plu, Canwen Xu, Teven Le Scao, Sylvain Gugger, Mariama Drame, Quentin Lhoest, and Alexander Rush. 2020. Transformers: State-of-the-art natural language processing. In *Proceedings of the 2020 Conference on Empirical Methods in Natural Language Processing: System Demonstrations*, pages 38–45, Online. Association for Computational Linguistics.

Atsuki Yamaguchi, Gaku Morio, Hiroaki Ozaki, and Yasuhiro Sogawa. 2022. Hitachi at SemEval-2022 task 2: On the effectiveness of span-based classification approaches for multilingual idiomaticity detection. In *Proceedings of the 16th International Workshop on Semantic Evaluation (SemEval-2022)*, pages 135–144, Seattle, United States. Association for Computational Linguistics.

Lang Yu and Allyson Ettinger. 2020. Assessing phrasal representation and composition in transformers. In *Proceedings of the 2020 Conference on Empirical Methods in Natural Language Processing (EMNLP)*, pages 4896–4907, Online. Association for Computational Linguistics.

Ziheng Zeng and Suma Bhat. 2021. Idiomatic expression identification using semantic compatibility. *Transactions of the Association for Computational Linguistics*, 9:1546–1562.

A Annotation of Idiom Features

We manually annotate the `MultiCoPIE` idioms with additional features, such as part-of-speech of idiom head and semantic compositionality. The annotation is performed by one native speaker per language.

Part-of-Speech of Idiom Head The part of speech tag of an idiom is determined by its phrase head. We rely on lexicographic resources to determine the standard idiom form. However, we do not annotate idiom function within each sentence. We place the idioms in `MultiCoPIE` into four categories depending on the part-of-speech tag of the idiom phrase head: `verb phrase`, `noun phrase`, `prepositional phrase` and `other` (due to infrequency of other idiom types in the corpora).

Semantic Compositionality We annotate idioms in `MultiCoPIE` for their semantic compositionality. Semantic idiomaticity falls on a continuum, and there are multiple studies on the compositionality of multiword expressions with various degrees of granularity. An extensive review of compositionality prediction techniques and compositionality datasets can be found in (Ramisch, 2023).

In this work, we adopt a simplified approach to (non)-compositionality. A binary label is used to reflect whether each idiomatic expression belongs to the category of fully non-compositional idioms. For simplicity and efficiency, we apply the following operational definition of transparency: the idiom is considered fully non-compositional (or semantically opaque), if its dictionary definition does not contain any of the idiom's components, their synonyms, hyponyms, hyperonyms or other semantically related words. In this definition, we only consider dictionary entries for components that bear lexical meaning, without taking into account such categories as determiners. To illustrate in English, the dictionary definition of the idiom *red herring* does not contain words *red* or *herring*, nor does it contain any semantically related words. In contrast, a dictionary definition of the idiom *green with envy* would contain the word *envy* or its synonyms and therefore cannot be assigned to the category of fully non-compositional idioms. In the future, such approach can be automated, for example, by ranking similarity between contextual embeddings of idiom components and the idiom definition.

B Training Hyperparameters

To determine learning rate and batch size for fine-tuning, we first ran grid-search for each setting across three different data splits, with learning rates of 1e-5, 2e-5, 3e-5, 4e-5 and 5e-5 and batch sizes of 8, 16, 32 and 64. The same procedure was done for fine-tuning with the context. The performance of each parameter combination was averaged over three runs; the parameters that yielded lowest validation loss over three runs were selected for further fine-tuning. Table 6 shows the best parameters for each setting and Table 7 the data used for each configuration.

	Zero-shot		One-shot		Random	
	w/o context	with context	w/o context	with context	w/o context	with context
learning rate	2e-5	1e-5	1e-5	3e-5	1e-5	3e-5
batch size	64	32	64	64	32	64
val. loss	.34 ± .03	.35 ± .03	.36 ± .03	.36 ± .02	.21 ± .01	.21 ± .02
val. accuracy	.86 ± .02	.85 ± .02	.86 ± .02	.86 ± .02	.93 ± .003	.92 ± .01

Table 6: Best hyperparameters as defined by grid search. The table reports scores averaged over three different runs (on a different training-validation-test split) together with the standard deviation.

		Grid-search		Fine-tuning	
		Idioms	Instances	Idioms	Instances
Zero-shot	**training**	1102	26630 ± 657	1102	26302 ± 664
	validation	240	5432 ± 419	240	5956 ± 246
	test	240	5862 ± 431	240	5666 ± 563
One-shot	**training**	1582	26691 ± 345	1582	25656 ± 337
	validation	240	5608 ± 246	240	5986 ± 427
	test	240	5624 ± 134	240	6281 ± 527
Random	**training**	1528 ± 7	26124	1525 ± 8	26124
	validation	1168 ± 14	5900	1170 ± 13	5900
	test	1154 ± 2	5900	1174 ± 8	5900

Table 7: The sizes of data splits used for fine-tuning. The random setting is not type aware which leads to varying numbers of idioms per each data split.

C Cross-Lingual Analysis

	w/o context			with context		
	CA	IT	RU	CA	IT	RU
Accuracy	.90 ± .01	.88 ± .02	.86 ± .02	.91 ± .02	.87 ± .03	.86 ± .03
F1-score	.94 ± .01	.93 ± .01	.89 ± .01	.94 ± .01	.92 ± .02	.87 ± .04
Precision	.94 ± .01	.94 ± .01	.87 ± .03	.94 ± .02	.94 ± .01	.91 ± .03
Recall	.94 ± .03	.91 ± .03	.90 ± .02	.94 ± .03	.91 ± .05	.85 ± .08
F1-score (`literal`)	.73 ± .02	.63 ± .03	.82 ± .03	.76 ± .02	.63 ± .02	.83 ± .02
Precision (`literal`)	.74 ± .07	.61 ± .06	.85 ± .02	.77 ± .08	.60 ± .08	.80 ± .07
Recall (`literal`)	.73 ± .07	.67 ± .05	.80 ± .06	.76 ± .08	.67 ± .09	.87 ± .06

Table 8: Performance scores (mean and standard deviation) averaged over 10 runs after fine-tuning XLM-RoBERTa on the English data in the **zero-shot setting**.

	w/o context			with context		
	CA	IT	RU	CA	IT	RU
Accuracy	$.91 \pm .01$	$.87 \pm .01$	$.87 \pm .01$	$.90 \pm .01$	$.87 \pm .02$	$.85 \pm .02$
F1-score	$.94 \pm .00$	$.92 \pm .01$	$.89 \pm .01$	$.94 \pm .01$	$.92 \pm .01$	$.88 \pm .02$
Precision	$.95 \pm .01$	$.94 \pm .01$	$.89 \pm .03$	$.93 \pm .02$	$.93 \pm .01$	$.88 \pm .04$
Recall	$.94 \pm .01$	$.90 \pm .02$	$.90 \pm .02$	$.95 \pm .03$	$.92 \pm .04$	$.88 \pm .06$
F1-score (literal)	$.75 \pm .01$	$.64 \pm .02$	$.84 \pm .02$	$.72 \pm .03$	$.60 \pm .02$	$.82 \pm .02$
Precision (literal)	$.74 \pm .04$	$.59 \pm .04$	$.85 \pm .03$	$.78 \pm .08$	$.61 \pm .08$	$.83 \pm .06$
Recall (literal)	$.77 \pm .04$	$.70 \pm .05$	$.83 \pm .05$	$.67 \pm .09$	$.61 \pm .10$	$.81 \pm .07$

Table 9: Performance scores (mean and standard deviation) averaged over 10 runs after fine-tuning XLM-RoBERTa on the English data in the **one-shot setting**.

	w/o context			with context		
	CA	IT	RU	CA	IT	RU
Accuracy	$.90 \pm .01$	$.87 \pm .02$	$.87 \pm .01$	$.90 \pm .01$	$.87 \pm .01$	$.85 \pm .01$
F1-score	$.94 \pm .00$	$.92 \pm .01$	$.89 \pm .01$	$.94 \pm .01$	$.92 \pm .01$	$.87 \pm .01$
Precision	$.95 \pm .01$	$.94 \pm .01$	$.88 \pm .02$	$.94 \pm .01$	$.93 \pm .01$	$.88 \pm .03$
Recall	$.94 \pm .02$	$.90 \pm .03$	$.90 \pm .03$	$.94 \pm .02$	$.91 \pm .02$	$.86 \pm .04$
F1-score (literal)	$.75 \pm .02$	$.64 \pm .02$	$.83 \pm .01$	$.73 \pm .02$	$.60 \pm .02$	$.81 \pm .02$
Precision (literal)	$.74 \pm .05$	$.59 \pm .06$	$.85 \pm .03$	$.75 \pm .06$	$.58 \pm .04$	$.80 \pm .04$
Recall (literal)	$.76 \pm .06$	$.71 \pm .05$	$.82 \pm .04$	$.72 \pm .06$	$.64 \pm .06$	$.82 \pm .06$

Table 10: Performance scores (mean and standard deviation) averaged over 10 runs after fine-tuning XLM-RoBERTa on the English data in the **random setting**.

		shared and seen	not shared or not seen	F-statistic	p-value
CA	**Accuracy**	$.95 \pm .01$	$.90 \pm .01$	149.81	3.7e−10
	F1-score	$.97 \pm .01$	$.94 \pm .00$	122.38	1.9e−9
IT	**Accuracy**	$.95 \pm .01$	$.86 \pm .01$	289.77	1.5e−12
	F1-score	$.97 \pm .01$	$.92 \pm .01$	224.36	1.3e−11
RU	**Accuracy**	$.89 \pm .02$	$.87 \pm .01$	10.15	0.005
	F1-score	$.91 \pm .02$	$.89 \pm .01$	9.57	0.006

Table 11: Results of a one-way ANOVA test comparing two groups of idioms: 'shared and seen' and 'not shared or not seen' (see Section 5.2). The first two columns report the mean and standard deviation for each group, while the last two columns provide the F-statistic and p-value.

Named Entity Recognition for the Irish Language

Jane Adkins[1], Hugo Collins[2], Joachim Wagner[1], Abigail Walsh[1], Brian Davis[1]

[1]ADAPT Centre, Dublin City University, Dublin 9, Co. Dublin, Ireland
[2]School of Computing, Dublin City University, Dublin 9, Co. Dublin, Ireland

Abstract

The Irish language has been deemed 'definitely endangered' (Moseley, 2012) and has been classified as having 'weak or no support' (Lynn, 2023) regarding digital resources in spite of its status as the first official and national language of the Republic of Ireland. This research develops the first named entity recognition (NER) tool for the Irish language, one of the essential tasks identified by the Digital Plan for Irish (Ní Chasaide et al., 2022). In this study, we produce a small gold-standard NER-annotated corpus and compare both monolingual and multilingual BERT models fine-tuned on this task. We experiment with different model architectures and low-resource language approaches to enrich our dataset. We test our models on a mix of single- and multi-word named entities as well as a specific multi-word named entity test set. Our proposed gaBERT model with the implementation of random data augmentation and a conditional random fields layer demonstrates significant performance improvements over baseline models, alternative architectures, and multilingual models, achieving an F1 score of 76.52. This study contributes to advancing Irish language technologies and supporting Irish language digital resources, providing a basis for Irish NER and identification of other MWE types.

1 Introduction

Despite being the first official and national language of the Republic of Ireland, Irish faces a stark reality - it is 'definitely endangered' (Moseley, 2012). Furthermore, it is one of the two European Union languages classified as having 'weak or no support' regarding digital resources (Lynn, 2023). Recognising this challenge, the Digital Plan for Irish (Ní Chasaide et al., 2022) outlines a broad strategy aimed at strengthening technologies tailored to the Irish language. Central to this plan is the recognition of the urgent need for a Named Entity Recognition (NER) tool for Irish. Such a tool not only facilitates various natural language processing (NLP) tasks but also represents a crucial step in providing much-needed essential digital support for the Irish language community (Ní Chasaide et al., 2022). Existing research on Irish MWEs has also highlighted Named Entities (NEs) as requiring special attention (McGuinness et al., 2020), as treatment of these constructions mirrors other MWE types, such as noun compounds (Walsh, 2023). Our research aims to address this gap in Irish language technology by developing a base NER tool specifically tailored for the Irish language, and the construction of the first gold-standard NER-annotated corpus for Irish.

NER is an information extraction task involving the identification of portions of text that refer to NEs and the categorisation of these portions into predefined groups such as location, person, organisation, or other relevant categories. While NER may seem straightforward in its concept, it presents significant challenges. Determining the category of a NE relies not only on the entity itself but also heavily on the context it appears in (Marrero et al., 2013). State-of-the-art NER tools employ neural models that are pre-trained using language modeling tasks, which mitigates the need to have an abundance of annotated corpora (Peters et al., 2018).

For Irish, a NER tool represents a pivotal step towards improving digital content and interfaces in the language, leading to an increase in its use across digital environments. In the development of this tool, a small NER-annotated corpus has been constructed from existing contemporary Irish text. This corpus is to be utilised with pre-trained language models, such as gaBERT (Barry et al., 2022) for the NER task. Due to the size of this corpus and also the size of Irish text in the pre-training of multilingual language models, we use data augmentation approaches to enhance and enrich the

Proceedings of the 21st Workshop on Multiword Expressions (MWE 2025), pages 82–96
May 4, 2025

corpus. Furthermore, we add a conditional random fields (CRF) layer and a bidirectional long short-term memory (Bi-LSTM) CRF layer to leverage contextual understandings captured by the models while incorporating the sequential modelling capabilities of CRFs and Bi-LSTMs (Souza et al., 2020). In this report, we evaluate several BERT (Bi-directional Encoder Representation from Transformers) (Devlin et al., 2019) models for the NER task for Irish, both monolingual and multilingual, and compare the above strategies. The models are tested on both a mixed-length NE test set and also a multi-word NE (MW-NE) test set.

2 Background

2.1 Irish Resources Utilised

This research leverages the following Irish NLP resources:

2.1.1 Irish Universal Dependency Treebank

The Irish Universal Dependency Treebank (IUDT) (Lynn et al., 2023) was first constructed as a conversion of the Irish Dependency Treebank (Lynn, 2016) to the Universal Dependency labeling scheme (Nivre, 2015; Nivre et al., 2016). Each tree in the treebank is manually annotated to include part-of-speech information, syntactic dependencies, and morphological features. While Universal Dependencies do not typically capture NEs in their dependency labels, the IUDT included NE information as part of their annotations (McGuinness et al., 2020). Data from V2.8 of the the mixed-domain treebank was leveraged in our experiments (see Section 3).

2.1.2 gaBERT

gaBERT is a monolingual Irish BERT model trained on over 7.9 million Irish sentences and approximately 161 million words (Barry et al., 2022). It uses the original BERT pretraining parameters (Devlin et al., 2019) along with whole-word masking. Whole-word masking treats entire words as a single unit during the masking process, enabling the model to effectively handle languages with intricate inflection and compounding such as Irish (Barry et al., 2022). When evaluated against off-the-shelf BERT, mBERT and monolingual Irish WikiBERT model, the gaBERT model outperformed these other models in the tasks of dependency parsing and masked-token prediction for Irish (Barry et al., 2022). gaBERT was also fine-tuned for the downstream task of MWE identification (Walsh et al., 2022), achieving higher results compared to a similar fine-tuned mBERT model.

2.2 Techniques for Data Augmentation

2.2.1 Rule-Based Data Augmentation

Rule-based approaches to data-augmentation implement simple manipulations of the data. Multimodal Data Augmentation (Xu et al., 2021) introduces four simple yet effective rule-based data augmentation techniques: synonym replacement, random insertion, random swap, and random deletion. While this work primarily targets text classification, these methods have been widely adapted for NLP tasks due to their potential to enrich training datasets significantly (Xu et al., 2021). This approach was further extended by the introduction of Label-wise Token Replacement, a technique that improves data diversity by replacing a token with another of the same entity type at random (Dai and Adel, 2020). In a study on a different low-resource language—Filipino—researchers used a technique where entities were randomly inserted into sentences or entirely new sentences were crafted with these entities at their core (Chan et al., 2023). Additionally, training data augmentation was utilised by swapping the positions of two randomly selected words within sentences (Xu et al., 2021). Another innovative rule-based method is Entity List Augmentation, where an entity from a list is chosen and the list is expanded by adding other entities of the same type from the training dataset. This approach makes the entity list more comprehensive, thus exposing models to a broader array of entity types (Hu et al., 2023). Mention Replacement is a method proposed by Raiman and Miller for the task of question-answering (Raiman and Miller, 2017) and has been implemented for NER previously (Dai and Adel, 2020), where an entity of the same type is randomly selected to replace the original mention of the entity, similar to the approach of Entity List Augmentation (Hu et al., 2023).

2.2.2 Back-translation Data Augmentation

An innovative technique for augmenting low-resource NER data is described by (Yaseen and Langer, 2021), who employ Back-Translation (BT) on a simulated low-resource dataset of English-German text. The method involves translating a text into another language, and then back into the original language, to create paraphrased texts that retain the general meaning of the original sentence, while still containing the same NE labels. BT as a data-augmentation technique was also explored by (Sbaty et al., 2021), using Code-Switched data.

2.3 Architecture Augmentation

2.3.1 Addition of a Conditional Random Fields Layer

In recent studies, the incorporation of a CRF layer within BERT, positioned after the softmax layer, has demonstrated notable enhancements in NER performance (Arkhipov et al., 2019; Ge et al., 2022). Additionally, for sequence labelling tasks, the use of a Bi-LSTM-CRF on top of BERT has achieved higher performance than the addition of a linear CRF layer (Liu et al., 2023). Specifically, monolingual BERT models augmented with a CRF layer have exhibited superior performance in precision and F1 scores compared to multilingual BERT models with this augmentation, in the context of Portuguese language tasks (Souza et al., 2020). Furthermore, the integration of a word-level CRF layer has been identified as a method to further amplify the performance of these models (Arkhipov et al., 2019).

3 Data

The data we used for these experiments are comprised of 36,825 tokens and were collected from three sources: the IUDT training set, the IUDT test set (Lynn, 2022), and publicly available transcripts from Dáil proceedings (Houses of the Oireachtas, 2024).

NEs have previously been tagged in the IUDT datasets using a designated label in the morphological features; a simple script was used to filter out these sentences for use as data. The domain is balanced, containing text from news, books, websites, and other sources.

All sentences gathered from Dáil proceedings were published between October 2023 and February 2024 (Houses of the Oireachtas, 2024). This ensured the data postdated the training completion of gaBERT in 2021 (Barry et al., 2022), and so was very unlikely to have been included in the training data for this model. As the Dáil transcripts are largely English text, annotators manually filtered the text for Irish sentences, and identified sentences containing named entities from these for use as data. The Dáil text comprises of formal language often discussing proposed laws, government policies, national issues, and other parliamentary business.

While the IUDT data was tagged with a general "Named Entity" label, none of the above data sources had been previously labeled with fine-grained NE information. Annotation of the data collected was conducted using Label-Studio (Label Studio, 2020) by two annotators and carried out following specified annotation guidelines (see Appendix A), labelling entities as persons (PER), locations (LOC), and organisations (ORG), using an IOB2-tagging scheme (where B indicates the initial token of a named entity span e.g. B-LOC, I indicates a non-inital token of a named entity span e.g. I-PER, and O indicates the token is outside of a named entity span). IOB2 tagging was previously implemented in a similar task for Irish MWE identification (Walsh et al., 2022). The annotators both performed annotation on all 1,249 sentences; all discrepancies were discussed during the annotation process and a decision was made on how to annotate that token/tokens. Overall, there were very few discrepancies in the annotation.

- Training set: 1,009 sentences containing at least one named entity (758 from the IUDT training set and 251 from Dáil proceedings October - December 2023) (Lynn, 2022; Houses of the Oireachtas, 2024)
- Validation set: 100 sentences containing at least one named entity (40 from the IUDT test set and 60 from Dáil proceedings January - February 2024) (Lynn, 2022; Houses of the Oireachtas, 2024)
- Test set: 140 sentences containing at least one named entity (50 from the IUDT test set and 90 from Dáil proceedings January - February 2024) (Lynn, 2022; Houses of the Oireachtas, 2024)
- MWE-Test set: a subset of the test set containing 89 sentences, each containing at least one MW-NE (46 sentences are from the IUDT test set and 43 sentences are from the Dáil proceedings January - February 2024) (Lynn, 2022; Houses of the Oireachtas, 2024)

All datasets were curated carefully to have a balanced spread of named entity types within them. Additionally, the validation and test sets each contained a majority of unseen NEs (see Figure 1),

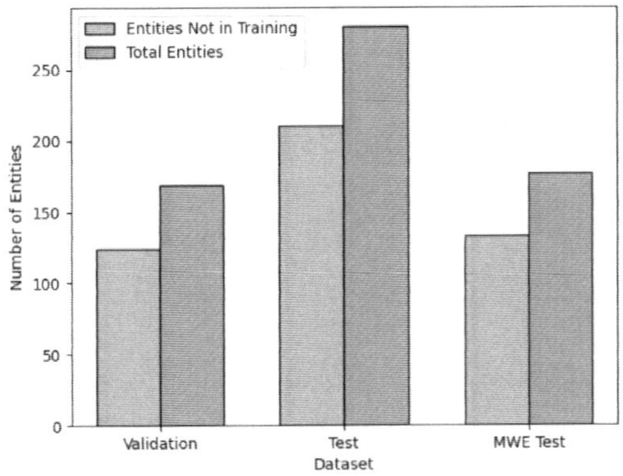

Figure 1: Named entities known or unknown from training in validation and both test sets

with approximately 75% of the NEs being unseen in the training data. This enables us to investigate the capability of testing on unseen NEs, mirroring the focus on unseen MWEs in the PARSEME Shared Task Edition 1.2 (Ramisch et al., 2020). Altogether there was an 80.79%/8.01%/11.20% train/validation/test split implemented for this task. While MW-NEs represent roughly 70% of the NEs in training, the number of single and two-word MW-NEs in the training set represent the majority of the NEs (38% single NEs and 30% two-word MW-NEs).

Table 1: Entity Counts across Datasets

Label	Train	Val	Test	(MWE-test)	Total
LOC	1444	99	275	(147)	1808
ORG	2271	177	225	(148)	2668
PER	1222	150	222	(177)	1590
O	24869	2507	3384	(2197)	30759
Total	29806	2933	4106	(2669)	36845

4 Models for the Task

We employ three BERT (Devlin et al., 2019) models (gaBERT, mBERT and XLMRoberta) to evaluate monolingual and multilingual models on the task of NER for Irish. gaBERT, a monolingual Irish BERT model, proved valuable to our research as it outperformed multilingual models on downstream tasks (Barry et al., 2022). mBERT (multilingual BERT) is a multilingual model containing Irish training data (Devlin et al., 2019). The third model used was XLMRoberta which has achieved state-of-the-art performance on sequence labelling tasks and has outperformed mBERT on cross-lingual classification on low-resource languages (Conneau et al., 2020). Irish is contained in the pre-training data for both mBERT and XLMRoberta, allowing us to evaluate their performances against monolingual gaBERT by fine-tuning these models on the NER task for the low-resource language Irish.

5 Experimental Set-Up

We utilised the AdamW optimiser (Loshchilov and Hutter, 2019) to fine-tune all parameters of the models. Weight-decay was implemented as a regularisation technique to prevent overfitting due to the small size of the training data. A learning rate of 3e-5 and an epsilon value of 1e-8 were chosen to strike a balance between convergence speed and stability during training. The weight decay rate was set to 0.01 for parameters subject to weight decay. Additionally, the maximum gradient norm was set to 1.0 to prevent exploding gradients. This scheduler adjusted the learning rate dynamically throughout the training process, starting with a warm-up phase of 0 steps and gradually linearly increasing the learning rate until reaching the total number of training steps. Training sentences were passed to the models randomly so that the sources of the data were shuffled. Validation and test sentences were passed to the model sequentially. Training epochs were set to 10 with a patience of 2 epochs. If the validation loss increased two times, training stopped and the epoch with the lower validation loss (before the two increases) was used for testing (Prechelt, 2012). The maximum sequence length was set to 256, with training batch size being 32. All models were trained using a T4 GPU in the Google Colab environment.

5.1 Data Augmentation

5.1.1 Random Data Augmentation

Our approach follows closely to that of Mention Replacement and Entity List Augmentation, where an entity pool is created from the entities in the training data and subsequently are added to the training data (Raiman and Miller, 2017; Hu et al., 2023). These entities are added to positions in the text following the IOB2-labelling scheme i.e. located a NE span where the previous and subsequent token are labelled O, then replaced the entire span with an NE or MW-NE (see Figure 2).

5.1.2 Data Augmentation using Back-Translation

To facilitate BT for augmenting our dataset, two models were selected from the Helsinki-

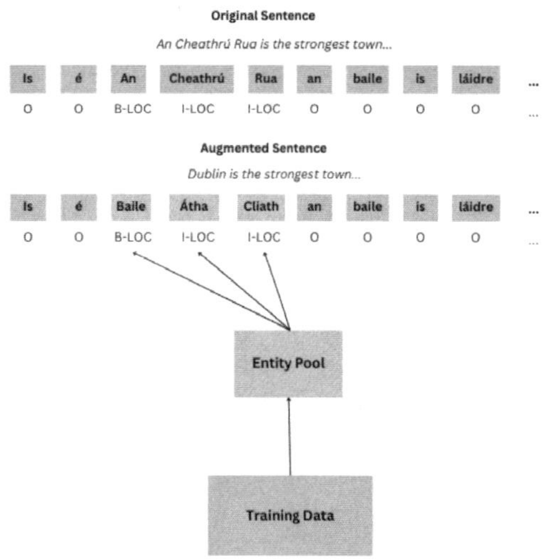

Figure 2: Random data augmentation example

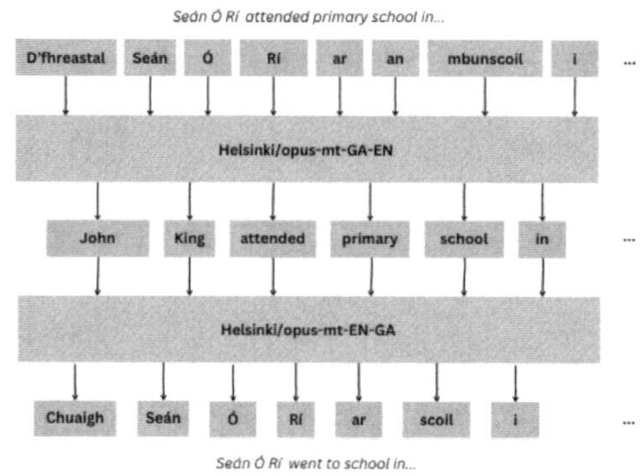

Figure 3: BT in action

NLP OPUS-MT project (Tiedemann and Thottingal, 2020). Specifically, we used the Helsinki-NLP/opus-mt-ga-en model for Irish-to-English translations and Helsinki-NLP/opus-mt-en-ga for the reverse translation from English back to Irish (Tiedemann and Thottingal, 2020). These models were selected based on their results when compared to similar models in the LoResMT 2021 Shared Task (Puranik et al., 2021; Ojha et al., 2021). The Helsinki-NLP/opus-mt-ga-en was used to translate Dáil sentences from the training set to English, and then the Helsinki-NLP/opus-mt-en-ga was used to translate them back to Irish. A total of 256 sentences sentences were backtranslated. Entities were mapped to their corresponding NE-label and the back-translated sentences were added to the training set. See Figure 3 to see backtranslation in action.

5.2 Addition of a CRF Layer

We experiment with adding a CRF layer and a BiLSTM CRF layer that are expected to improve the compatibility of predictions with the IOB2-tagging scheme (Ge et al., 2022). As previous work demonstrates, I- entities could not come before a B- entities (B-PER must always be before I-PER etc.) (Ge et al., 2022).

6 Evaluation

The main results from our experiments are presented in Table 2. All metrics were computed using the conlleval script[1] that considers only exact matches. This script focuses specifically on entity-level analysis, allowing for a detailed assessment of the model's ability to recognise distinct types of named entities and is similar to the seqeval (Nakayama, 2018) evaluation library utilised in a previous Irish MWE identification task (Walsh et al., 2022). It computes entity-level precision, recall, and the F1 score for each entity type, which measures the balance between precision and recall.

Additionally, it includes an overall accuracy score and a Non-O accuracy metric, which excludes the non-named entity labels from accuracy calculations to provide a deeper insight into the model's performance in identifying named entities.

7 Results

7.1 Comparison of the Baseline Models

gaBERT outperforms both mBERT and XLM-RoBERTa in most cases across the mixed-length test set and MW-NE test set, particularly excelling in the LOC-type and PER-type entities (see Table 2). While mBERT performs the best on the ORG-type entities across all metrics, XLMRoBERTa surpasses gaBERT on ORG-type entities in terms of recall and F1 scores, though not precision. Overall, monolingual gaBERT demonstrates superior performance compared to its multilingual counterparts, with mBERT and XLMRoBERTa trailing behind by a noticeable margin, except in their handling of the ORG tag.

[1]https://www.cnts.ua.ac.be/conll2000/chunking/output.html

Table 2: Table showing a subset of precision, recall and F-1 scores on the mixed-length NE test set. RDA, CRF, and BT pertain to random data augmentation, conditional random fields, and back-translation models respectively. Overall metrics include scores for O-tagged tokens.

Model	Overall			LOC			ORG			PER		
	P	R	F1	P	R	F1	P	R	F1	P	R	F1
gaBERT	71.74	**77.40**	74.46	76.61	77.51	77.06	61.11	72.79	66.44	76.88	**81.10**	78.93
gaBERT RDA CRF	**78.05**	75.05	**76.52**	**81.60**	78.70	**80.12**	**69.70**	67.65	68.66	**81.41**	77.44	**79.38**
mBERT	70.86	73.47	72.14	74.62	75.19	74.90	67.83	72.93	**70.29**	68.40	71.25	69.80
mBERT BT CRF	71.82	75.59	73.66	76.27	**80.56**	78.36	62.07	74.44	67.69	77.83	68.75	73.01
XLMRoberta	69.39	75.37	72.26	74.66	71.71	73.15	57.91	**77.78**	66.39	76.37	78.02	77.19
XLMRoberta RDA	69.18	74.02	71.52	70.13	71.05	70.59	60.16	74.40	66.52	77.92	77.59	77.75

mBERT records the highest number of false negatives, suggesting that it misclasses more tokens with an 'O' label than the other models. XLM-RoBERTa follows closely behind mBERT in identifying entity and non-entity tags, but it has a higher number of false positives. In contrast, gaBERT, though having the lowest true positives and negatives, exhibits fewer false positives and false negatives, reflecting its more conservative approach to entity prediction. While mBERT and XLM-RoBERTa show more balanced performance, they tend to miss certain entities, especially LOC-type entities. Notably, there are no sentences with common incorrect predictions across all three models, indicating the data is unlikely to contain "challenging" NE-types that are mis-categorised by all systems.

7.2 Performance by Entity Type

GaBERT-based models consistently outperform the multilingual models, with only the mBERT BT CRF model scoring higher for LOC-type entities (see Table 2) and mBERT RDA Bi-LSTM CRF scoring higher for ORG-type entities (recall of 79.32, see Appendix C). Additionally, gaBERT-based models appear to be the most robust across all entity types.

Titles or honorifics preceding PER NEs e.g. 'Bean' (Mrs. or Ms.) and 'Aire' (Minister) presented challenges for all models.

Overall, ORG-type entities were the most difficult for all models, particularly seen with low precision scores across all models. One recurring error for ORG-type NEs includes the difficulty models showed when correctly annotating the team names of regional teams e.g. 'Luimneach' (Limerick), which more commonly presents as a LOC-type entity.

MW-NE Test Set: Within multiword NEs, the same trend of gaBERT-based models dominating scores can be seen with PER-type MW-NEs category, with only one exception—mBERT RDA Bi-LSTM CRF achieves the highest precision for PER-type MW-NEs across all models on this test set (87.50, whereas the highest precision for PER achieved by a gaBERT-based model is 86.54 see Appendix D), meaning that this model is the most adept at reducing false positives for MW-NEs in this category. Additionally, mBERT variations appear to perform better on LOC-type and ORG-type MW-NEs rather than gaBERT (mBERT achieves the highest precision for LOC (76.72), mBERT BT CRF the highest recall for LOC (85.47), mBERT Bi-LSTM CRF the highest F1 score for LOC (80.11), both precision (64.84) and F1 score (71.30) for ORG, and mBERT RDA Bi-LSTM CRF the highest recall for ORG (83.89)), indicating that these models may be better at handling multi-word LOC-type and ORG-type MW-NEs than gaBERT-based models.

7.3 Effects of Data Augmentation Methods

Random data augmentation (RDA) negatively impacts recall across all models, with the most significant decline observed in mBERT, particularly for PER-type NEs, where the addition of RDA to mBERT led to the lowest results of all models for this category (precision of 66.51, recall of 58.75, and F1 score of 62.39). However, mBERT RDA sees a slight recall improvement for LOC (+4.61) due to an increase in true positives and decrease in false negatives. Precision also decreases (by 8.38 for the LOC-type NEs), suggesting that augmented data doesn't improve the model's predictive performance and makes them overconfident in their predictions. Exceptions are gaBERT RDA and XLMRoBERTa RDA, which show improvements for both the ORG- (+0.28 and +2.25 respectively and PER- (+3.50 and +1.55 respectively) type NEs. Consequently, F1 scores generally decline (see Appendix C), indicating that RDA does not enhance performance overall.

RDA on MW-NE Test Set: XLMRoBERTa RDA shows improved recall for LOC and PER, outperforming the baseline (+0.70 and +1.23 respectively) and BT (+2.09 and +0.62 respectively). In contrast, gaBERT RDA and mBERT RDA show recall degradation for PER and LOC (see Appendix D), suggesting that RDA can hinder performance for specific entity types, highlighting again that it can make models overconfident in their predictions. Notably, XLMRoBERTa maintains better precision at the overall level (+1.80 over baseline XLMRoBERTa and +1.86 over XLMRoBERTa BT), indicating it is more robust to any noise introduced by RDA.

Backtranslation (BT) leads to a more pronounced shift in model behaviour, particularly for recall, where substantial increases can be seen for mBERT on LOC-type NEs (+4.35) and gaBERT for PER-type NEs (+1.83). However, precision consistently drops across all models, particularly for mBERT (-4.35) and XLMRoBERTa on LOC-type NEs (69.74, the lowest recall for LOC of all models and a decrease of 1.97), where the models are showcasing more false positive predictions for this entity type. This highlights the fundamental trade-off with BT: it improves recall at the cost of precision, leading to more false positives. Overall F1 scores decrease due to the precision loss, although F1 scores improve for the PER tag across all models due to simultaneous increases in both recall and precision (see Appendix C).

BT on MW-NE Test Set: The inclusion of BT improves the accuracy of predictions for PER made by mBERT (76.62 vs 80.54). While precision doesn't universally improve, it does increase for PER in all models (+1.43, +3.92, and +3.35 for gaBERT BT, mBERT BT, and XLMRoBERTa BT respectively) and for ORG in XLMRoBERTa (+2.27), confirming that BT can be beneficial for specific entity types such as PER, especially where recall is prioritised, perhaps due to an increase in how often the label is seen during training.

7.4 Addition of CRF Layers

The addition of a CRF and Bi-LSTM CRF to gaBERT and mBERT yields varying improvements across both test sets. Although gaBERT generally performs well, the introduction of both a CRF or Bi-LSTM CRF leads to improvements at the overall level (increase in overall precision of 5.33 with the addition of a CRF and 2.13 with the addition of a Bi-LSTM CRF). For gaBERT, the CRF enhances precision and recall, particularly for LOC-type and PER-type NEs (see Appendix C).

CRF on MW-NE Test Set: The addition of a Bi-LSTM layer increases the F1 score for each model when compared to their baselines (increase of 2.53 for gaBERT and 1.98 for mBERT, with the overall F1 for gaBERT Bi-LSTM being the highest achieved of all models tested on this set (77.36)). While the addition of a CRF to mBERT does not yield performance improvements, a Bi-LSTM improves over the mBERT baseline overall and achieves a higher precision for LOC on the mixed-length test set (see Appenidx D).

CRF with Data Augmentation: When CRF and BiLSTM-CRF layers are added to models with RDA or BT, the impacts are more nuanced. For RDA, the CRF layer enhances recall, with improvements generally seen across all entity types with only a few exceptions (mBERT RDA Bi-LSTM recall on LOC-type NEs and precision on ORG-type NEs, gaBERT RDA CRF recall on ORG-type NEs, and gaBERT RDA Bi-LSTM CRF recall and F1 score on ORG-type NEs and precision on PER-type NEs). Similarly with mBERT RDA, the addition of a CRF yielded enhancements across all metrics, except recall on LOC-type NEs. The addition of a Bi-LSTM improves recall scores for both mBERT and gaBERT RDA models when calculated across all NE types (see Appendix C). Recall improvements are seen across the models with RDA at the overall level with the introduction of a Bi-LSTM CRF. Introducing CRFs helps to mitigate some of the precision loss associated with RDA and BT. Overall, the addition of CRFs generally enhances F1 scores across the models and particularly enhances performance on PER entities. The CRFs lead to a more balanced performance across both test sets and model variants. The best performing model for the mixed-length test set was gaBERT RDA CRF achieving a F1 score of 76.52. This model also performed well on the MW-NE test set, however it was outperformed by gaBERT Bi-LSTM CRF (75.09 vs 77.36).

On inspection of the results from gaBERT RDA, gaBERT RDA CRF, and gaBERT RDA Bi-LSTM CRF on the mixed-length test set, it is clear that the addition of a CRF outperforms the others by being more precise and accurate when predicting entities. The Bi-LSTM CRF architecture shows a similar performance, although it tends to produce more false positives. gaBERT RDA faces challenges in both over-predicting and missing entities compared to its CRF variants. Many of the errors made by gaBERT RDA are due to diverging from the integrity of the IOB2 tagging scheme. For almost all of these errors, both CRF variants did not make this mistake, as they were more consistent in maintaining the correct tagging structure, ensuring proper transitions between the tags (e.g. I-tagged tokens following B-tagged tokens).

7.5 MW-NEs

On further analysis, the majority of errors made on the mixed-length test set were due to incorrect predictions and divergence from the IOB2 tagging scheme. Investigation of the results show the majority of errors were made on MW-NEs with fewer words i.e. 2 words long. This is not surprising as the test set predominantly contains NEs of less than 3 words long (38% single-word NEs and 30% two-word NEs). As stated above; models have difficulty in maintaining accurate transitions between IOB2 tags, where entities are not always properly marked as part of a continuous sequence, titles and honorifics provide challenges for the PER-type NEs, and team ORG entities that are named for the location they are based in are predicted as the latter type.

The best performing model on the MW-NE test set is the gaBERT Bi-LSTM CRF with a F1 of 77.36 whereas the highest performing model for mixed-length NEs is gaBERT RDA CRF. It is interesting that a different model performed better on the MW-NE test set given that MW-NEs make up the majority of the entities in training. While this analysis did not reveal any entity-specific patterns for MW-NEs, it is hoped that on expansion of the datasets further insights can be gleaned on how MW-NEs are handled by these models.

8 Ethical Considerations

In the current climate of large language models, and massive data resources, the importance of data sovereignty and proper usage cannot be overlooked. The IUDT data (Lynn, 2022) was in part selected for the construction of the gold-standard NER-annotated corpus as it is under a CC BY-SA 3.0 license and comprises publicly accessible textual data sourced from the New Corpus of Ireland-Irish (NCII) (Kilgarriff et al., 2006), encompassing content from various sources such as websites, books, news articles, and other media. Additionally, it includes supplementary publicly available data available under the Open Data directive (European Parliament and Council of the European Union, 2019). The Dáil proceedings used are also publicly available under this directive (European Parliament and Council of the European Union, 2019). The lower energy demands of smaller BERT models is an argument for their continued usage in such experiments, particularly for exploratory studies such as this one. Insights from this work can be applied in future studies employing larger energy- and resource-hungry models.

9 Future Directions

Several avenues for advancing the scope and efficacy of NER for Irish present themselves after this research work. Firstly, acquiring more annotated data remains paramount given the scarcity of labelled corpora for low-resource languages such as Irish. Expanding the dataset used in this task could significantly bolster the performance of the models. A promising approach to this is self-training (Zhou et al., 2023) with Irish Wikipedia (Vicipéid). This semi-supervised approach would mitigate the labour-intensive manual annotation employed in this research (Zhou et al., 2023). Also, improving the data augmentation approach could be a focal point for future enhancement. Advanced techniques such as sentence-level resampling (Wang and Wang, 2022) could provide substantial benefits. This approach involves modifying existing sentences to create new training examples, which leads to different syntactic and semantic variations to improve the model's accuracy and generalisation capabilities (Wang and Wang, 2022). Additionally, a hybrid approach leveraging existing parsers should be considered (Lynn, 2016), using the parser to identify NEs in the text while BERT-based classifiers could be trained to predict the NE label. Newer models such as the UCCIX (Tran et al., 2024) monolingual Irish model are recently available for future experiments, and increases in performance can be weighed against the energy costs of training larger models. As mentioned in the European Language Equality Project's Report on the Irish Language (Lynn, 2023), the Gaois database of Irish-language surnames (Gaois, 2020) and the national placenames and biographies database (Gaois, 2008) could also be leveraged to build a NER tool.

[5]https://ga.wikipedia.org/wiki/Pr%C3%ADomhleathanach

Futhermore, the task of NER can be integrated into a larger study on machine translation capabilities of handling these challenging constructions (Ugawa et al., 2018). Additionally, a CRF model could be used to provide a baseline for comparison with the models utilised in this work. Finally, there is scope to combine this work with ongoing research in Irish MWE processing, and in particular research on noun compounds, as both constructions could be treated simultaneously.

10 Conclusion

We presented several architectures and training data setups for the NER for Irish task as well as a gold-standard NER-annotated corpus. We proposed and evaluated multiple NER models for Irish. Of these, the best-performing model is gaBERT with the implementation of random data augmentation and a CRF layer. Despite the limited amount of data available for fine-tuning, this model has demonstrated remarkable performance improvements compared to alternative architectures, including baseline gaBERT and the multilingual models mBERT and XLMRoberta on the task of Irish NER. With an F1 score of 76.52, the gaBERT RDA CRF model demonstrates robustness and accuracy in identifying both single- and MW-NEs in Irish text and generalises well to unseen data. Our findings further highlight several noteworthy observations. The incorporation of a CRF or BiLSTM CRF layer yielded notable performance improvements. Additionally, data augmentation strategies showed promising results at for different entity types and for general NE prediction. We hope that the gold-standard NER-annotated corpus for Irish can provide a benchmark for future research and valuable training data. Ultimately, our study sets the stage for continued progress in Irish NLP, offering a vital step forward in supporting the Irish language in the digital age.

Limitations

Due to time and resource constraints we were unable to implement the addition of CRFs to XLM-RoBERTa and only a small set of sentences were used for backtranslation. The data collection used text from transcriptions of Dáil proceedings, which represent a limited context of Irish language, e.g. formal language in a legal domain. Furthermore, as the text was filtered from a larger body of bilingual text, the Irish used likely represents a minority of speakers from the Dáil, which further narrows the scope of text type. Back-translation and random data augmentation provide a means for synthetically inflating training data in low-resource scenarios to improve model performance; however, it should be noted that these techniques can introduce new errors into the data. Future work includes exploring the impact of these data-augmentation techniques on the quality of the text (e.g. semantic coherence of the sentence, co-reference, etc.).

Acknowledgements

This research and future work on text processing for Irish is sustained through funding from the Department of Tourism, Culture, Arts, Gaeltacht, Sport and Media, Research Ireland, and Údarás na Gaeltachta. The authors would also like to thank the reviewers for their detailed feedback, many of whose comments were incorporated into the final paper.

References

Mikhail Arkhipov, Maria Trofimova, Yuri Kuratov, and Alexey Sorokin. 2019. Tuning multilingual transformers for language-specific named entity recognition. In Proceedings of the 7th Workshop on Balto-Slavic Natural Language Processing, pages 89–93, Florence, Italy. Association for Computational Linguistics.

James Barry, Joachim Wagner, Lauren Cassidy, Alan Cowap, Teresa Lynn, Abigail Walsh, Mícheál J. Ó Meachair, and Jennifer Foster. 2022. gaBERT — an Irish language model. In Proceedings of the Thirteenth Language Resources and Evaluation Conference, pages 4774–4788, Marseille, France. European Language Resources Association.

K. Chan, K.A Las Alas, C. Orcena, D.J. Velasco, Q.J. San Juan, and C. Cheng. 2023. Practical approaches for low-resource named entity recognition of Filipino telecommunications domain. In Pacific Asia Conference on Language, Information and Computation.

Alexis Conneau, Kartikay Khandelwal, Naman Goyal, Vishrav Chaudhary, Guillaume Wenzek, Francisco Guzmán, Edouard Grave, Myle Ott, Luke Zettlemoyer, and Veselin Stoyanov. 2020. Unsupervised cross-lingual representation learning at scale. In Proceedings of the 58th Annual Meeting of the Association for Computational Linguistics, pages 8440–8451, Online. Association for Computational Linguistics.

Xiang Dai and Heike Adel. 2020. An analysis of simple data augmentation for named entity recognition. Preprint, arXiv:2010.11683.

Jacob Devlin, Ming-Wei Chang, Kenton Lee, and Kristina Toutanova. 2019. BERT: Pre-training of deep bidirectional transformers for language understanding. In Proceedings of the 2019 Conference of the North American Chapter of the Association for Computational Linguistics: Human Language Technologies, Volume 1 (Long and Short Papers), pages 4171–4186, Minneapolis, Minnesota. Association for Computational Linguistics.

European Parliament and Council of the European Union. 2019. Open data directive - data.gov.ie. Data.gov.ie https://data.gov.ie/pages/open-data-directive.

Gaois. 2008. Placenames database of Ireland. logainm.ie.

Gaois. 2020. Database of Irish-language surnames. Gaois research group https://www.gaois.ie/en/surnames/info.

Yao Ge, Yuting Guo, Yuan–Chi Yang, Mohammed Ali Al–Garadi, and Abeed Sarker. 2022. A comparison of few-shot and traditional named entity recognition models for medical text. In 2022 IEEE 10th International Conference on Healthcare Informatics (ICHI), pages 84–89.

Houses of the Oireachtas. 2024. Dáil transcripts.

Xuming Hu, Yong Jiang, Aiwei Liu, Zhongqiang Huang, Pengjun Xie, Fei Huang, Lijie Wen, and Philip S. Yu. 2023. Entity-to-text based data augmentation for various named entity recognition tasks. In Findings of the Association for Computational Linguistics: ACL 2023, pages 9072–9087, Toronto, Canada. Association for Computational Linguistics.

A. Kilgarriff, M. Rundell, and E. Uí Dhonnchadha. 2006. Efficient corpus development for lexicography: Building the new corpus for Ireland. Language Resources and Evaluation, 40:127–152.

Label Studio. 2020. Label studio – open source data labeling. https://labelstud.io/.

Yafei Liu, Siqi Wei, Haijun Huang, Qin Lai, Mengshan Li, and Lixin Guan. 2023. Naming entity recognition of citrus pests and diseases based on the bert-bilstm-crf model. Expert Systems with Applications, 234.

Ilya Loshchilov and Frank Hutter. 2019. Decoupled weight decay regularization. In International Conference on Learning Representations, New Orleans, Louisiana, United States.

Teresa Lynn. 2016. Irish dependency treebanking and parsing. Phd thesis, Dublin City University, Dublin, Ireland. Available at https://doras.dcu.ie/21014/.

Teresa Lynn. 2022. Universaldependencies/ud irish-idt. https://github.com/UniversalDependencies/UD_Irish-IDT.

Teresa Lynn. 2023. Language report Irish. In European Language Equality Cognitive Technologies. Springer, Cham, Switzerland, pages 163–166. Accessed 10/12/2024.

Teresa Lynn, Jennifer Foster, Sarah McGuinness, Abigail Walsh, Jason Phelan, and Kevin Scannell. 2023. Universal Dependencies Irish Dependency Treebank (v2.12).

Mónica Marrero, Julián Urbano, Sonia Sánchez-Cuadrado, Jorge Morato, and Juan Miguel Gómez-Berbís. 2013. Named entity recognition: Fallacies, challenges and opportunities. Computer Standards I& Interfaces, 35(5):1–13. https://api.semanticscholar.org/CorpusID:2635684.

Sarah McGuinness, Jason Phelan, Abigail Walsh, and Teresa Lynn. 2020. Annotating MWEs in the Irish UD treebank. In Proceedings of the Fourth Workshop on Universal Dependencies (UDW 2020), pages 126–139, Barcelona, Spain (Online). Association for Computational Linguistics.

Christopher Moseley. 2012. The UNESCO Atlas of the World's Languages in Danger: Context and Process. World Oral Literature Project, University of Cambridge Museum of Archaeology and Anthropology.

Hiroki Nakayama. 2018. seqeval: A python framework for sequence labeling evaluation. Software available from https://github.com/chakki-works/seqeval.

J. Nivre. 2015. Towards a universal grammar for natural language processing. Computational Linguistics and Intelligent Text Processing, 9041:3–16.

Joakim Nivre, Marie-Catherine de Marneffe, Filip Ginter, Yoav Goldberg, Jan Hajič, Christopher D. Manning, Ryan McDonald, Slav Petrov, Sampo Pyysalo, Natalia Silveira, Reut Tsarfaty, and Daniel Zeman. 2016. Universal dependencies v1: A multilingual treebank collection. In Proceedings of the Tenth International Conference on Language Resources and Evaluation (LREC'16), pages 1659–1666.

Ailbhe Ní Chasaide, Neasa Ní Chiaráin, Elaine Uí Dhonnchadha, Teresa Lynn, and John Judge. 2022. Digital plan for the Irish language speech and language technologies 2023-2027. https://assets.gov.ie/241755/e82c256a-6f47-4ddb-8ce6-ff81df208bb1.pdf.

Atul Kr. Ojha, Chao-Hong Liu, Katharina Kann, John Ortega, Sheetal Shatam, and Theodorus Fransen. 2021. Findings of the LoResMT 2021 shared task on COVID and sign language for low-resource languages. In Proceedings of the 4th Workshop on Technologies for MT of Low Resource Languages (LoResMT2021), pages 114–123, Virtual. Association for Machine Translation in the Americas.

Matthew E. Peters, Mark Neumann, Mohit Iyyer, Matt Gardner, Christopher Clark, Kenton Lee, and Luke Zettlemoyer. 2018. Deep contextualized word representations. Preprint, arXiv:1802.05365.

Lutz Prechelt. 2012. Early stopping — but when? In Neural Networks: Tricks of the Trade: Second Edition, pages 53–67. Springer, Berlin, Heidelberg, Berlin, Heidelberg.

Karthik Puranik, Adeep Hande, Ruba Priyadharshini, Thenmozi Durairaj, Anbukkarasi Sampath, Kingston Pal Thamburaj, and Bharathi Raja Chakravarthi. 2021. Attentive fine-tuning of transformers for translation of low-resourced languages @LoResMT 2021. In Proceedings of the 4th Workshop on Technologies for MT of Low Resource Languages (LoResMT2021), pages 134–143, Virtual. Association for Machine Translation in the Americas.

Jonathan Raiman and John Miller. 2017. Globally normalized reader. In Proceedings of the 2017 Conference on Empirical Methods in Natural Language Processing, pages 1059–1069, Copenhagen, Denmark. Association for Computational Linguistics.

Carlos Ramisch, Agata Savary, Bruno Guillaume, Jakub Waszczuk, Marie Candito, Ashwini Vaidya, Verginica Barbu Mititelu, Archna Bhatia, Uxoa Iñurrieta, Voula Giouli, Tunga Güngör, Menghan Jiang, Timm Lichte, Chaya Liebeskind, Johanna Monti, Renata Ramisch, Sara Stymne, Abigail Walsh, and Hongzhi Xu. 2020. Edition 1.2 of the PARSEME shared task on semi-supervised identification of verbal multiword expressions. In Proceedings of the Joint Workshop on Multiword Expressions and Electronic Lexicons, pages 107–118, online. Association for Computational Linguistics.

C. Sbaty, I. Omar, F. Wasfalla, M. Islam, and S. Abdennadher. 2021. Data augmentation techniques on Arabic data for named entity recognition. Procedia Computer Science, 189:292–299.

Fábio Souza, Rodrigo Nogueira, and Roberto Lotufo. 2020. Portuguese named entity recognition using bert-crf. Preprint, arXiv:1909.10649.

Jörg Tiedemann and Santhosh Thottingal. 2020. OPUS-MT – building open translation services for the world. In Proceedings of the 22nd Annual Conference of the European Association for Machine Translation, pages 479–480, Lisboa, Portugal. European Association for Machine Translation.

Khanh-Tung Tran, Barry O'Sullivan, and Hoang D. Nguyen. 2024. Uccix: Irish-excellence large language model. Preprint, arXiv:2405.13010.

Arata Ugawa, Akihiro Tamura, Takashi Ninomiya, Hiroya Takamura, and Manabu Okumura. 2018. Neural machine translation incorporating named entity. In Proceedings of the 27th International Conference on Computational Linguistics, pages 3240–3250, Santa Fe, New Mexico, USA. Association for Computational Linguistics.

Abigail Walsh. 2023. The Automatic Processing of Multiword Expressions in Irish. Phd thesis, Dublin City University.

Abigail Walsh, Teresa Lynn, and Jennifer Foster. 2022. A BERT's eye view: Identification of Irish multiword expressions using pre-trained language models. In Proceedings of the 18th Workshop on Multiword Expressions @LREC2022, pages 89–99, Marseille, France. European Language Resources Association.

Xiaochen Wang and Yue Wang. 2022. Sentence-level resampling for named entity recognition. In North American Chapter of the Association for Computational Linguistics.

Nan. Xu, W. Mao, P. Wei, and D. Zeng. 2021. MDA: Multimodal data augmentation framework for boosting performance on sentiment/emotion classification tasks. IEEE Intelligent Systems, 36(6):3–12.

Usama Yaseen and Stefan Langer. 2021. Data augmentation for low-resource named entity recognition using backtranslation. In Proceedings of the 18th International Conference on Natural Language Processing (ICON), pages 352–358, National Institute of Technology Silchar, Silchar, India. NLP Association of India (NLPAI).

Ran Zhou, Xin Li, Lidong Bing, Erik Cambria, and Chunyan Miao. 2023. Improving self-training for cross-lingual named entity recognition with contrastive and prototype learning.

Appendix

A Gitlab

The scripts and annotation guidelines used in this research can be found in the GitHub repository: Named Entity Recognition for the Irish Language Gitlab Repo.

B Annotation Guidelines

- **Tags Discussed:** Person (PER), Location (LOC) and Organisation (ORG)
- **Tagging Scheme:** IOB2

B.1 Person

- A person's name or family name (real or fictional even if spelled incorrectly) e.g. Micheál (B- PER) Martin (I-PER)
- Gods (when having a single reference and capitalised)

(1) Buíochas le Dia (B-PER)

Thanks to God (B-PER)

- A person's initials e.g. M.M. (B-PER)

- Do not tag titles as a name or part of a name

(2) Chonaic (O) mé (O) Dr.(O) O'Sullivan (B-PER) inné (O), An(O) Taoiseach (O) Leo (B-PER) Varadkar (I-PER), An (O) tUasal (O) Mac (B-PER) Gabhann (I-PER), Mary (B-PER) Lou (I-PER) McDonald(I-PER) T.D. (O)

I saw Dr. (O) O'Sullivan (B-PER) yesterday (O), the (O) Prime (O) Minister (O) Leo (B-PER) Varadkar (I-PER), Mr. (O) Mac (B-PER) Gabhann (I-PER), Mary (B-PER) Lou (I-PER) McDonald (I-PER) T.D. (O)

- Do tag if used as a name mention

(3) Dúirt (O) An (O) Taoiseach (B-PER) go (O) bhfuil (O) . . .

The (O) Prime (B-PER) Minister (I-PER) said that ...

B.2 Location

- Geographical places, facilities or buildings e.g. countries, cities, towns, airports, hotels, roads etc.
- When two locations are consecutive, tag separately

(4) Tá (O) mé (O) i (O) mo (O) chónaí (O) i (O) Sord (B-LOC), Baile (B-LOC) Átha (I-LOC) Cliath (I-LOC)

I (O) live (O) in (O) Swords (B-LOC), Dublin (B-LOC)

- Tag whole postal addresses as one

(5) 27 (B-LOC) Bóthar (I-LOC) na (I-LOC) Foraoise (I-LOC), Caisleán (I-LOC) an (I-LOC) Chomair (I-LOC), Cill (I-LOC) Chainnigh (I-LOC)

27 (B-LOC) Forest (I-LOC) Road (I-LOC), Castle (I-LOC) Comer(I-LOC), Kilkenny (I-LOC)

B.3 Organisation

- Named collections of people (organisations, institutions, firms, political parties, unions, groups)

(6) Is (O) é (O) Simon (B-PER) Harris (I-PER) ceannaire (O) Fhine (B-ORG) Gael (I-ORG)

Simon (B-PER) Harris (I-PER) is (O) the (O) leader (O) of (O) Fine (B-ORG) Gael (I-ORG)

(7) Fáiltím (O) roimh (O) an (O) nuacht (O) is (O) deireanaí (O) a (O) chuala (O) muid (O) ar (O) maidin (O) ó (O) Citylink (B-ORG) go (O) mbeidh (O)...

I (O) welcome (O) the (O) latest (O) news (O) that (O) we (O) heard (O) this (O) morning (O) from (O) Citylink (B-ORG) that (O) there (O) will (O) be (O)...

- Names of places when they act as administrative units or sports teams

(8) Chaill (B-ORG) Baile (I-ORG) Átha (I-ORG) Cliath (I-ORG) in (O) aghaidh (O) Gaillimh (B-ORG) an (O) seachtain (O) seo (O) caite (O)

Dublin (B-ORG) lost (O) against (O) Galway (B-ORG) last (O) week (O)

- Include corporate designators like Co. and Ltd. as part of the name

(9) Is (O) gnólacht (O) dlí (O) iad (O) Johnson (B-ORG) & Co. (I-ORG)

Johnson (B-ORG) & Co. (I-ORG) is (O) a (O) law (O) firm

- Only tag brands if referring to the organisation itself, not as a brand label

(10) Tá (O) bróga (O) nua (O) eisithe (O) ag (O) Nike (B-ORG).

And not in the following:
Ghortaigh (O) mé (O) mo (O) chosa (O) mar (O) chaith (O) mé (O) Nike (O)

Nike (B-ORG) has (O) released (O) new (O) shoes (O).
And not in the following:
I (O) hurt (O) my (O) foot (O) because (O) I (O) wore (O) Nike (O)

Other points to note: Inclusion of non-name tokens should be tagged

(11) Nua-Eabhrac-bhunaithe (B-LOC)

New-York-based (B-LOC)

C Results on Mixed-Length Test Set

D Results on MW-NE Test Set

Table 3: Results on Mixed-Length Test Set

Model	Accuracy	Overall			LOC			ORG			PER		
		P	R	F1	P	R	F1	P	R	F1	P	R	F1
gaBERT	94.84	71.74	**77.40**	74.46	76.61	77.51	77.06	61.11	72.79	66.44	76.88	81.10	78.93
gaBERT CRF	95.25	77.07	75.27	76.16	80.37	77.51	78.92	65.00	66.91	65.94	**84.52**	79.88	82.13
gaBERT Bi-LSTM CRF	94.82	73.87	76.55	75.18	77.50	73.37	75.38	67.97	76.47	**71.97**	75.72	79.88	77.74
gaBERT RDA	94.72	71.11	75.05	73.03	71.51	75.74	73.56	61.39	71.32	65.99	80.38	77.44	78.88
gaBERT RDA CRF	**95.44**	**78.05**	75.05	**76.52**	**81.60**	78.70	**80.12**	**69.70**	67.65	68.66	81.41	77.44	79.38
gaBERT RDA Bi-LSTM CRF	95.02	74.59	76.97	75.76	79.88	77.51	78.68	63.89	67.65	65.71	78.41	84.15	81.18
gaBERT BT	94.67	69.19	76.12	72.49	67.20	73.96	70.42	61.15	70.59	65.53	78.61	82.93	80.71
gaBERT BT CRF	95.15	74.59	76.97	75.76	75.00	76.33	75.66	63.01	67.65	65.25	84.34	**85.37**	**84.85**
gaBERT BT Bi-LSTM CRF	94.59	72.08	73.77	72.92	73.78	71.6	72.67	60	63.97	61.92	80.7	84.15	82.39
mBERT	93.28	70.86	73.47	72.14	74.62	75.19	74.90	67.83	72.93	70.29	68.40	71.25	69.80
mBERT CRF	93.02	69.05	72.13	70.56	76.96	72.63	74.74	61.69	71.43	66.20	66.54	72.08	69.20
mBERT BiLSTM CRF	93.33	73.22	72.24	72.73	79.13	74.68	76.84	65.97	71.43	68.59	72.81	69.17	70.94
mBERT RDA	92.22	64.10	69.68	66.77	66.24	79.80	72.39	58.90	64.66	61.65	66.51	58.75	62.39
mBERT RDA CRF	93.57	72.28	74.14	73.20	77.27	78.26	77.76	62.34	72.18	66.90	77.31	69.58	73.25
mBERT RDA Bi-LSTM CRF	92.90	69.42	74.24	71.70	77.28	75.70	76.49	58.61	**79.32**	67.41	73.49	65.83	69.45
mBERT BT	93.01	68.81	74.02	71.32	74.58	79.54	76.98	60.45	70.68	65.16	69.62	68.75	69.18
mBERT BT CRF	93.41	71.82	75.59	73.66	76.27	**80.56**	78.36	62.07	74.44	67.69	77.83	68.75	73.01
mBERT BT Bi-LSTM CRF	92.60	68.72	69.79	69.25	75.60	72.89	74.22	57.70	71.80	63.99	73.89	62.50	67.72
XLMRoberta	93.44	69.39	75.37	72.26	74.66	71.71	73.15	57.91	77.78	66.39	76.37	78.02	77.19
XLMRoberta RDA	93.63	69.18	74.02	71.52	70.13	71.05	70.59	60.16	74.40	66.52	77.92	77.59	77.75
XLMRoberta BT	93.87	67.59	72.41	69.92	69.74	69.74	69.74	58.04	71.5	64.07	75.11	76.72	75.91

Table 4: Results on MW-NE Test Set

Model	Overall				LOC			ORG			PER		
	Accuracy	P	R	F1	P	R	F1	P	R	F1	P	R	F1
gaBERT	95.05	70.39	79.85	74.83	71.00	83.53	76.76	57.58	74.03	64.77	81.90	81.13	81.52
gaBERT CRF	95.49	73.33	77.99	75.59	74.44	78.82	76.57	57.61	68.83	62.72	86.41	83.96	85.17
gaBERT Bi-LSTM CRF	94.99	74.06	**80.97**	**77.36**	74.42	75.29	74.85	62.63	80.52	70.45	84.26	**85.85**	85.05
gaBERT RDA	94.86	67.21	76.49	71.55	64.15	80.00	71.20	54.08	68.83	60.57	83.17	79.25	81.16
gaBERT RDA CRF	**95.65**	**75.09**	77.61	76.33	75.82	81.18	78.41	61.9	67.53	64.6	85.29	82.08	83.65
gaBERT RDA Bi-LSTM	95.08	71.77	78.73	75.09	72.04	78.82	75.28	57.61	68.83	62.72	83.49	85.85	84.65
gaBERT BT	94.77	65.92	77.24	71.13	58.88	74.12	65.62	54.55	70.13	61.36	83.33	84.91	84.11
gaBERT BT CRF	95.49	72.79	79.85	76.16	72.92	82.35	77.35	58.24	68.83	63.10	85.05	85.85	85.45
gaBERT BT Bi-LSTM CRF	94.89	70.73	75.75	73.15	67.74	74.12	70.79	55.56	64.94	59.88	86.54	84.91	**85.71**
mBERT	94.08	71.54	77.64	74.46	**76.72**	81.01	78.80	62.30	79.87	70.00	76.62	71.95	74.21
mBERT CRF	93.76	68.85	76.83	72.62	73.96	79.33	76.55	58.38	77.18	66.47	75.62	73.78	74.69
mBERT Bi-LSTM CRF	94.49	73.63	79.47	76.44	76.26	84.36	**80.11**	**64.84**	79.19	**71.30**	80.79	74.39	77.46
mBERT RDA	93.29	62.90	71.34	66.86	60.76	80.45	69.23	55.38	72.48	62.79	78.57	60.37	68.28
mBERT RDA CRF	94.35	72.81	77.85	75.25	71.77	83.80	77.32	62.92	75.17	68.50	87.05	73.78	79.87
mBERT RDA Bi-LSTM CRF	93.71	68.95	77.64	73.04	72.86	81.01	76.72	55.07	**83.89**	66.49	**87.50**	68.29	76.71
mBERT BT	93.96	69.31	78.05	73.42	71.77	83.80	77.32	58.16	76.51	66.09	80.54	73.17	76.68
mBERT BT CRF	93.98	70.83	78.46	74.45	73.56	**85.47**	79.07	59.79	77.85	67.64	81.82	71.34	76.22
mBERT BT Bi-LSTM CRF	93.59	67.97	74.19	70.94	72.45	79.33	75.73	55.98	78.52	65.36	80.30	64.63	71.62
XLMRoberta	93.65	67.86	76.36	71.86	69.43	76.22	72.67	55.15	77.78	64.54	79.87	75.46	77.60
XLMRoberta+data_aug	94.23	69.66	77.07	73.18	65.48	76.92	70.74	60.67	77.78	68.16	83.33	76.69	79.87
XLMRoberta+backt	93.65	67.8	75.65	71.51	63.69	74.83	68.81	57.42	76.07	65.44	83.22	76.07	79.49

Author Index